Civil Rights,
The White House,
and the Justice Department
1945–1968

A 20 volume Series of Key Documents in Facsimile

Edited with Introductions by

Michal R. Belknap
Professor of Law
California Western School of Law

A Garland Series

CONTENTS OF THE SERIES

VOLUME 16

Justice Department Civil Rights Policies Prior to 1960

Crucial Documents from the Files of Arthur Brann Caldwell

Introduction by
Michal R. Belknap

Garland Publishing, Inc.
New York & London 1991

The editor and publisher are grateful to the Harry S. Truman, Dwight D. Eisenhower, John Fitzgerald Kennedy, and Lyndon Baines Johnson Libraries, and to the University of Arkansas for permission to reproduce the documents included in this series.

Library of Congress Cataloging-in-Publication Data

Justice Department civil rights policies prior to 1960 : crucial documents from the files of Arthur Brann Caldwell.
p. cm. — (Civil rights, the White House, and the Justice Department, 1945–1968 ; v. 16)
ISBN 0-8240-3384-1 (alk. paper)
1. Civil rights—Government policy—United States—History—20th century—Sources. 2. United States. Dept. of Justice—History. I. Caldwell, Arthur Brann, 1906–1987. II. Series.
KF4749.J87—dc20
342.73'085—dc20
[347.30285]   91-3612

Design by Marisel Tavárez

Printed on acid-free, 250-year-life paper.
Manufactured in the United States of America

INTRODUCTION

Attorney Arthur Brann Caldwell joined the United States Department of Justice in 1941 and, with the exception of a period of World War II service with the War Department's Military Intelligence Division, remained with that agency until 1968. From 1952 until 1957 he headed the Civil Rights Section of the department's Criminal Division. After Congress created a separate Civil Rights Division in 1957, Caldwell served for more than a decade as an assistant to the Assistant Attorney General in charge of that division. Among the highlights of a long career in the civil rights field was his work as a behind-the-scenes intermediary between the federal government and officials in his native Arkansas during the Little Rock school integration crisis of 1957.

After retiring from the Justice Department, A. B. Caldwell donated his personal papers to the library of his alma mater, the University of Arkansas. With its permission, Garland Publishing is reproducing in this series many of the most important documents in that valuable collection. In this volume readers will find two items of particular significance. The first, located in box 2 of the collection, is a notebook in which Caldwell kept Justice Department directives and other memoranda containing instructions to the Federal Bureau of Investigation and United States Attorneys, as well as most of the important correspondence between the Attorney General and F.B.I. Director J. Edgar Hoover concerning policies to be followed in investigating alleged violations of civil rights. The second item, "A Civil Rights Division Manual," is also found in box 2 of the Caldwell Papers. It contains directives issued by the Department of Justice concerning procedures to be followed by the Civil Rights Division, the F.B.I., and U. S. Attorneys. Also included are complete legislative histories of both the Civil Rights Act of 1957 and the Civil Rights Act of 1960.

Additional documents from the University of Arkansas' Caldwell collection appear in other volumes in this series. For their excact locations, see the list that appears at the end of this volume.

Because of a legibility problem document 20, a memorandum from the F.B.I. Director to the Attorney General, September 12, 1946, is included as a facsimile and as a typed transcript.

I would like to express my sincere appreciation to my research assistants: Richard Nover, Erin Gilland-Roby, Jane Ritter, Alicia Borrego, Michael B. Horrow, and Avigal Hoffman. Their hard work and dedication made the assembling of this collection possible.

I would also like to thank California Western School of Law for its financial support of this project.

Michal R. Belknap

CROSS REFERENCE GUIDE

There are other items from the Arthur Brann Caldwell collection in volumes 1, 7, and 12 of this series. The locations of these documents are listed below. The volume number precedes the colon, the document number follows it.

1:79 Letter to A.B. Caldwell from John Anderson, September 14, 1960

7:40 Chronology of events in Little Rock, Ark.

7:41 Memo for the files by Caldwell, May 28, 1957

7:42 Letter from Caldwell to Judge House, July 24, 1957

7:43 Report from Caldwell to Warren Olney III, July 24, 1957

7:44 Memorandum from Caldwell to Warren Olney III, August 12, 1957

7:45 Memo for the Files by Caldwell, August 21, 1957

7:46 Summary of Conference from Caldwell to Warren Olney III, August 30, 1957

7:47 Letter from Caldwell to A.F. House, September 1, 1957

7:48 Memo from Caldwell to Warren Olney III, September 3, 1957

7:49 Memorandum from Caldwell to Warren Olney III, September 5, 1957.

7:50 Memo from the Director, FBI, to the Attorney General, September 9, 1957

7:52 Memo from Olney to the Attorney General, September 13, 1957

7:53 Memorandum from Warren Olney III to Director, FBI, September 19, 1957

7:55 Memo from Caldwell to Warren Olney III, September 23, 1957

7:57 Memorandum from Warren Olney III to Director, FBI, October 1, 1957

12:17 "The Civil Rights Act of 1957"

12:18 Memorandum from A.B. Caldwell to Harold R. Tyler, August 15, 1960

CONTENTS

II. Civil Rights Division Manual

A. Organization

B. Jurisdiction

C. Procedure and Policy

D. Correspondence

E. Pleadings and Forms

Memoranda of policy sent to the Federal Bureau
of Investigation concerning the procedure to be followed in
Civil Rights Complaints and related matters.

        This volume contains copies of U. S. Department of Justice
directives and other memoranda containing instructions to the
Federal Bureau of Investigation and the U. S. Attorneys as well as
most of the important correspondence between the Attorney General
and the Director of the Federal Bureau of Investigation, Mr. J. Edgar
Hoover with especial reference to the policy to be followed in
the conduct of investigations of Civil Right matters.

        The originals of these documents are in the files of the
Deaprtment of Justice under the file numbers that appear on these
copies.   While none are classified as "Secret" or even "Confidential"
in the true sense, their contents should not be released to the
press, but can be made available to serious students performing
research in this field and this period of time.

        Much of the material here was reviewed and served as source
material for Dr. John T. Elliff, Asst. Professor of Politics at
Brandeis University, for his article, " Aspects of Federal Civil
Rights Enforcement: The Justice Department and the F.B.I.-1939-1964."
    Dr. Elliff's article appears in " Law in American History", published
by The Charles Warren Center for Studies in American History, Harvard
University. (Little Brown & Co. Boston, 1971) "Law in American History "
is Volume V of Perspectives in American History, published annually
by the Charles Warren Institute for Studies in American History,
Harvard University, Cambridge, Mass.

        For a similar and much more extensive discussion of the
relationship of the Federal Bureau of Investigation and the Department of Justice in Civil Rights Matters, see Dr. John T Elliff's
Doctoral (Harvard) thesis, Volumes 1 & 2,, entitled, " The United
States Departmant of Justice and Individual Rights--1937-1962", which
is a part of this collection of papers donated to the University
of Arkansas,
        by

                    Arthur B. Caldwell,
                    Class of 1929.

FOR IMMEDIATE RELEASE

DEPARTMENT OF JUSTICE

February 3, 1939

Attorney General Murphy announced today the establishment of a separate unit in the Criminal Division of the Department of Justice to be known as the Civil Liberties Unit. The Order creating the unit described the functions as follows:

"* * * to make a study of the provisions of the Constitution of the United States and Acts of Congress relating to civil rights with reference to present conditions, to make appropriate recommendations in respect thereto, and to direct, supervise and conduct prosecutions of violations of the provisions of the Constitution or Acts of Congress guaranteeing civil rights to individuals."

In making the announcement concerning the new unit, the Attorney General said:

"In a Democracy, an important function of the law enforcement branch of Government is the aggressive protection of the fundamental rights inherent in a free people. In America these guarantees are contained in express provisions of the Constitution and in Acts of Congress. It is the purpose of the Department of Justice to pursue a program of vigilant action in the prosecution of infringements of these rights.

"It must be borne in mind that the authority of the Federal Government in this field is somewhat limited by the fact that many of the Constitutional guarantees are guarantees against abuses by the Federal Government itself, or by the State governments, and are not guarantees against infringement by individuals or groups of individuals."

2

OFFICE OF THE ATTORNEY GENERAL

WASHINGTON, D. C.

February 3, 1939.

ORDER NO. 3204

Effective this date there is established within the Criminal Division of the Department of Justice a unit to be known as the Civil Liberties Unit.

The function and purpose of this unit will be to make a study of the provisions of the Constitution of the United States and Acts of Congress relating to civil rights with reference to present conditions, to make appropriate recommendations in respect thereto, and to direct, supervise and conduct prosecutions of violations of the provisions of the Constitution or Acts of Congress guaranteeing civil rights to individuals.

FRANK MURPHY

Attorney General.

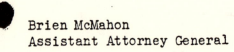

Brien McMahon
Assistant Attorney General

DEPARTMENT OF JUSTICE
Washington

February 3, 1939.

 O R D E R

    Pursuant to the Order of the Attorney General
numbered 3204, dated February 3, 1939, establishing
a Civil Liberties Unit within the Criminal Division
of the Department of Justice, Mr. Henry A. Schweinhaut, Special Assistant to the Attorney General, is
hereby designated as Chief of such unit.

                        Brien McMahon,
               Assistant Attorney General.

Henry A. Schweinhaut is 37 years of age and a native of the District of Columbia. He attended the local public schools and was graduated in 1924 from the National University Law School. He was in the general practice in Washington, D. C., from 1924 until 1934 when he was appointed an Assistant United States Attorney. He served in that office until 1936 when he was appointed a Special Assistant to the Attorney General. Since then he has been a member of the Trial Section of the Criminal Division. He is a former Vice President of the D. C. Bar Association and has been on the faculty of the Washington College of Law since 1932.

Mr. Schweinhaut took an important part in the Harlan County prosecution and has also been associated in the presentation of the evidence to the grand jury in the matter of the Jersey City difficulties.

OFFICE OF THE ATTORNEY GENERAL

WASHINGTON, D. C.

October 26, 1939

CIRCULAR NO. 3301

In the interpretation and application of the Hatch law, a number of cases have arisen under Section 9 (a) in which doubt has been expressed and the Department has been called upon to make a ruling. In issuing this circular, it is the aim of the Department merely to summarize these rulings for the benefit and information of government employees and the public generally. It is not the purpose to enumerate or describe all the activities and positions to which the law may or may not apply.

Accordingly, the circular should not be regarded as a complete or comprehensive statement of all the positions and activities to which Section 9 (a) applies. The law is general in scope and (with a few prominent exceptions) forbids all officers and employees of the executive branch of the Federal Government to take any active part in political management or political campaigns.

The pertinent provisions of Section 9 are as follows:

"No officer or employee in the executive branch of the Federal Government, or any agency or department thereof, shall take any active part in political management or in political campaigns. All such persons shall retain the right to vote as they may choose and to express their opinions on all political subjects."

I.

It has been ruled that the following officers and employees in the executive branch of the Federal Government, among others, are affected by the provisions of Section 9 of the Hatch Act:

(OVER)

1. United States Attorneys and Marshals, their assistants and deputies.

2. Special Attorneys of the Department of Justice and Special Assistants to the Attorney General.

3. Temporary employees, substitute employees, and per diem employees, during the period of their active employment.

4. Reserve officers of the United States Army, Navy, and Marine Corps during the period of their active duty.

5. Furloughed employees and employees on leave, whether with or without pay.

6. Officers and employees of governmental agencies such as the Home Owners Loan Corporation, the Reconstruction Finance Corporation, and the Public Works Administration.

7. Officers and employees occupying administrative and supervisory positions in the Work Projects Administration, the National Youth Administration, and the Civilian Conservation Corps.

> Note: Persons employed in any administrative or supervisory capacity by any agency of the Federal government whose compensation or any part thereof is paid from funds authorized by the Emergency Relief Appropriation Act of 1939 should consult Section 31 of that Act, which limits their public expression of opinions on political subjects more strictly than does the Hatch Act.

II.

Section 9 of the Hatch Act has been construed as not applying to the following:

1. Officers and employees of the legislative branch of the Federal Government, including secretaries and clerks to members of Congress and Congressional committees.

2. Officers and employees of the judicial branch of the Federal Government, including United States Commissioners, Clerks of United States

Courts, Referees in Bankruptcy, and their secretaries, deputies, and clerks.

3. Officers and employees of State and local governments, even though their employment involves the expenditure of Federal funds.

4. Persons who are retained from time to time to perform special services on a fee basis and who take no oath of office, such as fee attorneys, inspectors, appraisers, and management brokers for the Home Owners Loan Corporation and special fee attorneys for the Reconstruction Finance Corporation.

5. Persons who receive benefit payments, such as old age assistance and unemployment compensation under the Social Security Act, rural rehabilitation grants, and payments under the Agricultural Conservation Program.

6. Retired employees.

III.

It has been ruled that the following acts constitute taking an "active part in political management or in political campaigns" within the meaning of Section 9 of the Hatch Act:

1. Holding office in a political party or a political club.

2. Attending political conventions as a delegate or alternate.

3. Serving on committees of a political party or a political club.

4. Distributing buttons or printed matter in support of any candidate or party.

5. Serving at party headquarters or as watchers at the polls, or otherwise assisting a party or candidate in any primary or election campaign, whether or not Federal offices are involved.

6. Being a candidate for elective office--Federal, State, or local.

7. Soliciting funds for a political organization or campaign fund.

(OVER)

Note: Severe penalties are provided under Section 5 of the Hatch Act for those who solicit or receive any assessment, subscription, or contribution for any political purpose from a person known to be receiving compensation, employment, or other benefit provided for or made possible by any Act of Congress appropriating funds for work relief or relief purposes. Such persons include the administrative and supervisory personnel of relief agencies as well as the actual recipients of relief.

IV.

The following activities are not considered to be prohibited by the Hatch Act:

1. Holding membership in a political organization and attending its meetings otherwise than as an officer or delegate.

2. Participating in the activities of civic associations and educational groups, provided the activities in question are divorced from the campaigns of particular candidates or parties.

3. Holding a State or local office (but see III (6) above).

Note: An executive order of January 17, 1873 forbids persons holding a Federal civil office by appointment from holding any State or municipal office, with the exception of positions such as justice of the peace, notary public, commissioner to take acknowledgment of deeds or bail or to administer oaths, and positions on boards of education, school committees, public libraries, and in religious or eleemosynary institutions. Special exceptions are made in subsequent executive orders.

Circulars summarizing additional rulings will be issued as the necessity arises.

FRANK MURPHY,

Attorney General.

OFFICE OF THE ATTORNEY GENERAL

WASHINGTON, D. C.

Sec 2—
File 72-012

April 6, 1940

CIRCULAR NO. 3354

Violations of the provisions of Sections 1-7, inclusive, of the Hatch Act (Public No. 252, 76th Congress, approved Aug. 2, 1939) constitute criminal offenses and will be handled by the Department of Justice accordingly.

Section 9 of the Hatch Act, which prohibits officers and employees in the executive branch of the Government from taking active part in political management or in political campaigns, is enforceable administratively by the heads of the executive departments and other executive agencies, and not by the Department of Justice or through the courts.

It is open to the head of any executive department to require the opinion of the Attorney General on any questions of law arising in the administration of his department (U.S. Code, Title 5, Section 304). On the other hand it has been found unsatisfactory for the Department of Justice to continue to answer inquiries, often on inadequate statements of fact, from others than the heads of the executive departments as to matters which by the terms of the statute must be ultimately determined by such department heads.

Interpretations of the act which have been previously issued by the Department indicate in a general way the scope of the act. These interpretations are not revoked. The practice of issuing rulings under the Hatch Act at the request of interested parties other than heads of executive departments is hereby discontinued.

ROBERT H. JACKSON,

Attorney General.

10

DEPARTMENT OF JUSTICE
WASHINGTON 25, D. C.

April 10, 1940.

CIRCULAR NO. 3356

TO ALL UNITED STATES ATTORNEYS:

The Criminal Division has in preparation a memorandum
on the application of Sections 51 and 52 of Title 18 of the U. S.
Code, intended to be transmitted to United States Attorneys for
their use in dealing with civil liberties cases coming within
their jurisdiction. To assure comprehensiveness of this memorandum
each United States Attorney is requested to have the files of his
office examined for cases tried in his district under these statutes
and to forward to the Criminal Division not later than April 20th
a brief description of each such case. It is particularly desired
that cases within the last ten years be noted and that reference
be made to the outcome of any pleadings filed such as demurrers
and motions to quash.

O. JOHN ROGGE,

Assistant Attorney General.

11

DEPARTMENT OF JUSTICE
WASHINGTON 25, D. C.

May 21, 1940.

CIRCULAR NO. 3356

Supplement No. 1

TO ALL UNITED STATES ATTORNEYS:

Attached is a memorandum on Federal civil liberties prosecutions, prepared by the Civil Liberties Section of the Criminal Division. This memorandum is intended for the assistance of United States Attorneys and their staffs in responding to complaints and in supervising investigations of alleged violations of Federal law in civil liberties matters. Because of the importance of unified and consistent legal theory and prosecution policy in this field, it is requested that no indictments under 18 U.S.C. §§ 51, 52 be presented without clearance from the Department. Since crimes under these statutes are infamous, cases under these statutes should never be prosecuted by information.

In any case under these statutes where it is felt necessary to initiate immediate arrest or other preliminary proceedings the Department should be notified as soon thereafter as possible. In anticipation that indictments in these cases will be cleared with Washington, this memorandum contains no discussion of numerous detailed problems of pleading and law which are likely to arise in the extension of civil liberties jurisdiction to new fields, e.g.,

12

the exclusive procedure provisions of the Wagner Act, the meaning

of "color of law" and the application of the doctrine of official

immunity in 18 U.S.C. § 52, the constitutional arguments on the

problem of State inaction, etc., which may present special

difficulties of drafting or briefing in particular cases but will

normally not affect the selection of cases for prosecution or the

supervision of investigation therein.

Respectfully,

O, JOHN ROGGE,

Assistant Attorney General.

FEDERAL CRIMINAL JURISDICTION OVER

VIOLATION OF CIVIL LIBERTIES

TABLE OF CONTENTS

- i -

TABLE OF CASES

- v -

TABLE OF TEXTS

- vi -

FEDERAL CRIMINAL JURISDICTION OVER VIOLATION OF
CIVIL LIBERTIES

"Civil liberties" is not a technical legal term, but a phrase of popular currency applied somewhat indiscriminately to a miscellaneous group of rights, interests and situations. Typical "civil liberties" cases involve such varied matters as freedom of speech, press, assembly and ballot; and unreasonable searches and seizures; religious freedom; censorship of the arts; racial, labor, pacifist, and alien rights. Perhaps their one common characteristic is a tendency to give rise to charges, well or ill-founded, of conduct offensive to moral or political ideals stated or suggested in the Constitution. It is usually not difficult to cite something in the Constitution that sounds as though it bears on a given "civil liberties" problem, be it "due process of law", "equal protection of the laws", "freedom of speech", or "cruel and unusual punishments". It is this invocation of the Constitution which gives the phrase "civil liberties" its honorific character.

Hopeful complainants are too often unaware that the underlying conception of the Federal Government as one of delegated powers operating against a background of reserved States' rights leave the Federal Constitution largely unconcerned with the social and governmental situations which give rise to civil liberties problems. The label "civil liberties" sometimes raises but never answers the question whether a particular situation comes within the protection of the Constitution. Its use herein will therefore be purely descriptive, referring to the miscellaneous group of situations roughly covered in the list stated above. There is no law of civil liberties as such.

I. Statutes Covering Specific Violations of Civil Liberties

There are at present few statutes which make Federal crimes out of specific violations of civil liberties. In the late eighteen hundreds there was a body of Federal legislation in terms addressed to fraud and intimidation at elections for Federal office, but this has been off the books for more than forty years, and was only partly resurrected last year in the Hatch Act. Similarly, the mass of detailed civil rights legislation of the Reconstruction period has been with few exceptions repealed or declared unconstitutional. At present, the only specific statutes applicable in civil liberties situations appear to be: -

Now Sec. 243.

1. 8 U.S.C. § 44 - DISQUALIFICATION OF JURORS.

   This statute makes it a Federal crime for a judge or bailiff, State or Federal, to fail to summon or to exclude otherwise qualified jurors because of race, color or previous condition of servitude. The case sustaining its constitutionality, under the equal protection clause of the Fourteenth Amendment, ex parte Virginia, [1] is a leading case on the proposition, very important for Federal civil liberties jurisdiction, that a State official can be Federally prosecuted for violating rights secured by the Constitution against infringement by the States, even if he acts in violation of State law.

2. 18 U.S.C. § 61(c) (Hatch Act § 4) - INTIMIDATION OF FEDERAL BENEFICIARIES

   This statute makes it a Federal crime to deprive or attempt to deprive a person of Federal relief or work

---

[1] 100 U. S. 339 (1879)

relief benefits. It is a generalized and permanent form of § 30 (b) of the Emergency Relief Act of 1939, which was applied in a group of Minneapolis W.P.A. strike cases, involving violent picketing of a W.P.A. project. The prosecution aroused considerable public controversy, on the question whether the Government was depriving the strikers of the right to picket. Convictions were obtained against a number of persons responsible for extreme violence and the rest of the cases were nolle prossed. The same statute was sought to be applied in Alabama, where a Farm Security Administration supervisor was charged with attempting to force two negro clients to give up the benefits of a farm security loan as a result of a personal dispute with them, but the grand jury refused to return a true bill.

3. 18 U.S.C. § 61 (Hatch Act § 1) -
   INTIMIDATION AT FEDERAL ELECTIONS.

The opening section of the Hatch Act makes it unlawful to intimidate or attempt to intimidate any voter at a Federal election. Its importance has gone largely unnoticed in the political controversy over other sections of the statute. It has yet to be applied, but no particular difficulties are to be anticipated in its use in elections or registration therefor. Its extention to primaries is doubtful, depending to some extent on whether the doctrine of the prevailing opinion in Newberry

v. <u>United States</u>,[2] that a primary is not an election,
is still law.

4. 18 U.S.C. §§ 443, 444 - <u>SLAVERY AND PEONAGE</u>.

The peonage statute is well known and has been the
subject of numerous prosecutions. In consequence, in
recent years the Department has received relatively few
complaints of the common form of peonage, viz., holding
a person to compel him to work out a debt or other obligation. There is, however, a recent development of two
practices worked out in attempted evasion of the peonage
statute, apparently under advice of counsel. In one form,
a contractual relationship is initiated, typically with
ignorant persons, by virtue of a debt, and the debtor is
forced to work, although at wages, on the false representation that the original debt survives and has never
been paid. This should fall within the peonage statute,
notwithstanding the original debt has in fact been paid.
The other variation involves no debt; the laborer is
paid part or all of his wages, but is beaten or subjected
to some other extra-legal compulsion to prevent him from
changing employment. This latter practice appears to be
subject to prosecution under the slavery statute, simply
as a form of involuntary servitude. Several such cases
are now under investigation by the FBI.

2/ 256 U. S. 232 (1921).

5. 18 U.S.C. §§ 53(a), 630, 631 - SEARCHES AND SEIZURES.

The constitutional prohibition against unreasonable searches and seizures is implemented by these statutes, which apply only to action under Federal authority. Section 53(a) penalizes search of a private dwelling without a warrant, except when as an incident to arrest, etc. Search of any other kind of building or property without a warrant is penalized only if the search is malicious and without reasonable cause. Section 631 partially overlaps the second clause of Section 53(a) by penalizing a Federal officer who willfully exceeds his authority in executing a search warrant or uses unnecessary severity in the execution. Section 630 penalizes a person who maliciously and without probable cause procures the issue of a (Federal) search warrant.

6. 18 U.S.C. §§ 241(a), 242 - INTIMIDATION OF FEDERAL WITNESSES.

These statutes cover intimidation of witnesses before Federal courts or Federal investigative and administrative committees and agencies. Section 241(a), applying to committees and agencies, includes obstruction or attempts to obstruct administration of the statutes under which the investigative body acts and should, therefore, cover intimidation of prospective witnesses -- e.g., informers.

No especial discussion need be here made of Federal statutes
which may apply fortuitously in civil liberties situations, such as violence addressed to a Federal officer or occurring on a Federal reserva-
tion. The mail and income tax fraud jurisdiction, similarly, are essentially irrelevant to typical civil liberties situations.

II. General Statutes.

In the absence of other specific statutes, resort must be had to
two very general statutes, Sections ~~51~~ 241 and ~~52~~ 142 of Title 18 of the United
States Code, both Reconstruction laws and clearly intended to apply to
civil liberties. Although there is some overlapping in their application, the chief practical distinction between them is that Section 51
applies to private individuals and public officers alike, while Section
52 is, subject to fairly speculative exceptions, restricted to cases
where public officials are defendants. Since Section ~~51~~ 241 has been the
subject of far more case law than Section 52 and the Section 51 cases
throw light on Section 52, it will be convenient to discuss Section 51
first, as the statute available for prosecution of private persons.

1. Violations by Private Persons.

18 U.S.C. § 51:

"If two or more persons conspire to injure, oppress,
threaten, or intimidate any citizen in the free exercise
or enjoyment of any right or privilege secured to him by
the Constitution or laws of the United States, or because
of his having so exercised the same, or if two or more
persons go in disguise on the highway, or on the premises
of another, with intent to prevent or hinder his free exercise or enjoyment of any right or privilege so secured,
they shall be fined not more than $5,000 and imprisoned
not more than ten years, and shall, moreover, be thereafter ineligible to any office, or place of honor, profit
or trust, created by the Constitution or laws of the
United States."

Three obvious limitations may be noted from the face of the statute: 1. since it is a conspiracy statute, it is not available against offenses committed by a single person; 2. since it refers to rights of citizens, it is not available for aggression against aliens; [3/] 3. since the gravamen of the crime is aggression against one in the exercise of, or because of his having exercised, his Federal rights, the deprivation of rights must be the purpose of the conspiracy, not an incidental consequence. Experience with this statute, however, has demonstrated that the primary limitation on its application to civil liberties cases arises from its requirement that the right invaded be secured by the Federal Constitution or statutes, for such rights figuring in civil liberties cases are few in number.

a. Statutory Rights

The chief utility of Section 51 for enforcement of statutory rights has been as a criminal sanction for an otherwise sanctionless statute, and it is as a similar criminal catch-all that it appears susceptible of application in the civil liberties field. The reported cases dealing with the application of Section 51 to enforce Federal statutory rights are all homestead cases, involving Section 51 prosecution of persons who intimidated homesteaders in order to cause them to leave their homesteads. [4/] The homestead laws, although they provide a machinery for obtaining title to land in the public domain on compliance with statutory conditions, do not contain specific criminal provisions penalizing

---

3/ Baldwin v. Franks, 120 U. S. 678 (1887).

4/ The leading case is United States v. Waddell, 112 U. S. 76 (1884)

27

interference with homesteaders. The theory of these cases is that the homesteader has a Federal statutory right to acquire title on compliance with conditions including the residence requirement, and that running him off the homestead deprives him of this right, and hence falls within Section 51.

This theory appears susceptible of generalization to any case of coercion of a person who has acquired personal rights under a Federal Statute, if the purpose of the coercion is to cause him to renounce his statutory benefits. Recent Federal legislation has made Federal beneficiaries of some classes of people who have in the past been particularly subject to private intimidation through thugs and vigilantes. Industrial labor, for example, which had previously been denied Section 51 protection against lawless interference with its efforts to organize, [5/] now has acquired through the Wagner Act under certain circumstances a Federally-protected right to organize for collective bargaining. Criminal sanctions to punish attacks by private persons or public officials upon the exercise of this right, absent in the Wagner Act, appear to be available in Section 51 because of the invasion of a right "secured . . . by the . . . laws of the United States".

An indictment drawn on this theory has been sustained in the District Court against demurrer, in the (unreported) Harlan County case, and a similar indictment has been returned and is now pending in Georgia. Both cases involve the use of hired thugs against union activity, in the one case beating employees, in the other beating an organizer who was the

5/ United States v. Moore, 129 Fed. 630 (C.C.N.D. Ala. 1904)

accredited bargaining representative of employees. In cases of this sort the necessity of establishing that the victims have been intimidated in exercising rights under the Wagner Act will ordinarily require proof tantamount to that of a Wagner Act proceeding; and it may, therefore, be found helpful in the preparation and trial of such cases to consult local National Labor Relations Board attorneys on such specialized points as the proof of interstate commerce, the effect of chamber of commerce or trade association policies, and the position of labor organizers under the Wagner Act.

A further but less important application of Section 51 is its use as a conspiracy statute in statutory right cases even where there is a specific criminal penalty for the main violation, as in Federal election and relief intimidation cases under the Hatch Act §§ 1, 4(a), discussed above. In aggravated cases of this sort where the two-year imprisonment penalty of the 18 U.S.C. §88, the regular Federal conspiracy statute, is felt insufficient, the ten-year imprisonment provision of Section 51 may be availed of.

b. Constitutional Rights

The use of Section 51 in civil liberties cases turning on invasion of rights secured "by the Constitution . . . of the United States" is limited by the fact that there are comparatively few constitutional rights which run against individuals. The Constitution deals primarily with relationships between governmental authorities and between private people and the authorities, rather than with the relationships of private people to one another. Consequently, although the phrase "rights or privileges secured . . . by the Constitution or laws of the United States" in effect incorporate the Constitution by reference, in the absence of special facts the ordinary outbreak of ruffian, vigilante or Ku Klux Klan activity, whether directed against reds, nazis, negroes, soap-box speakers, Jehovah's Witnesses, Jews or Catholics, is not within Section 51. While such aggressions may constitute, according to the facts in the case, deprivation of freedom of speech, freedom of assembly, freedom of religion, unlawful searches and seizures, or similar invasions of personal rights mentioned in the Constitution or read into it by the courts, these constitutional rights are rights <u>against official action only</u> and do not extend to private action.

The limitation is largely a matter of grammar. This may be illustrated by the three Reconstruction amendments. The <u>Thirteenth</u> Amendment says "Neither slavery nor involuntary servitude . . . shall exist . . .": it is accordingly a general prohibition operative against the States, the Federal Government or any private persons who practices slavery, and it has in fact been held enforceable against private persons by prosecution under Section 51.[6] The Fourteenth Amendment says "No State shall . . ." and accordingly cannot be enforced except against States and their agents.[7] The Fifteenth Amendment prohibits discriminatory abridgment or denial of voting rights "by the United States or by any State" and is accordingly enforceable against both the Federal and State governments

---

[6] <u>Smith</u> v. <u>United States</u>, 157 Fed. 721 (C.C.A. 8th, 1907), cert. den., 208 U.S. 618 (1908); <u>Peonage Cases</u>, 123 Fed. 671 (M.D. Ala. 1903); cf. <u>Hodges</u> v. <u>United States</u>, 203 U.S. 1 (1906).

[7] U. S. v. <u>Harris</u>, 106 U. S. 629 (1882); <u>Civil Rights Cases</u>, 109 U. S. 3 (1883); <u>U. S.</u> v. <u>Wheeler</u>, 254 U. S. 281 (1920).

and their agents, but not against private persons.[8] In consequence,
the "liberal" civil liberties decisions of the Supreme Court which by
reading most of the Federal Bill of Rights into the Fourteenth Amendment
have made it unconstitutional under the due process clause of that Amendment for a State (municipality) to punish without fair trial,[9] to prevent hand-bill distribution,[10] to set up capricious impediments to picketing or holding meetings,[11] or to discriminate on grounds of color,[12] are
of no effect in establishing constitutional rights against individuals.
The Constitution prohibits the States (and the Federal Government) from
doing these things, but it leaves mobs free to do them -- except under
highly special circumstances.

The nature of such special circumstances was indicated in dictum
in United States v. Cruikshank,[13] the earliest and still leading case on
Section 51, and has been established by holdings in succeeding cases.
In the Cruikshank case a group of private individuals prevented negroes[14]

8/ James v. Bowman, 190 U. S. 127 (1903).

9/ Chambers v. Florida, 308 U.S. ___ (1940); Brown v. Mississippi, 297
U.S. 278 (1936); Powell v. Alabama, 287 U.S. 45 (1932); Mooney v.
Holohan, 294 U.S. 103 (1935); Moore v. Dempsey, 261 U.S. 86 (1923).

10/ Lovell v. Griffin, 303 U. S. 444 (1938); Schneider v. State, 308
U.S. 147 (1939).

11/ Carlson v. California, 308 U.S. ___ (1940); Thornhill v. Alabama,
308 U.S. ___ (1940); Hague v. CIO, 307 U.S. 496 (1939).

12/ Norris v. Alabama, 294 U.S. 587 (1935); Nixon v. Herndon, 273 U.S. 536
(1927); State of Missouri ex rel. Gaines v. Canada, 305 U.S. 337 (1938).

13/ 92 U.S. 542 (1875).

14/ The color question was raised in another count, alleging infringement
of the right to vote secured by the Fifteenth Amendment, but this went
off on the pleading point, 92 U.S. at 555-556.

from attending meetings. This was pleaded under Section 51 as a conspiracy to hinder citizens in the free exercise and enjoyment of their "lawful right and privilege to peaceably assemble together with each other and with other citizens of the said United States for a peaceable and lawful purpose.". The Supreme Court held this indictment invalid, on the ground that although the right to assemble is guaranteed by the First Amendment, that guarantee runs only against the Federal Government.[15] The Court pointed out, nevertheless, that had the meeting in question been a meeting "peaceably to assemble for the purpose of petitioning Congress for a redress of grievances, or for anything else connected with the powers or the duties of the national Government", Section 51 would have applied, for the reason that "the very idea of a government, republican in form, implies a right on the part of its citizens to meet peaceably for consultation in respect to public affairs and to petition for a redress of grievances". Thus it is not the fact that freedom of assembly is expressly mentioned in the Constitution but the fact that certain kinds of assembly are treated by the Court as essential to the effective functioning of the Federal Government that makes the right to assemble to discuss Federal affairs - an implied right - a Federal constitutional right which can be protected by Section 51 even against private action.

15/ The Court in the Cruikshank case had no occasion to discuss whether the right of assembly is protected against State action by the Fourteenth Amendment. (It is only within the last few years that the Fourteenth Amendment has been expanded to include the right of assembly.) The Court dismissed general counts drawn on the due process and equal protection clauses of the Fourteenth Amendment with the remark -- which is still sound constitutional law -- that the Amendment "adds nothing to the rights of one citizen as against another".

The dictum of the Cruikshank case has never been tested on its facts; no reported Section 51 case involves an assembly to discuss Federal affairs or to petition the Federal Government. The doctrine of the dictum has, however, become law in numerous other cases involving interference with voting at Federal elections [16] and intimidation of Federal witnesses and informers, [17] on the theory that the fair conduct of a Federal election and the safety of Federal witnesses, although not specifically mentioned in the Constitution, are matters so essential to the effective operation of a Federal Government whose Constitution has provided for Federal elections and Federal courts that the individual citizen has a derivative right to cast his vote and to give unintimidated testimony.

The most recent case on Section 51 is Powe v. United States, [18] where a newspaper editor was blackmailed by operators of gambling establishments because of his publication of news articles and editorials exposing gambling and calling upon State prosecutors to act. The Circuit Court of Appeals for the Fifth Circuit, after a conviction in the trial court, ordered the sustaining of demurrers which the trial court had

---

16/   See subdivision 3, infra, page 27

17/   In re Quarles and Butler, 158 U.S. 532, (1894); Motes v. United States, 178 U. S. 458 (1900); Foss v. United States, 361 Fed. 881 (C.C.A. 9, 1920). On the same principle Section 51 may be used against conspiracies to injure Federal officers and persons in their custody. Logan v. United States, 144 U. S. 263 (1892); United States v. Patrick, 54 Fed. 338 (C. C. M. D. Tenn. 1893).

18/   109 F. (2d) 147 (C. C. A. 5, 1940), cert. den. 308 U.S. ____ (1940).

overruled. In its opinion, which is an excellent summary of the present state of the law in this field, the Court pointed out the irrelevance of the guarantees of the freedom of the press stated in the First Amendment and implied in the Fourteenth, put the case on the basis of rights implied from Federal necessities, and held that there was no Federal right to discuss a local matter, although it conceded in dictum that there would be a Federal right to discuss a Federal election, a Federal law, or the operations or officers of the Federal Government. The Supreme Court denied the Government's petition for certiorari, which petition had suggested that disclosure of local crime was not necessarily a local matter, but might have national interest because of the possibility of revealing violations of Federal laws, e.g., income tax fraud, or suggesting Federal legislation to cover the Federal aspects of the crime.

To sum up the law on prosecution of private persons under Section 51 is may be said: (1) that the only square holdings applying the statute in civil liberties matters are in situations involving slavery, fraud and intimidation at Federal elections, intimidation of Federal informers and witnesses, and one sort of statutory right cases -- homestead cases; (2) that the dicta indicate and the theory of the decisions permits the use of the statute in other statutory right cases, and in those freedom of speech and press and assembly cases where the discussion relates to a Federal, rather than a local, subject.

Further extension to elections of State officers and freedom of speech on public although local issues involves overruling the doctrine of the Powe case. Similarly, extension to voting rights at primaries involves overruling the doctrine of the Newberry case, that there is no

Federal interest in a primary. These entreprises do not appear impossible, but should be attempted only on exceptionally persuasive sets of fact.

2. Violations by Public Officers

18 U.S.C. § 52:

> "Whoever, under color of any law, statute, ordinance, regulation, or custom, willfully subjects, or causes to be subjected, any inhabitant of any State, Territory or District to the deprivation of any rights, privileges, or immunities secured or protected by the Constitution and laws of the United States, or to different punishments, pains, or penalties, on account of such inhabitant being an alien, or by reason of his color, or race, than are prescribed for the punishment of citizens, shall be fined not more than $1,000, or imprisoned not more than one year, or both."

Two of the restrictions noted above in Section 51 are missing in Section 52: Section 52 applies to "inhabitants", a broader class than "citizens", and Section 52 is not a conspiracy statute and hence can be violated by a single person. Since the scope of Section 52 is restricted to defendants who act "under color of any law, statute, ordinance, regulation, or custom", it is at least applicable to public officers, the very class of people characterized by reference to action under color of law, statute, or ordinance, and this has been its application in the two reported cases.[19] It may also have a limited application to private persons, as in circumstances where private individuals impersonate an officer or act pursuant to "custom". These speculative cases, however, raise constitutional questions of the same sort as those discussed above in connection with prosecution of private individuals under Section 51: i.e., Section 52, if it is applicable to private persons at all, can be used

[19] United States v. Buntin, 10 Fed. 730 (S.D. Ohio, 1882); United States v. Stone, 188 Fed. 836 (D. Md. 1911).

against them, like Section 51, only for infringement of distinctively Federal rights.

a. Not Restricted to Negro Cases

Section 52 breaks into two parts: one relates to deprivation of Federal constitutional and statutory rights in general; the other, relating to discriminatory punishments, turns on race, color or alienage and is presumably designed for negro cases. In both of the reported cases under Section 52, involving discrimination against negroes on ballot and educational privileges, no question of "different punishments, pains, or penalties" was involved. The opinions in these cases unnecessarily confuse the two distinct parts of the statute by gratuitous discussion of the race, color and alienage clause. Reference to that clause except in connection with discriminatory punishment reads impossible grammar into the statute. The statute should, therefore, be regarded as available to all comers, not merely to negroes and aliens, and any contrary indications in the language of these opinions (both District Court cases) may be safely disregarded.

b. Possible Restriction to State Officials.

Section 52 is drawn generally, in terms which appear to comprehend any official. Its application in the past has been to State and municipal officials. Its heading in the Code is "Depriving Citizens of Civil Rights under Color of State Laws", but under the doctrine that titles do not affect substance, this may be disregarded.[20] Its original intent cannot

---

[20] Lapina v. Williams, 232 U.S. 78 (1914); Cornell v. Coyne, 192 U.S. 418 (1904); United States v. Oregon & C.R. Co., 164 U.S. 526 (1896); Sutherland, Statutes and Statutory Construction § 210 (1891).

be determined from its legislative history, but in view of its close connection with the Fourteenth Amendment and the standard interpretation of the Fourteenth Amendment as a restriction only on the States, it is by no means certain that the section will be held to apply to Federal officers. Nevertheless, in the absence of any decision on the point, Section 52 may be regarded as applicable alike to Federal, State and local officers. The discussion herein, although in terms of State officers, is in large measure pertinent to situations involving Federal officers.

c. Broad Scope of Rights Protected.

Section 52, in referring to "deprivation of any rights, privileges, or immunities secured or protected by the Constitution and laws of the United States" covers, along with other things, all rights which have been construed to lie within the Fourteenth Amendment. It has been noted above that this Amendment, by judicial construction over the last fifteen years, has been made the chief vehicle for constitutional protection of civil liberties against State action. Each of these notable Fourteenth Amendment cases, whether arising on habeas corpus, reversal of a conviction of crime, injunction to restrain enforcement of a statute, or any other procedure, is a holding that there is a constitutional right, generally under the due process clause but occasionally under the equal protection or privileges and immunities clause, against State action depriving of a fair trial, infringing on the freedom of speech or press, discriminating on grounds of race or religion, etc., as the case may be. The broad scope of those Fourteenth Amendment rights makes Section 52 a powerful weapon against misconduct of State officer.

Of the two other amendments in addition to the Fourteenth which deal with State action and hence afford a springboard for Section 52 prosecutions, only the Fifteenth (negro voting rights) Amendment is likely to have practical importance, for it will cover cases of deprivation of negro voting rights at State or local elections. The Nineteenth (women's suffrage) Amendment is not likely to become important, because of widespread current acquiescence in its policy.

Section 52 appears also available for enforcing against State officials the distinctively Federal rights which Section 51 enforces against conspiracies of individuals. One of the two reported Section 52 prosecutions and several of the unreported cases have involved rights of this sort -- deprivation of negro voting rights at Federal elections. Similarly, for cases under the Thirteenth (slavery) Amendment, which runs both against States and individuals, Section 52 offers a supplementary count, in addition to counts under the peonage statute and Section 51, for sheriffs and magistrates who connive in peonage schemes.

d. Willfullness.

Because of the statutory requirement of willfullness in Section 52, the mere fact that a given statute may be unconstitutional or that a given act of a public official may deprive a defendant of a fair trial does not mean that the official who has enforced the statute or committed the act is subject to prosecution under Section 52.

Several possible classes of cases of official action under Section 52 should be distinguished, as representing varying degrees of statutory "color" and also as involving different sorts of proof of the requisite "willfull" action by the defendant. These are: (1) where the officer's acts are specifically required by statute, such as the grandfather clause statutes, requiring election officers to discriminate against negroes;[21] (2) where the statute sets up a general standard, leaving the officer to fill in legislative details, as in ordinaces prohibiting public meetings without licenses to be issued in the discretion of the police chief; (3) where the statute sets up general duties but leaves executive details as to the enforcing officer, as in the ordinary ordinance setting up a police force to keep the peace and arrest for crimes; (4) where a statute prohibits the officer from committing the act, but it is his office which causes or enables him to commit the act. Under the doctrine of ex parte Virginia,[22] all of these situations involve State action and hence probably involve action "under color of any law . . . .", but they vary considerably as to "willfullness".

The term "willfull" has not been construed in Section 52. Its ordinary construction as importing malice or at least conscious recognition of the consequences of the act should carry over to Section 52;[23] yet the elusiveness of the term throughout criminal law makes it difficult to predict what it may be held to require in this statute. Because of the obvious impropriety of prosecuting an officer merely for his joyful

Has now in Screws

21/ Cf. Guinn v. United States, 238 U. S. 347 (1915).

22/ Supra, note 1.

23/ United States v. Murdock, 290 U.S. 389 (1933); Felton v. United States, 96 U.C. 699 (1878); Potter v. United States, 155 U.S. 438 (1894); Spurr v. United States, 174 U.S. 728 (1899); 1 Bishop Criminal Law (9th ed. 1923) Sec. 428.

acquiescence in the policy of a statute he may be enforcing, any practical construction of "willfull" should include not only the element of "evil intent" but also the element of "without justifiable excuse". If so, Section 52 can normally be invoked in cases of enforcement of unconstitutional statutes only where a statute substantially identical with the statute in question (or the statute itself) has been declared unconstitutional, and it can be invoked for unfair administrative action only where administrative acts substantially identical with the act in question have been declared unconstitutional. Only then does the law enforcement officer know, or as a public official may be find it difficult to convince a jury that he does not know, that the statute or action is unconstitutional, i.e., that his action is not privileged.

e. State Inaction

Sometimes it is the failure of State officers to afford protection to persons which results, in fact, in deprivation of life, liberty, or property, or in denial of the equal protection of the laws. A chief of police, for example, refuses to send his men against a lynching mob or against bands attacking meetings of strikers or reds; a district attorney refuses to prosecute persons who have committed acts of violence upon negroes or labor organizers. Willoughby's text on constitutional law[24] suggests that there is ground for regarding such dereliction in the performance of official duties as State violations of the due process and equal protection clauses. There appears to be no case foreclosing this interpretation. It is on this theory that various anti-lynching bills have

---

24/ 3 Willoughby, The Constitutional Law of the United States (2d ed. 1929) pp. 1834-1835.

been proposed in Congress. If the theory of these bills is constitutionally sound, prosecution of the officers for "willfull" failure, under Section 52, is likewise sound without such legislation. Nevertheless, since such prosecution may arouse antagonism on States' rights grounds, for jury reasons and perhaps also as a matter of constitutional law it should not be resorted to except in cases of flagrant and persistent breakdown of local law enforcement either in general or with respect to a particular type of cases.

The due process approach in such cases turns on the position that the State officer has willfully caused punishment without proper accusation and trial. The equal protection approach turns on the position that the officer, while providing the protection of the police or courts to some persons, has willfully withheld the same protection from others. Although there are too few decisions on the whole question of State inaction to permit a confident prediction of the success of either approach, such authority as exists points in the direction of Federal jurisdiction. In a proper case Federal prosecutors ought not to hesitate to raise the contention that State officers who persistently shut their eyes to certain kinds of mob violence, such as that inflicted upon negroes, labor organizers, or radicals, deprive those persons of rights secured by the Fourteenth Amendment.

f. Cooperation between Official and Private Person.

Another avenue of Federal criminal sanction against private violation of civil liberties is by way of the concept of official action, through involvement of the official as a co-conspirator. The doctrine

that all members of a conspiracy are principals to the separate crime of
conspiracy leads to the rule that conspiracy counts are good against
persons who did not and could not have committed the crime in chief.[25]
Hence if an official cooperates with a private person in deprivation of
civil liberties protected by an appropriate official-action guaranty of
the Constitution, both official and private person should fall under Section 51, notwithstanding, as indicated above, Section 51 would be inapplicable to private citizens alone. Even should Section 51 be inapplicable, as in a case where the victim is not a citizen, if the official
is responsible under Section 52 the private person becomes responsible
under Section 88 as a conspirator, or under Section 550 for aiding and
abetting.

Some lynching cases seem susceptible of this treatment. The
standard situation where the mob takes its victim from the custody of the
State officer, by overpowering the officer, has been held beyond the scope
of Section 51 as not involving State violation of the right of fair trial.[26]
trial. The attempt to bring in State action here through the sophisti-
cated theory that the lynching has prevented the State from fulfilling its
obligations under the Fourteenth Amendment has also failed.[27] But these
were cases where there was no showing of default of duty by the State

25/ United States v. Rabinowich, 238 U.S. 780 (1915); Israel v.
United States, 3 F. (2d) 743 (C. C. A. 6, 1925); United States v.
Inman, 190 Fed. 414 (D. Oregon, 1911).

26/ United States v. Powell, 212 U. S. 564 (1909), aff'g (C.C. N.D. Ala.
1907) 151 Fed. 648.

27/ United States v. Harris, supra note 7.

'official and are no authority against a holding that "willfull" cooperation by an official would subject him to responsibility under Section 51 or
Section 52, and would permit prosecution of the mob under Sections 51, 88,
or 550. Should the jailer by prearrangement turn over the keys to the
lynchers or should the constable agree to be conveniently absent at the
time when a meeting is to be broken up or the hooded knights are to ride,
the official's failure to protect amounts to discriminatory action in
unleashing unlawful force as a direct consequence of his unique position
as an official, and both he and the private parties appear subject to
Federal prosecution.

This reasoning has been applied in a case now pending on demurrer
in New Orleans, arising out of the 1940 primary. There a commercial pho+o-
tographer hired by the anti-administration faction arrived at a polling
place to take pictures of alleged voting irregularities; a city policeman, after warning the photographer against taking pictures, held him
and prevented him from adequately defending himself while he was set
upon and beaten by administration supporters. Although there was no
Federal jurisdiction over the primary as such, the policeman was indicted
under Section 52 for depriving the photographer of his right, under the
Fourteenth Amendment, to engage in a lawful occupation, and the private
citizens were indicted under Section 550 as aiders and abettors.   Cowan.

5.   Application of Sections 51 and 52 to Elections

Election cases, which constitute a large segment of the Section 51
litigation, involve many of the problems which arise in the enforcement
of Sections 51 and 52. They are treated separately herein, although at

the risk of repetition of a portion of the general discussion above, as illustrated of the variety of approaches to Federal criminal jurisdiction over a civil liberties situation, depending on slight changes in the facts. A similar analysis could readily be made for labor cases, free speech cases, or any other class of civil liberties cases, although there are fewer decisions in these fields.

It was in an early election case sustaining the conviction of Klansmen for conspiring to intimidate negroes from voting for a member of Congress, ex parte Yarbrough, [28] that the Supreme Court first found an opportunity to apply the Federal necessities doctrine suggested in the Cruikshank case. Despite the constitutional power of the States to prescribe the qualifications for voters, the right to vote at elections for Federal officers was regarded as one "essential to the healthy organization of the Federal Government itself", and, therefore, a "right conferred by the Constitution of the United States". Curiously, notwithstanding the parallel reasoning the Yarbrough case does not cite the Cruikshank case.

After repeal in 1894 of the extensive regulations for the conduct of Federal elections which had been enacted during the Reconstruction era, the argument was repeatedly advanced that Section 51 no longer applied to election offenses since Congress by the repeal had demonstrated its intention to return the conduct of elections to the exclusive control of the States. In United States v. Mosley [29] this argument failed and the broad language of Section 51 was held to embrace a conspiracy wherein

---

28/ 110 U. S. 651 (1884).

29/ 238 U. S. 383 (1915).

election officers failed to count some of the votes cast for a congressional candidate. A few years later, however, in the Bathgate case,[30]
holding that Section 51 could not be used to punish bribery of voters,
the Supreme Court appeared to attach more weight to the argument, but
avoided a square decision on it.[31] Instead the Court developed a new
line of doctrine, emphasizing the personal nature of the right protected
by Section 51. A direct conflict with the Yarbrough and Mosley cases was
avoided by holding that the rights to vote and to have the vote counted,
but not the right to an honest election, were the kind of "definite,
personal right" required by Section 51. Thus, since the Bathgate case,
the Federal Government is empowered by Section 51 to prosecute conspirators who prevent a qualified voter from casting his ballot at an election
for Federal officers or who tamper with the ballot boxes in such a manner
as to prevent the vote from being accurately recorded; but, in the absence of new legislation, the Federal Government is powerless to deal
with bribery of voters, voting by persons not properly qualified, and
any other corrupt practice which the Court may choose not to label a
violation of a "definite, personal right." The harm to the "healthy
organization of the government" is, of course, no less serious in the
latter situations than in the former.

Although in the Mosley case the Supreme Court had taken a broad
view of the scope of Section 51, declaring " . . . we cannot allow the

---

30/ United States v. Bathgate, 246 U.S. 220 (1918).

31/ The argument has less validity today, since the passage of
the Hatch Act.

past so far to affect the present as to deprive citizens of the United States of the general protection which on its face § 19 most reasonably affords", in the Gradwell case,[32] decided a year before Bathgate, the Court was already beginning to restrict the section in its application to voting matters. The defendants were indicted for conspiring to injure certain candidates for the Republican nomination for United States Senator by inducing illegal voting at a State primary. The Court refused to extend Section 51, characterized as "originally enacted for the protection of the civil rights of the then lately enfranchised negro", to the rights of candidates at a State nominating primary. Despite a general intimation in the opinion that Section 51 does not apply to offenses committed in the conduct of primary elections, the language and the holding of the case relate only to the rights of candidates. The Gradwell case thus leaves still undecided the availability of Section 51 to protect the rights of qualified voters at primary elections.

In the Gradwell case the Court deliberately avoided taking a position on the question of the power of Congress to regulate primary elections, but later in the Newberry case,[33] which arose not under Section 51 but under the Corrupt Practices Act of 1910, as amended in 1911, four members of the Court held that the Constitution conferred no such power. A fifth member joined them in holding the Act unconstitutional as applied to a senatorial candidate in a primary election, but reserved the question of the power of Congress to enact such legislation after the adoption

32/ United States v. Gradwell, 243 U.S. 476 (1917).

33/ Supra note 2.

of the Seventeenth Amendment. In the prevailing four-judge opinion,

the Gradwell case was cited with deference, in a passage which apparently

stands for the proposition that the sole source of congressional authority

over elections is the specific election clauses of Article I. The

Yarbrough and Mosley cases were cited, discussed, and held inapplicable

as overridden by the proposition that a primary is not an election. Four

members of the Court, concurring in the decision on procedural grounds

only, argued that Congress derived power to control the conduct of nomina-

ting primaries not merely from Section 4 of Article I but also from the

"necessary and proper" clause in Section 8 of Article I. The fact that

Mr. Justice Holmes, the writer of the Mosley decision, joined in the

prevailing Newberry opinion indicates the extent of the reaction in the

Court. The vote of the Court is so confused, however, that it offers

little guidance in predicting whether Section 51 is applicable to prima-

ries. Details of theory aside, it is at least clear that a majority of

the Court anticipated the unrealistic treatment of a primary as the

private function of a political party, rather than as an integral part

of the electoral process, which has been more recently manifested on an

entirely different legal problem in the third Texas primary case, Grovey

v. Townsend. 34/   In consequence it is possible, although by no means certain,

that the present Court would hold Section 51 inapplicable to private

interference with primaries on the ground that a primary is not an elec-

tion and hence not within the rule of the Yarbrough and Mosley cases.

Any application of Section 51 or Section 52 in a primary situation should,

---

34/   295 U. S. 45 (1935).

therefore, be regarded as a test case.

Where only State offices are in contest, the rule of the Yarbrough and Mosley cases does not apply, and in general neither the vote nor the count is within the protection of the Federal Government. Theoretically a Federally-protected right to vote at State and local elections might be derived from the constitutional guaranty to the States of a republican form of government, but this could be accomplished only by reversing a decision, contemporary with Cruikshank, which excluded Federal jurisdiction over State elections. [35] In a more recent Circuit Court of Appeals case a conviction under Section 51 was set aside because of the prosecution's failure to prove that the voters who were intimidated intended to cast their ballot for Federal officers and not merely for State officers. [36] Similarly, where ballots at a general election for both State and Federal officers were tampered with, the conviction of candidates for the State legislature who were responsible was set aside in the Circuit Court of Appeals because their intention was to falsify the vote for State offices only. [37] In the recent Kansas City election cases, [38] although indictments for conspiracy to make fraudulent returns of the vote for members of Congress were sustained, the Circuit Court of Appeals for the Eighth Circuit held invalid the counts based upon interference with the right

---

35/ United States v. Reese, 92 U. S. 214 (1875).

36/ United States v. Kantor, 7 F. (2d) 710 (C.C.A. 2, 1935).

37/ Steedle v. United States, 85 F. (2d) 867 (C.C.A. 3, 1936).

38/ Walker v. United States, 93 F. (2d) 355 (C.C.A. 8, 1938).

to vote for Presidential electors on the ground that such electors are wholly creatures of the State. Earlier cases do not recognize this distinction, which stems from the same kind of unrealistic thinking responsible for the Gradwell and Newberry decisions.

The rights of voters just discussed are those enforceable against private as well as official infringement, i.e., primarily subjects of prosecution under Section 51. The prohibitions on discrimination in suffrage based upon race, color or sex contained in the Fifteenth and Nineteenth Amendments, on the other hand, secure rights enforceable only against the State and Federal governments, i.e., primarily subjects of prosecution under Section 52. These latter, however, are enforceable not only at Federal elections, but also at State and local elections and, unless the doctrine of the Newberry case be extended, at primaries as well.

In Nixon v. Herndon, 39/ the first Texas primary case, the Supreme Court chose to rely upon the equal protection clause of the Fourteenth Amendment rather than upon the Fifteenth Amendment to protect the right of a negro to be free from State discrimination in voting at a primary election. The Herndon case, as well as Nixon v. Condon, 40/ which followed it, demonstrate the occasional availability of the Fourteenth Amendment for the protection of voting privileges at State-sponsored primaries and a fortiori at State elections. The subsequent refusal of the Supreme Court in Grovey v. Townsend to recognize a violation of the equal protection clause where the exclusion of negroes from the primaries rested upon

---

39/ Supra note 12.

40/ 286 U. S. 76 (1932).

the private regulations of a political party, rather than upon State legislation, suggests the pitfalls which surround Federal jurisdiction over primary elections.

Aside from problems of discrimination, there are other interesting possibilities in the application of the Fourteenth Amendment to the conduct of State elections and primaries. The implication of State officers affords a basis for Federal jurisdiction over such matters as intimidation of voters by policemen or election officers and official suppression of efforts (such as taking pictures of polling places) to guard the honesty of elections by lawful means. Unless the public officials can justify the restrictions which they place upon the freedom of the citizenry, their actions may constitute an infringement of rights secured by the due process clause of the Fourteenth Amendment and, if willfull, afford grounds for prosecution under Section 52. The private parties who act in collusion with the officers, such as machine politicians and strong-arm squads can be prosecuted as aiders and abettors under Section 550 or as conspirators under Section 51 or Section 88.

Although it has been assumed herein that Section 51 is appropriate legislation for the enforcement not merely of rights secured against private infringement, but also of rights secured only against violation by public officers, one Circuit Court of Appeals has held in Karen v. United States [41/] that the statute, being directed at the acts of individuals, is broader than the powers of Congress under the Fifteenth Amendment and cannot be used to enforce rights derived from that Amendment. The --

---

41/ 121 Fed. 250 (C.C.A. 6, 1903)

reasoning of the Court equally applies, of course, to rights secured by the Fourteenth and Nineteenth Amendments and the Bill of Rights. We question the soundness of the Karem decision, which runs counter to the reasoning of the Supreme Court in Guinn v. United States.[42] The fact that the election involved in the Guinn case embraced Federal offices, as well as State offices, appears to have borne no weight in the decision, the conviction under Section 51 of State election officers who discriminated against negroes being sustained as a violation of rights secured by the Fifteenth Amendment. In any event, if Section 51 is not available for enforcement of rights secured only against infraction by public officials, the combination of Sections 52 and 88 will accomplish approximately the same result.

[42] Supra note 21.

DEPARTMENT OF JUSTICE
WASHINGTON, D. C.

August 8, 1940.

CIRCULAR NO. 3404

Circular No. 3354, issued April 6, 1940, called attention to the fact that Section 9 of the Hatch Act (Public No. 252, 76th Congress, approved August 2, 1939), which prohibits officers and employees (with a few exceptions) in the executive branch of the Government from taking active part in political management or in political campaigns, is enforceable administratively by the agencies with which such officers or employees are connected, and not by the Department of Justice or through the courts.

Section 12(a) of the Hatch Act, as amended by the Act of July 19, 1940 (Public No. 753, 76th Congress), applies similar restrictions to the political activities of officers and employees of state or local agencies in cases in which the principal employment is in connection with any activity financed in whole or in part by loans or grants made by the United States or by a Federal agency.

Section 15 of the Hatch Act, as amended, incorporates by reference thereto the determinations of the United States Civil Service Commission as to what constitutes prohibited political activity. For

the convenience of interested officers and employees, and as
generally indicative of the applicable determinations made by the
Commission, reference is made to Civil Service Commission Circular
Form 1236, entitled "Political Activity and Political Assessments
of Federal Officeholders and Employees", which is available at the
United States Government Printing Office, Washington, D. C., at five
cents per copy. It is understood that the Civil Service Commission
plans to prepare a new edition of Circular Form 1236 which will include such changes as are necessary to bring this document up to date
in relation to current legislation.

In relation to the administration of the Hatch Act, as amended,
the Department of Justice has no administrative functions except insofar as the statute relates to its own personnel.

For a brief period following enactment of the original Hatch
Act, it was the practice of the Department of Justice to answer
general queries with respect to its meaning and interpretation in
particular situations. This practice was discontinued, however, and
no further rulings are being issued by this Department except upon
the request of the President or the heads of the several executive
departments, in accordance with Sections 303 and 304 of Title 5 of
the United States Code, which read as follows:

"303. <u>Opinions and advice of Attorney General;
to President.</u> The Attorney General shall give
his advice and opinion upon questions of law,
whenever required by the President."

"304. <u>Same; to heads of executive departments.</u>
The head of any executive department may require
the opinion of the Attorney General on any question of law arising in the administration of his
department."

Certain provisions of the Hatch Act apply generally and
add many new enactments to the Criminal Code of Laws of the United
States. There are many provisions of the Act, the violations of
which constitute criminal offenses and such violations have been
and will accordingly be handled by the Department of Justice.

These criminal offenses are as follows:

"Sec. 1. It shall be unlawful for any person
to intimidate, threaten, or coerce, or to
attempt to intimidate, threaten, or coerce,
any other person for the purpose of interfering
with the right of such other person to vote or
to vote as he may choose, or of causing such
other person to vote for, or not to vote for,
any candidate for the office of President,
Vice President, Presidential elector, Member
of the Senate, or Member of the House of Representatives at any election held solely or in
part for the purpose of selecting a President,
a Vice President, a Presidential elector, or any
Member of the Senate or any Member of the House
of Representatives, Delegates or Commissioners
from the Territories and insular possessions."

"Sec. 2. It shall be unlawful for (1) any person employed in any administrative position by

the United States, or by any department, independent agency, or other agency of the United
States (including any corporation controlled by
the United States or any agency thereof, and
any corporation all of the capital stock of which
is owned by the United States or any agency thereof), or (2) any person employed in any administrative position by any State, by any political subdivision or municipality of any State, or by any
agency of any State c any of its political sub-
divisions or municipalities (including any corporation controlled by any State or by any such political
subdivision, municipality, or agency, and any corporation all of the capital stock of which is owned
by any State or by any such political subdivision,
municipality, or agency), in connection with any
activity which is financed in whole or in part by
loans or grants made by the United States, or by any
such department, independent agency, or other agency
of the United States, to use his official authority
for the purpose of interfering with, or affecting,
the election or the nomination of any candidate for
the office of President, Vice President, Presidential
elector, Member of the Senate, Member of the House
of Representatives, or Delegate or Resident Commissioner from any Territory or insular possession."

"Sec. 3. It shall be unlawful for any person,
directly or indirectly, to promise any employment,
position, work, compensation, or other benefit,
provided for or made possible in whole or in part
by any Act of Congress, to any person as consideration,
favor, or reward for any political activity or for
the support of or opposition to any candidate or any
political party in any election."

55

"Sec. 4. Except as may be required by the provisions of
subsection (b), section 9 of this Act, it shall be unlawful
for any person to deprive, attempt to deprive, or threaten
to deprive, by any means, any person of any employment, position,
work, compensation, or other benefit provided for or made possible
by any Act of Congress appropriating funds for work relief or relief purposes, on account of race, creed, color, or any political
activity, support of, or opposition to any candidate or any political party in any election."

"Sec. 5. It shall be unlawful for any person to solicit or receive or be in any manner concerned in soliciting or receiving
any assessment, subscription, or contribution for any political
purpose whatever from any person known by him to be entitled to
or receiving compensation, employment, or other benefit provided
for or made possible by any Act of Congress appropriating funds
for work relief or relief purposes."

"Sec. 6. It shall be unlawful for any person for political
purposes to furnish or to disclose, or to aid or assist in
furnishing or disclosing, any list or names of persons receiving
compensation, employment, or benefits provided for or made possible by any Act of Congress appropriating, or authorizing the
appropriation of, funds for work relief or relief purposes, to
a political candidate, committee, campaign manager, or to any
person for delivery to a political candidate, committee, or campaign manager, and it shall be unlawful for any person to receive any such list or names for political purposes."

"Sec. 7. No part of any appropriation made by any Act, heretofore or hereafter enacted, making appropriations for work relief,
relief, or otherwise to increase employment by providing loans and
grants for public-works projects, shall be used for the purpose of, and
no authority conferred by any such Act upon any person shall be
exercised or administered for the purpose of, interfering with,
restraining, or coercing any individual in the exercise of his
right to vote at any election."

Any person who is convicted of violating
any of the above provisions of Sections 1, 2, 3,
4, 5, 6, or 7, is subject to a fine of not more
than $1,000 or imprisonment for not more than
one year, or both.

"Sec. 13. (a) It is hereby declared to be a pernicious political activity and it shall hereafter be unlawful, for any person, directly or indirectly, to make contributions in an aggregate amount in excess of $5,000, during any calendar year, or in connection with any campaign for nomination or election, to or on behalf of any candidate for an elective Federal office (including the offices of President of the United States and Presidential and Vice Presidential electors), or to or on behalf of any committee or other organization engaged in furthering, advancing, or advocating the nomination or election of any candidate for any such office or the success of any national political party. This subsection shall not apply to contributions made to or by a State or local committee or other State or local organization.

"(b) For the purposes of this section--

"(1) The term 'person' includes an individual, partnership, committee, association, corporation, and any other organization or group of persons.

"(2) The term 'contribution' includes a gift, subscription, loan, advance, or deposit of money, or anything of value, and includes a contract, promise, or agreement, whether or not legally enforceable, to make a contribution.

"(c) It is further declared to be a pernicious political activity, and it shall hereafter be unlawful for any person, individual, partnership, committee, association, corporation, and any other organization or group of persons to purchase or buy any goods, commodities, advertising, or articles of any kind or description where the proceeds of such a purchase, or any portion thereof, shall directly or indirectly inure to the benefit of or for any candidate for an elective Federal office (including the offices of President of the United States, and Presidential and Vice Presidential electors) or any political committee or other political organization engaged in furthering, advancing, or advocating the nomination or election of any candidate for any such office or the success of any national political party: Provided, That nothing in this sentence shall be construed to interfere with the usual and known business, trade, or profession of any candidate.

"(d) Any person who engages in a pernicious political activity in violation of any provision of this section, shall upon conviction thereof be fined not more than $5,000 or imprisoned for not more than five years. In all cases of violations of this section by a partnership, committee, association, corporation, or other organization or group of persons, the officers, directors, or managing heads thereof who knowingly and willfully participate in such violation, shall be subject to punishment as herein provided.

"(e) Nothing in this section shall be construed to permit the making of any contribution which is prohibited by any provision of law in force on the date this section takes effect. Nothing in this Act shall be construed to alter or amend any provisions of the Federal Corrupt Practices Act of 1925, or any amendments thereto."

"Sec. 20. No political committee shall receive contributions aggregating more than $3,000,000, or make expenditures aggregating more than $3,000,000 during any calendar year. For the purposes of this section, any contributions received and any expenditures made on behalf of any political committee with the knowledge and consent of the chairman or treasurer of such ommittee shall be deemed to be received or made by such committee. Any violation of this section by any political committee shall be deemed also to be a violation of this section by the chairman and the treasurer of such committee and by any other person responsible for such violation. Terms used in this section shall have the meaning assigned to them in section 302 of the Federal Corrupt Practices Act, 1925, and the penalties provided in such Act shall apply to violations of this section."

Applicable penalties as set forth in Section 252 of Title 2 of the United States Code subject any person who violates the provisions of Section 20 to a fine of not more than $1,000, or imprisonment for not more than one year, or both. Any person who willfully violates any of the provisions of Section 20 shall be fined not more than $10,000 and imprisoned not more than two years.

"Sec. 5. (Act of July 19, 1940) (a) No person or firm entering into any contract with the United States or any department or agency thereof, either for the rendition of personal services or furnishing any material, supplies, or equipment to the United States or any department or agency thereof, or selling any land or building to the United States or any department or agency thereof, if payment for the performance of such contract or payment for such material, supplies, equipment, land, or building is to be made in whole or in part from funds appropriated by the Congress, shall, during the period of negotiation for, or performance under such contract or furnishing of material, supplies, equipment, land, or buildings, directly, or indirectly, make any contribution of money or any other thing of value, or promise expressly or impliedly to make any such contribution, to any political party, committee, or candidate for public office or to any person for any political purpose or use; nor shall any person knowingly solicit any such contribution from any such person or firm, for any such purpose during any such period. Any person who violates the provisions of this section shall, upon conviction thereof, be fined not more than $5,000 or imprisoned not more than five years.

"(b) Nothing in this section shall be construed to permit any action which is prohibited by any provision of law in force on the date this section takes effect."

ROBERT H. JACKSON,
Attorney General.

59

CIRCULAR NO. 3416

TO ALL UNITED STATES ATTORNEYS

On August 8, 1940 you received Circular No. 3404, which set forth the additions to the Criminal Code of the United States as contained in the Hatch Act, as amended (Public No. 252, 76th Congress, approved August 2, 1939) as amended (Public No. 753, 76th Congress, approved July 19, 1939).

Because of the newness of this legislation and the necessity of correct and uniform interpretation of its provisions before porsecutive action is taken, you are hereby instructed to clear through the Department all future complaints of violations of the terms of the Hatch Act, as amended, both in relation to the criminal sections and in relation to violations of Sections 9 and 12. The same instructions apply to complaints of violations of the terms of Sections 29 to 31, inclusive, of the Emergency Relief Appropriation Act of 1939 (Public No. 24, 76th Congress); Sections 28 to 30, inclusive, of the Emergency Relief Appropriation Act, fiscal year 1941 (Public No. 88, 76th Congress); The Federal Corrupt Practices Act, Sections 241 and 256, inclusive, Title 2, United States Code; and to Sections 208 and 213, inclusive, Title 18, United States Code.

Especial care should be taken not to render rulings, interpretations or opinions with respect to the meaning and interpretation of above designated statutes.

ROBERT H. JACKSON,

Attorney General.

OFFICE OF THE ATTORNEY GENERAL

WASHINGTON, D. C.

December 12, 1941

CIRCULAR NO. 3591

TO ALL UNITED STATES ATTORNEYS:

Re: Involuntary Servitude,
Slavery, and Peonage

A survey of the Department files on alleged peonage violations discloses numerous instances of "prosecution declined" by United States Attorneys, the chief reason stated as being the absence of the element of debt. It is apparent that these determinations were reached after considering the facts at hand only in accordance with the case law under Section 444, Title 18, U.S. Code, which holds that debt is the "basal element of peonage." It is further disclosed that only in a negligible number of instances was consideration given these complaints in the light of:

(a) Section 443, Title 18, U.S. Code, which punishes for causing persons to be held in involuntary servitude, regardless of the existence of a debt.

(b) Section 51, Title 18, U.S. Code, which punishes for conspiracy to deprive citizens of rights secured to them by the Constitution, particularly the right to be free from slavery and involuntary servitude.

(c) Section 52 Title 18, U.S. Code, which punishes persons vested with official authority who aid or cause others to suffer deprivation of rights secured to them by the Constitution, particularly the right to be free from slavery and compulsory servitude.

(d) Section 88, Title 18, U.S. Code, the general conspiracy statute, which may be employed in combination with Section 443 or Section 52.

It is the purpose of these instructions to direct the attention of the United States Attorneys to the possibilities of successful prosecutions stemming from alleged peonage complaints which have heretofore been considered inadequate to invoke federal jurisdiction. It is requested that the spelling out of peonage under Section 444 be deferred in favor of building the cases around the issue of involuntary servitude and slavery under Sections 443, 51 and 52, disregarding entirely the element of debt. If, however, it is found that a claimed debt is the basis of the intimidation to compel one to the service of another, a separate count under Section 444 should be included in the

61

indictment. Evidence of such debt, of course, may likewise be employed as an additional circumstance to prove intimidation under the counts based on Sections 443, 51, and 52. In any event the Government should henceforth emphasize and depend upon the issue of involuntary servitude and slavery in lieu of peonage (debt plus involuntary service) in prosecuting this type of case.

The United States Attorneys are instructed, therefore, to consider such complaints in accordance with the following statutes and authorize prosecutions where any one or more of the following conditions exist, regardless of the existence of debt real or claimed:

(a) Section 443, Title 18, U.S. Code

carrying or enticing of any person from one place to another in order that he may be held in slavery or involuntary servitude;

causing another by force, fraud or intimidation to enter and remain in another's employment;

causing one to be held by threats, as well as held by force, and whether such threats are of prosecution, arrest or imprisonment or by threats of bodily harm;

holding another by threats of prosecution, even under a valid law; the validity of the law not justifying its use for the criminal purpose of causing compulsory service by intimidation;

deliberately causing one who has deserted his employment to be arrested with the intent of producing on the mind of the servant or employee a condition which leaves him no choice but to return to his employment or suffer prosecution and incarceration;

where one does not stay in his employment of his own free will but only in accordance with the will of his master or employer, involuntary service exists. -- "service" does not necessarily mean labor, i.e., a man may be in that state if he is held to be made to work but escapes before he has begun such work;

by falsely accusing another of crime and carrying him before a magistrate in order that he may be convicted and put to hard labor, in consequence of which such person is convicted and put to hard labor, the false accuser at the time having the purpose or design to hire such person or to enable some other person to hire him.

(b) Section 51, Title 18, U.S. Code

If two or more persons conspire or combine to do any of the acts outlined above, they are guilty of a conspiracy to deprive the person, if he is a citizen of the United States, of the free exercise or enjoyment of the right and privilege secured to him by the Constitution of the United States to be free from involuntary servitude, and are indictable accordingly.

(c) Section 52, Title 18, U.S. Code

This section is applicable to public officers, judges, sheriffs, local constabulary, etc., who act under color and in the name of their authority in perpetrating any of the acts listed above in violation of a person's rights to be free from involuntary servitude and slavery as secured to him by the Thirteenth Amendment to the Constitution.

For a discussion of the applicability of this Section to colorably official action, see Circular No. 3356, Supp. 1.

In the matter of control by one over the person of another, the circumstances under which each person is placed must be determined, i.e., the subservience of the will of one to the other. Open force, threats or intimidation need not be used to cause a person to go involuntarily from one place to another to work and to remain at such work; nor does evidence of kind treatment show an absence of involuntary servitude.

In the United States one cannot sell himself as a peon or slave -- the law is fixed and established to protect the weak-minded, the poor, the miserable. Men will sometimes sell themselves for a meal of victuals or contract with another who acts as surety on his bond to work out the amount of the bond upon his release from jail. Any such sale or contract is positively null and void and the procuring and causing of such contract to be made violates these statutes.

It is not necessary that the defendants be themselves charged with holding a person in a condition of compulsory servitude, a showing of aiding in holding or returning one to that condition is sufficient.

Procedure

1. The United States Attorneys should contact local law enforcement officials by letter, circular, conference, or any other means found effective for seeking state wide cooperation, and advise them that the practices outlined above will be prosecuted by the Federal Government.

2. In those states where legislatures have enacted criminal statutes to enforce labor contracts, United States Attorneys from the various districts therein should promptly notify the local magistrates, sheriffs, and other law enforcement officers, that such laws are repugnant to the provisions of the Thirteenth Amendment to the Constitution of the United States and that action to enforce such statutes may subject the local officials to federal prosecution.

Experience has shown that where United States Attorneys have pointed out to state and local officials that certain state statutes and local ordinances affecting the rights of persons conflicted with the provisions of the federal Constitution, the local authorities have readily ceased their active enforcement and in many instances have thereupon sought the outright repeal of the statutes or ordinances.

3. In the interest of consistency and uniformity in the method of investigation, the Federal Bureau of Investigation has been requested to direct all original complaints in this field to the Civil Rights Section of the Criminal Division of the Department for clearance and instruction before embarking upon a formal investigation. No investigation or prosecution of these cases should be commenced through the offices of the various United States Attorneys without Departmental sanction. Because of the importance of unified and consistent prosecution policy in these cases, it is further requested that no indictments under these statutes be sought without obtaining authority from the Department.

4. To assure emphasis upon the issue of involuntary servitude and slavery in considering these cases on the one hand and to minimize the necessity of relying upon the element of debt to fix jurisdiction on the other, the Federal Bureau of Investigation has been requested to change the title on its reports from "Peonage" to read "Involuntary Servitude and Slavery." Henceforth, Peonage will be considered as secondary to involuntary servitude and slavery investigations.

FRANCIS BIDDLE
Attorney General

DEPARTMENT OF JUSTICE
Washington, D. C.

April 4, 1942

CIRCULAR NO. 3356

Supplement No. 2

TO ALL UNITED STATES ATTORNEYS:

Much has been said concerning the status of civil rights during the present war. This Department will oppose any curtailment of those rights beyond that absolutely necessary to the efficient conduct of the military and economic war effort of the United States. Indeed, a further disregard for civil rights can only be viewed as distinctly injurious to national moral and subversive of the democratic ideals which this nation is seeking to defend.

To emphasize the Department's firm purpose to prevent a breakdown of those rights, this revision of the Civil Rights Circular with respect to Sections 51 and 52 of Title 18, United States Code, has been prepared by the Civil Rights Section of the Criminal Division. It embraces the recent law developed under Sections 51 and 52, as well as the general discussions found in the first supplement of the circular bearing this number.

Among the elements of liberty frequently infringed in war time without justification are freedom of speech and press. The words of the late Justice Holmes in Schenk v. United States, 249 U. S. 47, 52 (1919), are here repeated, both as a guide and limitation for judging the appropriateness of attempted control:

> "The most stringent protection of free speech
> would not protect a man in falsely shouting fire in
> a theatre and causing a panic. It does not even

(OVER)

64

protect a man from an injunction against uttering
words that may have all the effect of force. Gom-
pers v. Bucks Stove & Range Co., 221 U. S. 418,
439. The question in every case is whether the
words used are used in such circumstances and are
of such a nature as to create a clear and present
danger that they will bring about the substantive
evils that Congress has a right to prevent. It is
a question of proximity and degree. When a nation
is at war many things that might be said in time
of peace are such a hindrance to its effort that
their utterance will not be endured so long as men
fight and that no Court could regard them as protected by any constitutional right."

The existence of war must not be permitted to serve as an

excuse for the oppression of any racial, religious, economic, or po-

litical group. You are directed to employ every facility available

to your offices to secure the cooperation of state and local officials

to prevent and rectify situations constituting a threat to the Federally

secured civil rights herein discussed. In the interest of consistency

and uniformity in the conduct of investigations, the policy of direct-

ing all original complaints to the Civil Rights Section of the Criminal

Division for clearance and instruction before embarking on a full in-

vestigation will be continued. No investigation or prosecution of these

cases should be commenced through the offices of the United States At-

torneys without Departmental sanction and because of the importance of

maintaining consistent legal theory in these cases, it is requested

that proposed indictments be submitted to the Department for considera-

tion before undertaking prosecutive action.

Two very general statutes, Sections 51 and 52, Title 18,

United States Code, originating in the Enforcement Act of 1870, are applicable to punish infringements of rights secured to citizens and inhabitants of the United States by the Federal Constitution and laws. Those Federally secured rights are the civil rights referred to here-after.

I

Title 18, United States Code, Section 51

This statute in terms reaches conspiracies of either private individuals or public officials, and the following discussion is chiefly concerned with the problem of indicating what rights secured by the Constitution and laws of the United States are so secured as against invasion by conspiracies of private individuals. Considerable case law has been developed around Section 51, much of that law is applicable also to the companion statute, Section 52, which in terms applies to public officials.

Section 51 reads as follows:

> "If two or more persons conspire to injure, oppress, threaten, or intimidate any citizen in the free exercise or enjoyment of any right or privilege secured to him by the Constitution or laws of the United States, or because of his having so exercised the same, or if two or more persons go in disguise on the highway, or on the premises of another, with intent to prevent or hinder his free exercise or enjoyment of any right or privilege so secured, they shall be fined not more than $5,000 and imprisoned not more than ten years, and shall, moreover, be thereafter ineligible to any office, or place of honor, profit or trust, created by the Constitution or laws of the United States."

Three obvious limitations may be noted from the face of the statute: (1) since it is a conspiracy statute, the offense defined cannot be committed by a single person; (2) since it refers to rights of citizens,

(OVER)

it is not available for aggression against aliens;[1] (3) since the gravamen of the crime is aggression against one in the exercise of, or because of his having exercised, his Federal rights, the deprivation of rights must be the purpose of the conspiracy, not an incidental consequence. Experience with this statute, however, has demonstrated that the primary limitation on its application to civil rights cases arises from its requirement that the right invaded be secured to the victim by the Federal Constitution or statutes, for such rights figuring in civil rights cases are few in number.

A. Statutory Rights

The chief utility of Section 51 for enforcement of statutory rights has been as a criminal sanction for an otherwise sanctionless statute, and it is as a similar criminal catch-all that it appears susceptible of application in the civil rights field. The reported cases dealing with the application of Section 51 to enforce Federal statutory rights are all homestead cases, involving Section 51 prosecution of persons who intimidated homesteaders in order to cause them to leave their homesteads.[2] The homestead laws, although they provide a machinery for obtaining title to land in the public domain on compliance with statutory conditions, do not contain specific criminal provisions penalizing interference with homesteaders. The theory of these cases is that the homesteader has a Federal statutory right to acquire title on compliance with conditions including the residence requirement, and that running him off the homestead deprives him of this right, and hence falls within Section 51.

---

1. Baldwin v. Franks, 120 U.S. 678 (1887).

2. The leading case is United States v. Waddell, 112 U.S. 76 (1884).

This theory appears susceptible of generalization to any case of coercion of a person who has acquired personal rights under a Federal statute, if the purpose of the coercion is to cause him to renounce his statutory benefits. Recent Federal legislation has made Federal beneficiaries of some classes of people who have in the past been particularly subject to private intimidation through thugs and vigilantes. For example, the Social Security laws, the Wages and Hours law, and the Agricultural Adjustment Act of 1937, providing parity payments, confer certain benefits on persons who have a right to qualify for and to receive benefits. Industrial labor, which had previously been denied Section 51 protection against lawless interference with its efforts to organize,[3] now has acquired through the Wagner Act under certain circumstances a Federally-protected right to organize for collective bargaining. Criminal sanctions to punish attacks by private persons or public officials upon the exercise of this right, absent in the Wagner Act, appear to be available in Section 51 because of the invasion of a right "secured.....by the.....laws of the United States."

Indictments drawn on this theory have been sustained in the District Court against demurrer, in the Harlan County case (unreported), D. C., E. D. Ky. and in United States v. Fitzgerald (unreported), D. C., S. D. Ga.

---

3. United States v. Moore, 129 Fed. 630 (C. C. N. D. Ala. 1904).

4. The applicability of Sec. 51 to rights secured by the National Labor Relations Act is the subject of a special circular.

(OVER)

A further but less important application of Section 51 is its use as a conspiracy statute in statutory right cases even where there is a specific criminal penalty for the main violation, as in Federal election and relief intimidation cases under the Hatch Act, §§ 1, 4(a). In aggravated cases of this sort where the two-year imprisonment penalty of Title 18, United States Code, § 88, the regular Federal conspiracy statute, is felt insufficient, the ten-year imprisonment provision of Section 51 may be availed of.

B. Constitutional Rights

The use of Section 51 in civil rights cases turning on invasion of rights secured "by the Constitution......of the United States" is limited in its application to private persons by the fact that there are comparatively few constitutional rights which run against individuals. The Constitution deals primarily with relationships between governmental authorities and between private people and the authorities, rather than with the relationships of private people to one another. Consequently, although the phrase "rights or privileges secured....by the Constitution or laws of the United States" in effect incorporates the Constitution by reference, in the absence of special facts the ordinary outbreak of ruffian, vigilante activity, not participated in by public officials, whether directed against reds, nazis, negroes, soap-box speakers, or religious groups is not within Section 51. While such aggressions may constitute, according to the facts in the case, deprivation of freedom of speech, freedom of assembly, freedom of religion, unlawful searches and seizures, or similar invasions of personal rights mentioned in the

Constitution or read into it by the courts, these constitutional rights are rights <u>against official action only</u> and do not extend to private action.

The limitation is largely a matter of grammer. This may be illustrated by the three Reconstruction amendments. The Thirteenth Amendment said "Neither slavery nor involuntary servitude.....shall exist....": it is accordingly a general prohibition operative against the States, the Federal Government or any private persons who practice slavery, and it has in fact been held enforceable against private persons by prosecution under Section 51.[5] The Fourteenth Amendment says "No State shall...." and accordingly cannot be enforced except against States and their agents.[6] The Fifteenth Amendment prohibits discriminatory abridgment or denial of voting rights "by the United States or by any State" and is accordingly enforceable against both the Federal and State governments and their agents, but not against private persons.[7] However, there is a federally secured right to vote at a Federal election independent of the Fifteenth Amendment, which may be made the basis of a Section 51 prosecution[8] against private persons. Although civil rights decisions of the Supreme Court have read most of the Federal Bill of Rights into the Fourteenth Amendment and have made it unconstitutional under the due process clause of that Amendment for a State (municipality)

---

5. Smith v. United States, 157 Fed. 721 (C.C.A. 8, 1907), cert. den., 208 U. S. 618 (1908); Peonage Cases, 123 Fed. 671 (M.D.Ala. 1903); cf. Hodges v. United States, 203 U. S. 1 (1906).

6. United States v. Harris, 106 U. S. 629 (1882); Civil Rights Cases, 109 U.S. 3 (1883); United States v. Wheeler, 254 U.S. 281 (1920).

7. James v. Bowman, 190 U. S. 127 (1903).

8. United States v. Classic, 313 U. S. 299 (1941).

(OVER)

to punish without fair trial,[9] to prevent hand-bill distribution,[10] to set up capricious impediments to picketing or holding meetings,[11] or to discriminate on grounds of color,[12] these decisions are of no effect in establishing constitutional rights against <u>individuals</u>. The Constitution prohibits the States (and the Federal Government) from doing these things, but it leaves mobs free to do them — except under highly special circumstances. <u>United States</u> v. <u>Wheeler</u>, clearly points out the circumstances in which Section 51 is inapplicable.[13]

On the other hand the nature of the special circumstances making Sec. 51 applicable was indicated in dictum in <u>United States</u> v. <u>Cruikshank</u>,[14] the earliest and still leading case on Section 51, and has been established by holdings in succeeding cases. In the <u>Cruikshank</u> case a group of private individuals prevented negroes [15] from attending meetings.

---

9   <u>Chambers</u> v. <u>Florida</u>, 309 U. S. 227 (1940); <u>Brown</u> v. <u>Mississippi</u>, 297 U. S. 278 (1936); <u>Powell</u> v. <u>Alabama</u>, 287 U. S. 45 (1932); <u>Mooney</u> v. <u>Holohan</u>, 294 U. S. 103 (1935); <u>Moore</u> v. <u>Dempsey</u>, 261 U. S. 86 (1923).

10 <u>Lovell</u> v. <u>Griffin</u>, 303 U. S. 444 (1938); <u>Schneider</u> v. <u>State</u>, 308 U. S. 147 (1939).

11 <u>Carlson</u> v. <u>California</u>, 310 U. S. 106 (1940); <u>Thornhill</u> v. <u>Alabama</u>, 310 U. S. 28 (1940); <u>Hague</u> v. <u>CIO</u>, 307 U. S. 496 (1939).

12 <u>Norris</u> v. <u>Alabama</u>, 294 U. S. 587 (1935); <u>Nixon</u> v. <u>Herndon</u>, 273 U. S. 536 (1927); <u>State of Missouri ex rel Gaines</u> v. <u>Canada</u>, 305 U. S. 337 (1938).

13 254 U. S. 281 (1920).

14 92 U. S. 542 (1875).

15 The color question was raised in another count, alleging infringement of the right to vote secured by the Fifteenth Amendment, but this went off on the pleading point, 92 U. S. at 555-556.

This was pleaded under Section 51 as a conspiracy to hinder citizens in the free exercise and enjoyment of their "lawful right and privilege to peaceably assemble together with each other and with other citizens of the said United States for a peaceable and lawful purpose." The Supreme Court held this indictment invalid, on the ground that although the right to assemble is guaranteed by the First Amendment, that guarantee runs only against the Federal Government.[16] The Court pointed out, nevertheless, that had the meeting in question been a meeting "peaceably to assemble for the purpose of petitioning Congress for a redress of grievances, or for anything else connected with the powers or the duties of the national Government," Section 51 would have applied, for the reason that "the very idea of a government, republican in form, implies a right on the part of its citizens to meet peaceably for consultation in respect to public affairs and to petition for a redress of grievances." Thus it is not the fact that freedom of assembly is expressly mentioned in the Constitution but the fact that certain kinds of assembly are treated by the Court as essential to the effective functioning of the Federal Government that makes the right to assemble to discuss Federal affairs - an implied right - a Federal constitutional right which can be protected by Section 51 even against private action.

---

[16] The Court in the Cruikshank case had no occasion to discuss whether the right of assembly is protected against State action by the Fourteenth Amendment. (It is only within the last few years that the Fourteenth Amendment has been expanded to include the right of assembly.) The Court dismissed general counts drawn on the due process and equal protection clauses of the Fourteenth Amendment with the remark -- which is still sound constitutional law -- that the Amendment "adds nothing to the rights of one citizen as against another."

(OVER)

The dictum of the Cruikshank case has never been tested on its facts; no reported Section 51 case involves an assembly to discuss Federal affairs or to petition the Federal Government. The doctrine of the dictum has, however, become law in numerous other cases involving interference with voting at Federal elections[17] and intimidation of Federal witnesses and informers,[18] on the theory that the fair conduct of a Federal election and the safety of Federal witnesses, although not specifically mentioned in the Constitution, are matters so essential to the effective operation of a Federal Government whose Constitution has provided for Federal elections and Federal courts that the individual citizen has a derivative right to cast his vote, to have his vote counted as cast, and to give unintimidated testimony.

A recent case on Section 51 is Powe v. United States,[19] where a newspaper editor was blackmailed by operators of gambling establishments because of his publication of news articles and editorials exposing gambling and calling upon State prosecutors to act. The Circuit Court of Appeals for the Fifth Circuit, after a conviction in the trial court, ordered the sustaining of demurrers which the trial

---

[17] This is to be the subject of a special circular.

[18] In re Quarles and Butler, 158 U. S. 532, (1895); Motes v. United States, 178 U. S. 458 (1900); Foss v. United States, 266 Fed. 881 (C.C.A. 9, 1920). On the same principle Section 51 may be used against conspiracies to injure Federal officers and persons in their custody. Logan v. United States, 144 U. S. 263 (1892); United States v. Patrick, 54 Fed. 338 (C.C.M.D. Tenn. 1893).

[19] 109 F. (2d) 147 (C.C.A. 5, 1940), cert. den. 309 U. S. 679 (1940)

court had overruled. In its opinion, which is an excellent summary of the present state of the law in this field, the Court pointed out the irrelevance of the guarantees of the freedom of the press stated in the First Amendment and implied in the Fourteenth, put the case on the basis of rights implied from Federal necessities, and held that there was no Federal right to discuss a local matter, although it conceded in dictum that there would be a Federal right to discuss a Federal election, a Federal law, or the operations or officers of the Federal Government. The Supreme Court denied the Government's petition for certiorari, which petition had suggested that disclosure of local crime was not necessarily a local matter, but might have national interest because of the possibility of revealing violations of Federal laws, e.g., income tax fraud, or suggesting Federal legislation to cover the Federal aspects of the crime.

What has been said above concerning the limitations of Section 51 with respect to conspiracies of private individuals is not to be considered as denying its applicability to conspiracies of public officials or conspiracies of public officials with private individuals. Should public officers, Federal, state or local, in the exercise of their powers cooperate to injure or oppress a citizen in the exercise of a federally secured right, Section 51 would be an appropriate criminal sanction.[20] The numerous rights listed above as not being secured against private injury are clearly secured against action by governmental agents purporting to exercise governmental authority.

---

20 United States v. Classic, 313 U. S. 299, involves such a conspiracy of public officials.

(OVER)

Again, if private individuals conspire with public officials to injure or oppress a citizen because of his exercise of a right secured against governmental infringement, Section 51 appears to be applicable. Where private persons thus pervert governmental action their conduct should no longer be considered as private action; their use, or more properly abuse, of governmental power makes their acts assume the character of governmental action.

To sum up the law on prosecution of private persons under Section 51 it may be said: (1) that the only square holdings applying the statute in civil rights matters are in situations involving slavery, fraud and intimidation at Federal elections, intimidation of Federal informers and witnesses, and one sort of statutory right cases -- homestead cases; (2) that the dicta indicate and the theory of the decisions permits the use of the statute in other statutory right cases, and in those freedom of speech and press and assembly cases where the discussion relates to a Federal, rather than a local, subject; (3) individuals and officers conspiring through perversion of governmental powers to interfere with the exercise of rights secured from governmental infringement may be held responsible under Section 51 for the governmental action.

Further extension to elections of State officers and freedom of speech on public although local issues involves overruling the doctrine of the Powe case.

II

18 United States Code, Section 52

Section 52 of Title 18, United States Code, is aimed at
infringement of Federally secured civil rights by wrongful action
of state or Federal Governments, and reads as follows:

> "Whoever, under color of any law, statute,
> ordinance, regulation, or custom, willfully sub-
> jects, or causes to be subjected, any inhabitant
> of any State, Territory or District to the de-
> privation of any rights, privileges, or immuni-
> ties secured or protected by the Constitution
> and laws of the United States, or to different
> punishments, pains, or penalties, on account of
> such inhabitant being an alien, or by reason of
> his color, or race, than are prescribed for the
> punishment of citizens, shall be fined not more
> than $1,000, or imprisoned not more than one
> year, or both."

At the outset, it will be observed that two distinct offenses are defined by this Section: (1) the wilful subjection of
any inhabitant under color of law to a deprivation of rights secured
by the United States Constitution and laws; (2) the wilful subjection
of any inhabitant under color of law to discriminatory pains or punishments on account of race, color, or alienage.

United States v. Classic [21] has dispelled the confusion on
this point created by two early cases. [22]

---

[21] 313 U. S. 299 (1941).

[22] United States v. Buntin, 10 Fed. 730 (S. D. Ohio, 1832); United
States v. Stone, 188 Fed. 836 (D. Md. 1911).

(OVER)

Elements

Unlike Section 51, Section 52 is not a conspiracy statute; it may be violated by a single individual.

To be in violation of Section 52, the action resulting in a deprivation of Federally secured rights must be done "wilfully," and though that term, as used in this statute, has not been construed, it clearly means "with a purpose to bring about the deprivation."[23] When it appears that a public officer has subjected an inhabitant to a loss of Federally secured rights, and such was the natural and probable consequence of the officer's act, the presumption is that the result was intended.[24] If the offense is the subjection to different pains and punishments on account of alienage, race, or color, wilfulness is adequately shown when it is established that the discriminatory punishments were inflicted because of the alienage, race, or color of the victim.[25]

The Act proscribed must be committed "under color of law, statute, ordinance, regulation, or custom." This phrase is synonymous with "color of authority" and is intended to limit the application of the Act to persons occupying or purporting to occupy public office, Federal, state, and municipal, or persons who exercise governmental powers. The legislative history of this statute discloses that it

---

23 See discussion of "wilful" in Townsend v. United States, 95 Fed. (2d.) 352, 357, 359 (App. D.C., 1938), and cases there collected.

24 Cf. Dunlap v. United States, 70 Fed. (2d.) 35 (C.C.A., 7th., 1934)

25 Cf. United States v. Buntin; 10 Fed. 730, 732, where this concept was advanced in the charge to the jury, but observe that the Judge confused the two offenses defined by Section 52.

was originally framed to enforce against the agents of the several

states the inhibitions imposed on the states by the Fourteenth

Amendment,[26] but that on substantially reenacting the precursor of

Section 52 in the Revised Statutes of 1875, Congress substituted the

broader phrase "rights.....secured by the Constitution and laws of

the United States" for the less comprehensive description of the

rights in the old Section 16 of the Enforcement Act. Under this

broader language agents and officers of the Federal Government appear

to be subject to the sanctions of Section 52 if, under color of author-

ity, they infringe the rights secured to inhabitants as against the

Federal Government by the Constitution or infringe rights secured by

Federal laws.

The concept of "color of law" or "color of authority" in

civil and criminal cases involving federally guaranteed civil rights

has been the source of some confusion.

For example, the decision of the District Court for the

Eastern District of Tennessee in <u>International Union, etc.,</u> v. <u>Tennessee</u>

<u>Copper Co.</u> raised the question whether a complaint in a suit to enjoin

a violation of the Fourteenth Amendment sufficiently alleged that the

offending acts were committed under "color of state authority."[27]

The complaint set out that a corporation, an officer of the corporation,

a sheriff, and a justice of the peace conspired to deprive members of

the complaining union of their right of free speech. The court concluded

that as such a conspiracy on the part of the state officers would be

_____

26   91 Cong. Globe 3672 and 3690; Enforcement Act of May 31, 1870; Secs.
     16 and 17 (16 Stat. 140, 146).

27   31 Fed. Supp. 1015 (E. D. Tennessee, 1940).

(OVER)

illegal under state law and as there was no statutory authority for their action, it would be individual action not "conduct of a state or its officers under authority or color of authority." The same sort of contention, namely, that the offending action of a person who is a state official is not done under color of law because it is not authorized by state laws or is in direct violation of state laws has been raised in Section 52 prosecutions.

Much of this confusion was disspelled by the discussion of this point in the Classic case and in United States v. Sutherland.[28] In the former, it is stated: "Misuse of power, possessed by virtue of State law and made possible only because of the wrongdoer is clothed with the authority of state law, is action taken 'under color of' state law." In the Sutherland decision, in overruling a demurrer, the Court declared "the indictment charges in sufficiently specific language that defendant was acting under authority of a state law creating the office of policeman and detective and prescribing the duties of such office; that under color of such law and authority, he committed the unlawful acts * * *." Both decisions cite Home Tel. & Tel. Co. v. Los Angeles,[29] which rules that it was irrelevant whether the state had authorized the wong done by its agent, and the Sutherland case cites Iowa-Des Moines Bank v. Bennett,[30]

---

28 Classic case, 313 U. S. 299 (1941); Sutherland case, 37 Fed. Supp. 344 (N.D. Ga. 1940); see also for discussion as to what constitutes state action, Ex parte Virginia, 100 U. S. 339 (1879); Home Tel. & Tel. Co. v. Los Angeles, 227 U. S. 278, 287 (1913); Iowa-Des Moines Bank v. Bennett, 284 U. S. 239, 245, 246(1931); Mooney v. Holohan, 294 U. S. 103 (1935); Hague v. C. I. O., 307 U. S. 496 (1939); footnote 20 at p. 512.

29 Supra, Note 28

30 Supra, Note 28

which stated that Federal rights could be so violated by a state officer even where he disregarded express commands of state laws.

In the Copper Company case, supra, the sheriff and justice of the peace were acting under color of the laws creating their respective offices and prescribing their duties, and their unlawful action pursuant to the conspiracy with the corporation and its officers was a misuse of power possessed by virtue of those statutes. Hence, under the rule laid down in the cases cited above, the District Court should have upheld Federal jurisdiction.

The formula approved in the Sutherland case, namely, that an officer acts under color of the law creating his office and prescribing its duties will be found useful in Section 52 indictments. However, action under color of law can also mean action under a law which a public official executes or administers as in the case of a municipal officer who uses an ordinance as an excuse for unconstitutional action. A 52 indictment embodying this view of color of law has been upheld against demurrer in United States v. Curlin, et al., Eastern District of Arkansas (unreported), which is now pending trial.

Persons Subject to Section 52

The necessity for action under color of law reveals that Section 52 is primarily designed to punish public officials, Federal, state, and local, who misuse their powers as noted above. Its chief use will probably continue to be against state officers who violate rights secured by the Fourteenth Amendment.

The sanctions of Section 52 may possibly apply to persons pretending to be officers, although this is a highly conjectural application. Should the members of a mob represent themselves as a posse and thus compel a victim to submit to violence, prosecution may be possible. The word "color" seems

(OVER)

clearly to include pretended authority.

Persons acting under color of a "custom" are expressly subject to the sanctions of Section 52. What is meant by custom is not clear. It should undoubtedly embrace de facto officers. It should also embrace persons engaging in practices that have official sanction, or are recognized as law. Typical of such practices is the brutal Kangaroo Court that exists in many local jails throughout the country, or the custom of excluding qualified negroes from juries.

Though private individuals cannot by themselves violate Section 52, yet if they cooperate with a public official to accomplish a deprivation of Federally secured rights, they may be made defendants in an indictment based upon Section 88, Title 18, United States Code, charging a conspiracy to violate Section 52.[31] Such an indictment has been upheld against demurrer without opinion in United States v. Curlin, et al, supra. Similarly, private persons thus cooperating with public officials may be charged under Section 550, Title 18, United States Code, as aiders and abettors. Section 51 should be applicable also.

Persons protected

"Any inhabitant" may be the victim of a violation of Section 52 if a right secured to such an inhabitant by the Federal Constitution or laws can be made out. There is no limitation of the protection of Section 52 to "citizens" as is found in Section 51.

---

31 All members of a conspiracy are principals to the separate crime of conspiracy and this doctrine leads to the rule that conspiracy counts are good against persons who did not and could not have committed the crime in chief. United States v. Rabinowich, 238 U. S. 78 (1915); Israel v. United States, 3 F. (2d.) 743 (C.C.A. 6, 1925); United States v. Lyman, 190 Fed. 414 (D. Oregon, 1911).

Rights Protected

The gist of the offense defined by Section 52 in each case is the deprivation of a right secured by the Constitution or laws of the United States. Most important of those rights secured are defined in the Fifth and Fourteenth Amendments; i.e., the right not to be deprived by either state or Federal Governments of life, liberty or property without due process of law. The wilful taking of life by a person acting under color of authority and without due process would not only violate Section 52, but would also be murder under state laws. Ordinarily prosecution of such murder would be left to the several states; however, should it appear that no action would be taken by the state by reason of an apparent condonation of the offense, federal prosecutors should not hesitate to invoke Section 52. A wilful deprivation of property rights without due process of law under color of authority is likewise in violation of Section 52. Such tactics may be a part of an extortion scheme or it may consist of a confiscation of union files, or radical books, or religious literature. The right to conduct a lawful business has been called a property right protected by the Fourteenth Amendment, and wilful action of public officials to destroy a man's business would constitute a violation.[32]

The usual prosecution under this section will be concerned with deprivation of liberties. Liberty includes freedom from physical restraint, and other forms of assault and battery[33] freedom of

---

32 Truax v. Corrigan, 257 U.S. 312, 327-328 (1921); Pierce v. Society of Sisters, 268 U.S. 510 (1925).

33 See Meyer v. Nebraska, 262 U.S. 390 (1923); United States v. Sutherland, 37 Fed. Supp. 344 (N.D.Georgia, 1940) which involved 3rd degree torture.

(OVER)

speech[34] and of the press,[35] freedom to peaceably assemble,[36] to petition the Government,[37] to pursue a lawful calling,[38] to express and exercise religious beliefs,[39] to acquire and use knowledge,[40] to establish a home.[41] Akin to these rights is the right to move freely from state to state.[42] The intentional interference with such rights by public officials may be punished under Section 52.

---

34 DeJonge v. Oregon, 299 U.S. 353, 364 (1937); Herndon v. Lowry, 301 U.S. 242, 259 (1937); Lovell v. Griffin, 303 U.S. 444, 450 (1938); Hague v. C.I.O., 307 U.S. 496 (1939); Bridges v. California, Times-Mirror v. Superior Court, decided Dec. 8, 1941, ___ U.S. ___.

35 Grosjean v. American Press Co., 297 U.S. 233 (1936); Near v. Minnesota, 283 U.S. 697 (1931); Bridges v. California, supra, Note 34.

36 See Note 34 above.

37 Constitution of the United States, Amendment I, and cases cited above concerning the right of free speech.

38 United States v. Cowan et al., D. C. E. E. La. (1941), involving a Section 52 indictment charging a deprivation of this right was sustained against demurrer without opinion. And see Truax v. Raich, 239 U.S. 33 (1915); Allgeyer v. Louisiana, 165 U.S. 578, 589 (1897); Meyer v. Nebraska, supra, Note 33.

39 Pierce v. Society of Sisters, 268 U.S. 510 (1925); Hamilton v. Regents, 293 U.S. 245, 262 (1934); Cantwell v. Connecticut, 310 U.S. 296 (1940); Schneider v. State, 308 U.S. 147 (1939); Lovell v. Griffin, 303 U.S. 444 (1938).

40 Meyer v. Nebraska, supra, Note 33.

41 See Meyer v. Nebraska, supra, Note 33.

42 Cf. Crandall v. State of Nevada, 6 Wall. 35 (1867), and Edwards v. California, decided Nov. 24, 1941, ___ U.S. ___, 86 L. Ed. 133 holding California statutory restrictions on bringing indigent persons into the state were a burden on interstate commerce. There is, therefore, a right secured by the commerce clause, Article I, Section 8 of the Constitution or under the privileges and immunities clause as indicated by the concurring opinion of Mr. Justice Douglas and Mr. Justice Jackson.

The right to due process here includes the right to a fair trial which in turn encompasses a real, not a sham or pretended, hearing,[43] the right of a defendant in a criminal case to real representation by counsel,[44] the right to a jury from which members of the defendant's race have not been purposely excluded.[45]

The foregoing are rights secured against Federal, state and local officials alike. Section 52 to this extent merely translates into a criminal statute, the constitutional safeguards against governmental encroachment on fundamental rights of persons. However, the Classic case necessarily establishes that Section 52 is also applicable to punish official interference with rights secured against any infringement, individual or governmental. For example, the right not to be held as slave,[46] the right to vote at a federal election,[47] the right of access to the federal courts (whether or not the applicant is entitled to relief),[48] the right to inform federal officers concerning Federal offenses,[49] the right to be a witness in the Federal courts.[50]

In addition to the rights enumerated above, the first eight amendments set forth certain rights secured only as against infringement by the

---

43   Moore v. Dempsey, 261 U.S. 86; Mooney v. Holohan, 294 U.S. 103 (1935).

44   Powell v. Alabama, 287 U.S. 45 (1932).

45   Smith v. Texas, 311 U.S. 128 (1940).

46   Thirteenth Amendment.

47   United States v. Classic, 313 U.S. 299 (1941).

48   Ex parte Cleo Hull, 312 U. S. 583 (1941).

49   In re Quarles and Butler, 158 U.S. 532 (1895); Motes v. United States, 178 U.S. 458 (1900).

50   Cf. 18 U.S.C. 241 (a), 242.

(OVER)

Federal Government: the right not to be subjected to unlawful searches and seizures,[51] the right not to be twice put in jeopardy for the same offense,[52] the right in criminal cases to a speedy and public trial by an impartial jury,[53] the right not to be held under excessive bail nor be subjected to excessive fines or cruel and unusual punishment.[54]

The Fourteenth Amendment suggests the possibility that state officers could violate Section 52 by wilfully denying persons the right to equal protection of the laws. Yick Wo v. Hopkins, 118 U.S. 356 (1886) sets forth a fact situation which might well have given rise to criminal prosecution of the officials whose discriminatory administration of the laundry licensing ordinance was there successfully attacked.[55] It would be essential to establish an infringement of such a right to show discriminatory law enforcement based upon an invalid classification of persons or things to be protected. For example, if it could be established that a police officer ordinarily stopped street brawls that occurred in his presence or that were reported to him, but refused to intercede in cases of assaults on union organizers or Jehovah's Witnesses or political opponents, it is felt that this would constitute a denial of equal protection in violation of Section 52. Persistent breakdown of law enforcement would warrant use of this theory.

This equal protection approach appears to be the strongest basis for attacking state inaction. It should not be overlooked that inaction also

---

51 Fourth Amendment.

52 Fifth Amendment.

53 Sixth Amendment.

54 Eighth Amendment.

55 In the Classic case, it is felt that the Supreme Court would like to have considered the right of equal protection. It declined to do so since the point was not necessarily involved.

may in fact result in a deprivation of life, liberty or property, in violation of the due process clause. Willoughby's text on Constitutional Law suggests that there is ground for regarding such dereliction in the performance of official duties as state violations of the due process and equal protection clauses.[56] "Inaction" is somewhat of a misnomer. Actually some positive act is usually involved such as a refusal to give police protection, or the turning away from an attack when the officer knows that it is going on. If this is kept in mind, the so-called "inaction" theory becomes more substantial. It should also be borne in mind that Section 52 reads "willfully subjects, or causes to be subjected." The intentional refusal of officials to intercede frequently causes an inhabitant to be subjected to a deprivation of his liberties, and in lynching cases, his life.

Statutory rights which are entitled to protection under Section 52 are the same as those outlined in the discussion of the Section 51. Official interference with rights secured by the National Labor Relations Act is discussed in a special circular devoted to that Act.

It would be appreciated if, after consideration of this circular, the United States Attorneys would submit their suggestions and criticisms of the legal theories propounded. It is believed that the views of the United States Attorneys would contribute immeasurably to the sound development of Federal jurisdiction in Civil Rights matters.

FRANCIS BIDDLE
ATTORNEY GENERAL

---

56   3 Willoughby, "The Constitutional Law of the United States,"
     (2d Ed.) 1929, pp. 1934-1935.

COPY

April 6, 1942

MEMORANDUM FOR THE ATTORNEY GENERAL

There is attached a copy of a proposed Circular for United
States Attorneys relative to prosecution to enforce rights secured
by the National Labor Relations Act. This Circular aims to clarify
the Federal rights, as set forth in Section 7 of the National Labor
Relations Act (Section 157 of Title 29, United States Code). The
present issuance of this Circular is suggested at this time, in
view of the pending conference with United States Attorneys, in
that it will make more understandable certain conferences which
will take place, relative to the Civil Rights Statutes. Also, this
Circular indicates clearly to United States Attorneys the very
definite limitations of Section 157 of Title 29, United States Code,
in that the legislative history of the National Labor Relations Act
makes clear that interference which employees' rights must be the
interference of employers. Experience thus far has indicated that
nine out of ten reported labor difficulties do not indicate employer
participation and, accordingly, United States Attorneys are inclined
to waste considerable time in the consideration of possible labor
disputes, which are clearly without the Federal jurisdiction.

Accordingly, I recommend that the issuance of this Circular
be expedited.

Respectfully,

WENDELL BERGE
Assistant Attorney General

Enclosure
No. 337348

87

April 6, 1942

<u>MEMORANDUM FOR THE ATTORNEY GENERAL</u>

There is attached a copy of a proposed Circular
for United States Attorneys relative to prosecution to enforce
rights secured by the National Labor Relations Act. This
Circular aims to clarify the Federal rights, as set forth in
Section 7 of the National Labor Relations Act (Section 157 of
Title 29, United States Code). The present issuance of this
Circular is suggested at this time, in view of the pending
conferences with United States Attorneys, in that it will make
more understandable certain conferences which will take place,
relative to the Civil Rights Statutes. Also, this Circular
indicates clearly to United States Attorneys the very definite
limitations of Section 157 of Title 29, United States Code, in
that the legislative history of the National Labor Relations
Act makes clear that interference with employees' rights must
be the interference of employers. Experience thus far has
indicated that nine out of ten reported labor difficulties do
not indicate employer participation and, accordingly, United
States Attorneys are inclined to waste considerable time in
the consideration of possible labor disputes, which are clearly
without the Federal jurisdiction.

Accordingly, I recommend that the issuance of this
Circular be expedited.

Respectfully,

WENDELL BERGE
Assistant Attorney General

Enclosure
No. 337348

WB:VWR:rm

April 8, 1942

MEMORANDUM FOR MR. JAMES ROWE, JR.
ASSISTANT TO THE ATTORNEY GENERAL

Re: Prosecutions to Enforce
    Rights Secured by the National
    Labor Relations Act

We would like to have the attached circular,

which has been signed by the Attorney General, issued

and sent to all United States Attorneys.

Thirty-five (35) copies are essential for use

in conferences with United States Attorneys on Friday,

April 10, 1942, and expedited delivery by 10:00 a.m.

April 10, 1942 is accordingly requested.

Respectfully,

WENDELL BERGE
Assistant Attorney General

Enclosure
No. 287142

DEPARTMENT OF JUSTICE
Washington, D. C.
April 8, 1942

Circular No. 3673

TO ALL UNITED STATES ATTORNEYS:

Re: Prosecutions to Enforce Rights Secured
     by the National Labor Relations Act

The purpose of this Circular is to bring to the attention of
the United States Attorneys the power of this Department to enforce by
criminal prosecution the recognition of the rights of labor as secured
by the National Labor Relations Act.

Among the more serious and frequent violations of civil liberties are the denials of labor's right to organize, meet, strike, picket
and collectively to bargain. Occasionally the suppression of those
rights is carried out in the name of "law and order" and in certain
cases this means illegal violence and intimidation on the part of
employer groups, either directly or through the media of vigilantes,
special deputies or local police officers acting with the acquiescence
of the employers and often at their solicitation.

When the local administration of law collapses and there is
a consequent suspension of the recognition of the rights of individuals
secured by the Constitution and laws of the United States, it is the
province of the Federal Government to intervene. An instance of
individual rights directly guaranteed by Federal law is found in the
National Labor Relations Act of July 5, 1935. By Section 7 of that Act
certain fundamental rights are secured to employees engaged in indus-
tries affecting interstate commerce. In Section 8 unfair labor practices

90

on the part of the employer are defined. In Section 10 the power of the National Labor Relations Board to prevent the abuses described as unfair labor practices is outlined. This power is exercised by means of mandatory injunctions. The power of the Board is, thus, a preventative power directed against a single employer and restraining him from interfering with or coercing his employees.

There is also, however, the punitive power of the court to deal with a conspiracy to violate the rights secured by the National Labor Relations Act. Section 7 of that Act (Section 157 of Title 29, U. S. C.) provides:

> "Employees shall have the right to self-organization, to form, join, or assist labor organizations, to bargain collectively through representatives of their own choosing, and to engage in concerted activities, for the purpose of collective bargaining or other mutual aid or protection."

Recognition of these rights may be compelled by resort to the preventative measure of injunctions, but it may also be enforced by criminal prosecutions for conspiracy in violation of Section 51 of Title 18, U. S. C., which reads in part as follows:

> "If two or more persons conspire to injure, oppress, threaten, or intimidate any citizens in the free exercise or enjoyment of any right or privilege secured to him by the Constitution or laws of the United States, or because of his having so exercised the same * * * they shall be fined not more than $5,000 and imprisoned not more than ten years * * * etc."

It is thus apparent that the provisions of Section 51 seek to protect citizens in the exercise of any rights secured to them by any law of

the United States. Section 7 of the National Labor Relations Act is
such a law and secures certain enumerated rights to any employees engaged in businesses affecting interstate commerce.[*] Similar rights are
guaranteed to railway employees by the provisions of the Railway Labor
Act (Section 152 [Fourth] of Title 45, U.S.C.), and these should be
accorded the same protection.

---

[*] From a first reading of Section 7, it would appear to grant a right
to employees to be free from coercion or intimidation on the part of
anyone, including inter alia, employees, labor organizations or mobs not
connected with either. However, the right conferred has reference only
to acts by employers or persons acting for them. That such was the intent of the framers of the National Labor Relations Act is evidenced by
the hereinafter quoted statement by the author of the Act, Senator Robert
F. Wagner, before the Committee on Education and Labor, United States
Senate, 64th Congress 1st Session, during consideration of S. 1958 [Hear-
ings, Part 1, page 47]:

"SHOULD THE BILL PROHIBIT COERCION FROM ANY SOURCE?
Having outlined the main substantive provisions of the National Labor
Relations bill I want to direct attention to one criticism that has been
leveled against it. It has been claimed that in order to be fair, the
bill should prohibit employees and labor organizations, as well as employers, from coercing employees in their choice of representatives. This
argument rests upon a misconception of the needs which give rise to this
measure. Violence and intimidation by either employers or workers are
adequately prevented by the common law and do not require special treatment. This measure deals with the subtler forms of economic pressure.
Such pressure cannot be exerted by employees upon one another to an extent justifying congressional action. But it can be directed against
a worker by an employer who controls his job. It is this latter evil
which has grown to a magnitude requiring a new public remedy. Furthermore,
many courts have defined the term 'coercion' to embrace all strikes or
picketing, no matter how jusitifiable. They have drawn a line between
legal and illegal coercion. Thus to prohibit employees from coercing
their own side would not merely outlaw the undesirable action which the
word connotes to us, but would make the result reached in the loudly
condemned Hitchman Coal Case, 245 U.S. 229 (1917), the law of the land.
It would defeat the very freedom of self-organization which the bill is
designated to protect. All legislation strives not for an abstract or
paper equality but for conditions which will produce actual equality in
the light of concrete facts."

There is very little authority on this whole subject,
Reference, however, should be made to the unreported cases decided
by two District Courts wherein demurrers directed to indictments
drawn on the conspiracy theory were overruled. These are the cases
of United States v. Mary Helen Coal Co., et al, in the Eastern District of Kentucky, and United States v. Fitzgerald Cotton Mills,
et al, in the Southern District of Georgia. The briefs of both
sides in each case are on file in the Criminal Division of the Department. Both cases involve the use of henchmen hired by employers
to thwart union activity through beating and otherwise intimidating
employees. In each instance influential members of the community
and local government officials aligned themselves on the side of
the employer group to effect the objects of the conspiracy.

Upon receiving a complaint with respect to a violation of
the rights secured by Section 7 of the Act, you should report your
findings together with your recommendations to the Civil Rights Section of the Criminal Division of the Department. No prosecutions
should in any event be commenced through the offices of the various
United States Attorneys without departmental sanction.

In preparing an indictment for a violation of Section 51,
Title 18, U.S.C., against conspirators seeking to injure employees
in the exercise of rights secured by Section 157, Title 29, U.S.C.,
the following averments are essential:

1. That a conspiracy exists and that one party thereto is the employer or his duly authorized agent.

2. That the employees affected (or at least one of them) are citizens of the United States.

3. That such employees are engaged in a business affecting interstate commerce within the meaning of the National Labor Relations Act.

4. That the purpose of the conspiracy is to injure such employees in the free exercise of the rights secured by Section 7 of the Act.

If the employees have been intimidated in the exercise of their rights by the commission of any unfair labor practice, as outlined in Section 8 of the Act, any proof tantamount thereto would be proper under such an indictment and might constitute the gravamen of the offense. For this reason it is essential that the attorneys for the National Labor Relations Board in the nearest regional office be consulted for advice and guidance because that Board has preventative jurisdiction with respect to the instances of unfair labor practices mentioned in Section 8 of the Act. Further, access may be had, upon request, to the files of the Wage and Hour Division of the Department of Labor and to those of the National Mediation Board. Finally, investigations by the Federal Bureau of Investigation will, of course, be sought in the interest of consistency and uniformity in investigative matters. Before embarking upon these courses, however, the necessary clearance should be obtained from the Department.

FRANCIS BIDDLE
Attorney General

DEPARTMENT OF JUSTICE
WASHINGTON 25, D. C.

November 3, 1943

CIRCULAR NO. 3356

Supplement No. 3

TO ALL UNITED STATES ATTORNEYS:

Your attention is directed to the discussion in Department Circular No. 3356, Supplement No. 2, regarding the applicability of Sections 51 and 52, Title 18, United States Code, to invasions of constitutionally secured rights. Since the writing of that supplement there have been several cases clarifying the status of religious organizations with respect to leaflet peddling ordinances and compulsory public school flag salute requirements. Brief mention of these cases is made below and the Department's policy with regard to future complaints of interferences with religious liberty is set forth.

It will be recalled that the Supreme Court has held invalid ordinances and statutes requiring a permit as a condition precedent to the right to distribute religious pamphlets and literature when such permit regulations vested in a State official an arbitrary discretion to refuse a permit. Lovell v. Griffin, 303 U.S. 444 (1938); Schneider v. Irvington, 308 U.S. 147 (1939); Cantwell v. Connecticut, 310 U.S. 296 (1940). In the October, 1942, term the court followed the above cases in Jamison v. Texas, 318 U.S. 413 (1943), declaring to be void an ordinance absolutely forbidding the carrying of placards, advertisements, etc., on the city streets, and in Largent v. Texas, 318 U.S. 418 (1943); Murdock v. Pennsylvania, 319 U.S. 105 (1943); Douglas v. Jeannette, 319 U.S. 157 (1943), invalidating leaflet distribution permit ordinances. In Martin v. Struthers, 319 U.S. 141 (1943) an ordinance forbidding the ringing of doorbells or otherwise summoning the occupants of a residence to the door to receive leaflets, etc., was held unconstitutional. The court reversed its stand with regard to the applicability of peddlers' licensing taxes to distributors of religious literature in the case of Jones v. Opelika, etc., 319 U.S. 103 (1943), holding that such a tax was a burden on religious freedom in violation of the Fourteenth Amendment.

Taylor v. Mississippi, 319 U.S.   , involved a state statute making it an offense to teach or disseminate any doctrine tending to create an attitude of stubborn refusal to salute or honor the government of the United States.

(OVER)

95

The court held this could not constitutionally be applied to a person who was seeking to teach his religious conviction that the flag salute was in violation of the Biblical commandment against obiesance to a graven image.

In still another case, West Virginia State Board of Education v. Barnette, 319 U.S. (1943), the court reversed its ruling in Minersville District v. Gobitis, 310 U.S. 586 (1940), and held that it was a violation of the freedom of thought and religion secured by the Fourteenth Amendment to compel school children to perform the flag salute exercises on pain of expulsion when such exercises were contrary to the children's religious training and convictions.

The Department has received numerous complaints over a period of some three or four years involving the application of leaflet distribution ordinances and statutes against certain religious organizations. In a great many of these complaints it would appear that local state officials have acted in a manner which might be considered violative of Sections 51 and 52, Title 18, United States Code. Some of these complaints have originated since the above cases were decided. It has been reported to the Department that local school board officials are refusing to follow the clear mandate of the West Virginia State Board of Education case, supra, and are continuing to expel children who have asserted conscientious objections to the participation in flag salute exercises.

The Department does not desire to institute wholesale prosecutions against over-zealous public officials who have deprived others of their religious freedom by the unconstitutional application of leaflet distribution ordinances or by persisting in the enforcement of compulsory flag salute exercise regulations against school children whose consciences forbid their participation. Prosecutive action should be reserved for those cases where that remains the only means of alleviating the situation. When, therefore, complaints of interferences with religious liberty by state officials are called to your attention, you are requested to contact the appropriate, responsible state officials, pointing out to them the possibility that their actions may involve a denial of constitutional guarantees and seek their cooperation to the end that the activities complained of may be avoided. It is felt that most of the difficulties involving alleged state interference with religious freedom can be avoided through the prompt mediation of the United States Attorneys with the local authorities by letter or personal conference.

You are requested to continue to advise the Department of all complaints coming to you regarding alleged violations of Sections 51 and 52, Title 18, United States Code, and to inform the Department of the results of your efforts to prevent interference with religious freedom in accordance with the procedure suggested above.

TOM C. CLARK
Assistant Attorney General.

July 25, 1946

The Attorney General

Director - FBI

INVESTIGATION OF CIVIL RIGHTS CASES

    Our Atlanta, Georgia Office has advised that recently some misunderstandings have arisen betwen that office and the United States Attorneys for the Middle and Northern Districts of Georgia with regard to the institution of investigations of Civil Rights Cases. The established policy, as you know, is that investigations of Civil Rights Cases are conducted only upon authority of the Department. You will recall that when this policy was initiated several years ago the reason propounded was that by clearing all cases falling within this category through the Department a uniform and consistent policy with regard to the institution of investigations and prosecutions would result. Our Field Offices were instructed accordingly to conduct no investigations of Civil Rights Cases referred to them by United States Attorneys or anyone else without first receiving authority from the Department through the Washington headquarters of this Bureau. This procedure has been followed effectively for the past several years.

    According to information now received from the Special Agent in Charge of our Atlanta Office, Mr. Caudle recently advised United States Attorney John P. Cowart of Macon, Georgia, that the policy in connection with the investigation of Civil Rights Cases has been changed and that in the future requests for investigation should be referred by Mr. Cowart direct to our Field Office. As a result a misunderstanding has arisen in a few instances with regard to the proper procedure. It is understood, of course, that in connection with the recent primary election in Georgia, due to the number and frequency of the complaints received that Negroes were being denied the right to register to vote, an exception was made and that on authority of the Department all complaints received by the United States Attorneys were referred direct to our Atlanta and Savannah Field Offices for immediate investigation.

    I have not been informed, however, that there has been any change in the established policy with regard to the institution of Civil Rights Cases in general, and in the absence of advice from you that there has been a general change in policy our Field Offices in Georgia and elsewhere will continue to follow the practice of conducting investigations of Civil Rights Cases only after we have received specific authority from the Department.

Office Memorandum · UNITED STATES GOVERNMENT

TO : THE ATTORNEY GENERAL

DATE:

FROM : Director, FBI

September 12, 1946

SUBJECT:

I believe it would be well to give consideration to having a thorough and prompt review made of the Federal Statutes relating to Civil Liberties in order that a concise statement might be furnished to this Bureau for its guidance, in which there would be set forth specifically a statement as to the exact types of cases in which there would appear to be a potential violation of the Civil Liberties statute and an outline of the type and nature of the evidence necessary to support a criminal prosecution. I believe that at the present time the Bureau is expending a considerable amount of manpower investigating murders, lynchings and assaults, particularly in the Southern States in which there cannot conceivably be any violation of a Federal Statute. Generally, as a result of the aggressiveness of pressure groups or as a result of newspaper stories appearing prominently in newspapers, the Bureau is requested to initiate an investigation in a case for the purpose of determining whether there has been a violation of the Civil Liberties statutes. The improbability of such a violation existing is manifested by the large number of cases in which investigation is and has been conducted and the virtually non-existent prosecution in the Federal Courts. Nevertheless, the Bureau and the Department of Justice are publicized as entering these cases and are thereafter charged in the public mind and in the press with the responsibility for the solution of the cases. The vast majority of the public and the majority of the newspapermen do not understand the legal distinction between facts which would justify prosecution or a violation of the various Federal Statutes and the outright solution of a murder, assault or lynching case which would justify prosecution in the State courts. As a result, there is a feeling and belief that the Bureau has failed to "solve" many cases into which it has entered and the resulting feeling that the Department of Justice has been inadequate to the occasion. While within the Department we realize the fallacy of this conclusion, it nevertheless is a fact that the public judges the efficiency of a law enforcement and prosecuting organization upon the basis of prosecutions which it undertakes. While I, of course, do not subscribe to this fallacy, I again point out that it exists nevertheless.

I do not mean to infer that I condone the type of activities embraced in the average case referred to the Bureau for investigation as a Civil Liberties violation. On the contrary, I think it is incumbent to the effective working of democracy that the perpetrators of such offenses should be apprehended and prosecuted for their crimes. The responsibility for the solution and prosecutive action in these cases and the juris-diction for the accomplishment of these ends are in the State courts. Under the present circumstances it appears that the work of the Department and the Bureau is completely ineffective both as a deterrent and as a punitive force. Regardless of whether we like it is a fact that the Federal Statutes penalizing violations of Civil Liberties are an

I believe it would be well to give consideration to having a thorough and prompt review made of the Federal Statutes relating to Civil Liberties in order that a concise statement might be furnished to this Bureau for its guidance, in which there would be set forth specifically a statement as to the exact types of cases in which there would appear to be a potential violation of the Civil Liberties statute and an outline of the type and nature of the evidence necessary to support a criminal prosecution. I believe that at the present time the Bureau is expending a considerable amount of manpower investigating murders, lynchings and assaults, particularly in the Southern states in which there cannot conceivably be any violation of a Federal Statute. Generally, as a result of the aggressiveness of pressure groups or as a result of newspaper stories appearing prominently in newspapers, the Bureau is requested to initiate an investigation into a case for the purpose of determining whether there has been a violation of the Civil Liberties statutes. The improbability of such a violation existing is manifested by the large number of cases in which investigation is and has been conducted and the virtually non-existent prosecution in the Federal Courts. Nevertheless, the Bureau and the Department of Justice are publicized as entering these cases and are thereafter charged [in th]e public mind and in the press with the responsibility for the solution of the cases. [The] vast majority of the public and the majority of the newspapermen do not understand the legal distinction between facts which would justify prosecution or a violation of the nebulous Federal Statutes and the outright solution of a murder, assault or lynching case which would justify prosecution in the State courts. As a result, there is a feeling and belief that the Bureau has failed to "solve" many cases into which it has entered and the resulting feeling that the Department of Justice has been inadequate to the occasion. While within the Department we realize the fallacy of this conclusion, it nevertheless is a fact that the public judges the efficiency of a law enforcement and prosecuting organization upon the basis of prosecutions which it undertakes. While I, of course, do not subscribe to this fallacy, I again point out that it exists nevertheless.

I do not mean to infer that I condone the type of activities embraced in the average case referred to the Bureau for investigation as a Civil Liberties violation. On the contrary, I think it is incumbent to the effective working of democracy that the perpetrators of such offenses should be apprehended and prosecuted for their crimes. The responsibility for the solution and prosecutive action in these cases and the jurisdiction for the accomplishment of these ends are in the State courts. Under the present circumstances it appears that the work of the Department and the Bureau is completely ineffective both as a deterrent and as a punitive force. Regardless of whether we like it, it is a fact that the Federal Statutes penalizing violations of Civil Liberties are

...... weapon for efficient enforcement by the Department and I think, ..., that it is a mistake of policy for the Department to accept for ...... so many of these cases in which, as I have indicated, there is ...... of Federal prosecutive action and in which the Bureau and the ...... are merely assessed in the public mind with a responsibility which ...... Discharged nor executed.

I think it is essential to the prestige of the Department and the Bureau that ...... immediate step be taken to clarify this situation both in the policy of the ...... and in the public concept of the Department's responsibility in this

Mr. T. L. Caudle
Assistant Attorney General
Criminal Division

an inadequate weapon for efficient enforcement by the Department and I think, consequently, that it is a mistake of policy for the Department to accept for investigation so many of these cases in which, as I have indicated, there is [proba]bility of Federal prosecutive action and in which the Bureau and the Department are merely assessed in the public mind with a responsibility which [is neither] discharged nor executed.

I think it is essential to the prestige of the Department and the Bureau that some immediate step be taken to clarify this situation both in the policy of the Department and in the public concept of the Department's responsibility in this [   ].

Mr. T.L. Caudle
Assistant Attorney General
Criminal Division

144-012 Sec. 1

INFORMAL MEMORANDUM

September 18, 1946

TO: Mr. Caudle

FROM: Turner L. Smith

SUBJECT: Civil Rights Policy

At this writing Mr. Fred Folsom and I are in executive session discussing the attached copy of a memorandum from the Director to the Attorney General which discusses the civil rights situation in general. The original of this memorandum is being retained by us for answer as requested. This note to you merely contains some preliminary observations from us in regard to the overall situation.

First of all both of us heartily endorse the position taken by the Director. In fact, the contents of his memorandum is the very thing that all of us have discussed many times, that is, inadequate Federal legislation. We do believe, however, that Mr. Hoover oversimplifies the problem when he refers to establishing a policy of just what civil rights complaints we will investigate and those we will reject. Actually almost every complaint we get presents a potential violation. Only after a preliminary investigation can we say with more than guess work that a violation does not exist. The Georgia lynching case is an outstanding example. On the face of the newspaper favts we could not conclude positively that there was not some collusion by the peace officers at Monroe with the subsequent lynchings. Therefore the investigation. A similar situation is presented in almost every other civil rights complaint. Yet I feel that as a practical proposition Mr. Hoover is eminently correct for the reason that so very few investigations actually result in a case we can prosecute. A ratio of one case to 100 investigations would be a fair statement of our experience in the last six years.

At any rate we will give the Director a precise statement of the civil rights law for his guidance in directing investigations. In this connection we will also transmit to the Director lengthy memorandums beginning as early as March 1940 which fully and comprehensively outline the scope of the civil rights statutes and all major reported cases decided thereunder.

The main point of this immediate memorandum to you, however, is to state that we think Mr. Hoover's observations clearly support the Attorney General's announced public position that more Federal legislation is needed if we are to continue an effective civil rights organization. The Director's memorandum also provides an excellent springboard for the

report which the Attorney General has committed himself to
render to the next Congress outlining the type of complaints
we receive and the investigations conducted as to which no
prosecution can be undertaken.

I must point out to you that the preparation of such
proposed legislation and particularly the type of report we
think the Attorney General has in mind will call for very pains-
taking and time-consuming work by at least two attorneys for
a period of weeks. As you know, it is not physically possible
under existing conditions for us to handle the daily workload
of incoming mail and still find time for jobs such as those
before us in preparing this report and legislation.

I now reach a proposal for your consideration which has
come to Mr. Folsom like a dream in the middle of the night.
He points out that approximately two-thirds of our actual
efforts in the Civil Rights Section are essentially social and
public relations work rather than strictly prosecutive. In
addition to this a very large field of this work actually calls
for civil action rather than criminal action. Here there is a
complete vacuum so far as the Department of Justice policies are
concerned. Thus you have it: some prosecutive problems; some
civil problems (to afford any adequate relief to victims); and
some purely social, educational, and public relations problems.

It is therefore our recommendation that you and the Attorney
General give consideration to setting up a Division within the
Department answerable directly to the Attorney General with the
head thereof to be made an Assistant Attorney General and such
Division to be charged with the responsibility of all phases of
civil rights problems as we have outlined above. In this
connection it is our thought that the Attorney General should
go to Congress with this proposal and with request for sufficient
funds at the same time he goes to the Congress with his proposal
for new legislation and with his report of past experience. It
seems to us that such a proposal would emphasize the Attorney
General's great concern over these problems and his genuine
desire to see that something is done about it.

Let me add that I have, as you know, absolutely no
personal ambitions whatsoever to take on further responsibilities
such as would necessarily result from the above suggestion. The
Civil Rights field is a most exacting one and at the same time
a thankless job. People we are trying hardest to help are
frequently out bitterest critics. No lawyer enjoys representing
dissatisfied clients. My sole interest in this entire problem is
to see that the Department gets in position where it can accept
a given responsibility and have sufficient law to meet it.

144-012 Sec. 1

September 24, 1946

The Director, Federal Bureau of Investigation

RLC:FGF:BC

The Attorney General

Scope of the Civil Rights Statutes

Reference is made to your memorandum of September 12, 1946, requesting that the Bureau be furnished for its guidance a statement as to the exact types of cases in which there would appear to be a potential violation of the Civil Rights Statutes and an outline of the type and nature of the evidence necessary to support a prosecution.

The following documents are enclosed:

(1) Department of Justice Circular No. 3356, Supplement No. 1, dated May 21, 1940.

(2) Department of Justice Circular No. 3356, Supplement No. 2, dated April 4, 1942.

(3) Criminal Division memorandum concerning Ballot Frauds and Political Cases dated April 8, 1942.

These documents give a detailed picture of the manner in which offenses may arise under the Civil Rights Statutes and indicate the type and nature of the evidence which would be necessary to support a criminal prosecution.

Two additional cases have further defined the jurisdiction of the Federal Government under Sections 51 and 52. The first of these is United States v. Screws, 325 U.S. 91 (1945), in which the Supreme Court upheld the constitutionality of Section 52 as applied to police brutality but required that the Government establish the element of willfulness by strong proof that the officer had in mind the particular constitutional right he is charged with invading. Evidence of the duration character of the assault and the nature of the weapons used were indicated as important in the absence of expressed intent on the part of the officer. The second case is that of United States. v. Saylor, 322 U.S. 385 (1944) which held that the right to vote included not only the right to cast a ballot and have it counted as cast but also not to have the effect of that ballot diluted by ballot stuffing.

There is no question but that a large percentage of the investigations initiated in this field prove in the end to be fruitless but in each case the complaint made is indicative of the possibility of a violation and if we do not investigate we are placed in the position of having received a complaint of a

104

violation and of having failed to satisfy outselves that it is or is not such a violation. I know of no way to avoid at least a preliminary inquiry into the facts of a complaint which alleges a civil rights offense. I am sure you agree that we should not be in the position of avoiding such action.

It is my understanding that the Civil Rights Section of the Criminal Division has, as a matter of policy, requested only limited investigations in almost every case as a means of ascertaining sufficient facts upon which to base a determination to go forward or to close out each complaint. In many cases the United States Attorneys are requested to make the necessary initial inquiries through confidential sources available to them in order that the Department hay have a basis for appraising a complaint. Despite these precautions, we are frustrated in large measure and as you know it is my purpose to report these matters to Congress in the hopes of securing a broader and more substantial basis for Federal action. I would welcome any suggestions that your Bureau may wish to make.

Enclosure No. 279688

AG's note: Can't we work out some
policy that would protect the Bureau
on this. (Written beside second para.)
Sent to Criminal 10-7-46 (A. G. Clark)

The Attorney General   October 2, 1946

Director, FBI

SCOPE OF THE CIVIL RIGHTS STATUTES

Reference is made to your memorandum dated September 24,
1946, captioned as above. In that part of your memorandum
dealing with the initiation of investigations in the civil
rights field, you state that the policy of the Civil Rights
Section of the Criminal Division is to request only limited
investigations in almost every case as a means of ascertaining
sufficient facts upon which to base a determination to go
forward or to close out each complaint received.

I appreciate the fact that many complaints alleging a
violation of civil rights do not contain sufficient facts upon
which to determine whether or not a Federal violation is
involved. I wish to point out, however, that once inquiries are
instituted by the Bureau whether they are preliminary in nature
or a part of a complete and thorough investigation, the majority
of the public and the press are given the impression that we
have actively untered and are investigating the case. Local
law enforcement officers likewise gain the impression that by
our inquiries we have assumed jurisdiction and as a result they
withdraw from any investigation they may be conducting.

As you are aware, my attitude has always been to vigorously investigate any situation in which there are substantial
indications of a violation of Civil Rights Statutes or any
other Federal law over which this Bureau has jurisdiction. I
do not believe, however, that the Bureau should make inquiries
or conduct investigations in the nature of "fishing expeditions"
on the mere possibility that there have been infringements of
a Civil Rights Statute.

144-03

April 8, 1947
TLC:TLS:esw

Assistant Attorney General Theron L. Caudle

Turner L. Smith, Chief, Civil Rights Section

Departmental Clearance for Civil Rights Investigations

The attached memorandum from both of us to the Attorney
General results from the criticism which I understand was made
by the Director at the time of his appearance before the President's
Civil Rights Committee to the effect that the Bureau was handicapped in its investigation of civil rights cases because of the
time element involved in having to first get authorization for the
investigation from the Department.
Peyton Ford informed me that the Attorney General was
favorable to modifying this policy and authorizing "on the spot"
preliminary investigations if we did not consider it inadvisable.
I see no objection to it.

Some time is necessarily lost in the very mechanics of
clearing the incoming and outgoing memoranda through the Records
Division. Although, as you know, we resort to the use of the
telephone in any serious incident such as a lynching. At any
rate by having the additional facts which will result from an
immediate preliminary investigation, we can better evaluate the
case and more intelligently direct any further investigation that
should be conducted.

C O P Y

The Director, Federal Bureau of Investigation

April 10, 1947
TLC:TLS:esu
144-Q

The Attorney General

Departmental Clearance for Civil Rights Investigations

Since the time the Civil Rights Section was established in 1939 it has been the policy for the Bureau to submit civil rights complaints to that section in the Criminal Division for clearance and instructions before any investigation was undertaken.

I find that this practice necessarily involves delay before the Bureau is authorized to begin active investigations. In this interval it is possible that valuable evidence is lost or destroyed and your subsequent investigation accordingly made more difficult.

Effective immediately the Bureau is authorized to conduct preliminary investigations of any civil rights complaints or incidents upon its own motion without the necessity of first clearing the matter with the Department. As in the past, copies of your reports should be made available to the Criminal Division as rapidly as possible for guidance in any full-scale investigation which might follow.

Rewritten April 22, 1947

DEPARTMENT OF JUSTICE

Washington, D. C.

April 23, 1947.

CIRCULAR NO. 3356
Supplement No. 4

TO ALL UNITED STATES ATTORNEYS:

The policy hitherto followed of clearing all complaints of
civil rights violations with the Department before embarking on any
investigation is hereby modified to authorize the Federal Bureau of
Investigation to conduct preliminary investigations of any civil
rights complaints or incidents upon its own motion without the necessity
of first clearing the matter with the Department. Departmental clearance
and instruction will still be required for full-scale investigation or
before prosecutive action shall be commenced through the offices of the
United States Attorneys.

TOM C. CLARK

Attorney General

109

72-43-23 Sec. 6

Mr. McGregor   June 3, 1947

Turner Smith

Procedure in investigating civil rights
matters, particularly election complaints

You asked me to review old Department files and otherwise
attempt to ascertain the full history of the Department's policy in
handling and conducting investigations of civil rights complaints
which involved charges of election frauds. The following information
is based upon my study of all pertinent files I have been able to
locate on this subject. In addition thereto I have discussed the
question with a number of long-time Criminal Division employees. My
main informant is Hugh Fisher who, as you know, has been actively
connected with the Criminal Division for about 30 years and was First
Assistant during a substantial portion of that period.

I find that prior to January 1, 1939, any complaint or
incident involving a possible election crime under the Civil Rights
Statutes was handled in the Department and by the Criminal Division as
any other general crime. I find no special directice or special
order whatever by any Attorney General prior to 1939 which required
any special procedure for the handling of this type of complaint.
This likewise was the case in regard to any general civil rights matter.

Hugh Fisher cited any number of instances from his recollection
which substantiates the above. He stated that prior to the time the
Civil Rights Section was formally created in 1939 that all civil rights
incidents and election complaints were received and noted by the
Department as any other general crime, and that the United States
Attorneye and the FBI were free to act independently and on their own
motion in instituting an investigation or proceeding with prosecution
without any prior approval or clearance in the Department. In other
words, these cases were handled up to 1939 in a routine manner by the
Department, and United States Attorneys, and the Bureau, such as we
now handle common crimes as alcohol tax cases, bankruptcy frauds,
and the like.

On February 3, 1939, Attorney General Murphy set up a Civil
Rights Section in the Criminal Division. It is generally understood
that this was done at the specific suggestion of President Roosevelt
who was concerned with minority problems. From that point on civil
rights cases received special handling. Since our only jurisdiction
in election frauds is under the Civil Rights Statutes, these cases
likewise receive the same special handling as all other civil rights
matters. At the same time the Section was created the United States
Attorneys and the Bureau were directed that no investigations of
civil rights complaints were to be instituted or prosecutions under-

110

taken without the prior approval of the Department. This practice
has been consistently followed since that time up until April 23,
1947, at which time the present Attorney General modified this policy
by authorizing the Bureau and the United States Attorneys in
Circular No. 3356, Supp. No. 4, to institute preliminary investigations in civil rights matters on their own motion without the
necessity of specific approval or authorization by the Department.

Procedure employed by the Civil Rights Section in investigating
election fraud complaints. We have invariably followed the practice
of instituting preliminary investigations of election fraud complaints
before first determining upon a full-scale investigation or a petition
for an order impounding the ballots. When we receive communications
which we believe to be from substantial informants which charge an
election crime within the purview of the Civil Rights Statutes, we
promptly ask the Bureau to conduct a preliminary investigation by
interviewing our informants and following any pertinent leads obtained
from such source. When we have the results of this first investigation, we then determine if the matter merits a further and more
wide-scale investigation. If so, we immediately continue the investigation by appropriate memorandum to the Bureau and, if not, we
advise the Bureau to discontinue the investigation. We have found
from long experience that it is not profitable to have agents run off
in all directions investigating an election where our informants
cannot lead us into facts indicating possible Federal jurisdiction.

We have prepared in a separate memorandum a digest of a number
of election cases handled by this Section over the period of the last
several years which substantiates the above statements as to our
policy in conducting election investigations. The identical procedure outlined above was followed in the Kansas City Election
complaints, and this case was handled just as any other civil rights
matter within this Section. Notice of possible Federal election
frauds came to our attention through the press and through the United
States Attorney who related the formal request for an investigation
by the Kansas City Election Board. We immediately instituted our
usual preliminary investigation and directed the Bureau to interview
the informants, which they did. Through the Election Board, our
formal complainants, the Bureau gathered several hundred pages of
reports in this case, including the statements of thirteen or fourteen
hundred individuals who sought to throw some light on the irregularities complained of in this primary election.

When all of these reports became available to us, including the
results of the Kansas City Star investigation, and the investigation
by the House Committee, a staff of attorneys immediately analyzed the
data here in the Department, at which time the United States Attorney
and his staff was likewise making an analysis of the facts. All
Attorneys reached the positive and definite conclusion that the information accumulated did not disclose civil rights violations but did
disclose numerous xxxxgxixtixixx irregularities and possible State
election crimes. Inasmuch as we had "run out" all available information

-3-

and leads, the investigation by the Bureau was discontinued. During this interval the United States Attorney advised me that he had fully disclosed all of our evidence to three Federal Judges in Kansas City and that they stated to him that the matter did not in their opinion warrant the consideration of a grand jury nor would they sign an order impounding the ballots which were in the possession of the State election officials.

The matter, therefore, was a suspended one with the Department until it came to my attention that a State Grand Jury was conducting a further investigation and had the benefit of the ballots that were cast in this primary. We immediately xxx reopened the investigation by the Bureau, and it was directed to follow the State Grand Jury inquiries and any pertinent leads that might be developed therefrom which indicated any possible Federal crime. We directed that this be done under the active supervision of the United States Attorney because of the ever present possibility of local criticism of Federal agents meddling into what is almost exclusively a local problem for the State to handle. This xxxxix new investigation was reopened on April 22, 1947, and is continuing to the present moment.

June 12, 1947

The Attorney General

Director, FBI

DEPARTMENTAL CLEARANCE FOR
CIVIL RIGHTS INVESTIGATIONS

Reference is made to your memorandum dated April 22, 1947, captioned as above, in which it was stated that since 1939, when the Civil Rights Section in the Department was established, it had been the policy to submit civil rights complaints to the Criminal Division for clearance and instructions before any investigation was undertaken. Your memorandum advised that effective immediately the Bureau was authorized to conduct preliminary investigations of any civil rights complaints or incidents upon our own motion without the necessity of first clearing the matter with the Department.

I am assuming that the new instructions set forth in your memorandum are limited to the usual civil rights case, that is the case involving loss of life or threats to life as a result of beatings by law enforcement officers, and do not extend to complaints involving the denial of the right to vote and election frauds in general. If I am wrong in this assumption, I shall appreciate your instructions in this regard.

113

72-43-23 Sec. 6

June 13, 1947

The Attorney General

Turner L. Smith, Chief, Civil Rights Section
            Criminal Division

Kansas City Primary Case
(Screening of Civil Rights Complaints and
Preliminary Investigations)

      I have been studying the background of the policy initiated
in the Department following the time the Civil Rights Section was
set up providing for a clearance of civil rights complaints with
the Criminal Division before any active investigation was undertaken either by the FBI or the offices of the United States
Attorneys. In this connection, I bring to your attention a
memorandum from the Director of the Bureau to you dated September
12, 1946, and your reply thereto of September 24, 1946. I am
attaching photostats of these two memoranda and quoting below
the pertinent portion of these two memoranda which generally deal
with this problem of screening complaints and instituting preliminary investigations.

      Mr. Hoover, in his memorandum to you, pointed out:

      "Generally, as a result of the aggressiveness of pressure
groups or as a result of newspaper stories appearing prominently in
newspapers, the Bureau is requested to initiate an investigation
into a case for the purpose of determining whether there has been
a violation of the civil liberties statutes. The improbability
of such a violation existing is manifested by the large number of
cases in which investigation is and has been conducted and the
cirtually non-existent prosecution in the Federal courts. Nevertheless, the Bureau and the Department of Justice are publicized as
entering these cases and are thereafter charged in the public mind
and in the press with the responsibility for the solution of the
cases. The vast majority of the public and the majority of the
newspapermen do not understand the legal distinction...." between
facts which would justify state prosecution and not Federal
prosecution.

      Mr. Hoover further points out: "Regardless of whether we
like it, it is a fact that the Federal statutes penalizing violations
of civil liberties are an inadequate weapon for efficient enforcement by the Department and I think, consequantly, that it is a
mistake for the Department to accept for investigation so many of
these cases in which, as I have indicated, there is no probability
of Federal prosecutive action...."

114

-2-

-While I believe the Director had particularly in mind the lynching and police brutality incidents at the time this memorandum was prepared, nevertheless the observations he makes as to the limited scope of the Civil Rights Statutes (Secs. 51 and 52) apply in the same identical measure to the problem we have of getting sufficient facts to make out an election case under the Civil Rights Statutes. As you pointed out to him in your reply to him of September 24, 1946:

"There is no question but that a large percentage of the investigations initiated in this field prove in the end to be fruitless, but in each case the complaint made is indicative of the possibility of a violation and if we do not investigate we are placed in the position of having received a complaint of a violation and of having failed to satisfy ourselves that it is or is not a violation. I know of no way to avoid at least a preliminary inquiry into the facts of a complaint which alleges a civil rights offense. It is my understanding that the Civil Rights Section has, as a matter of policy, requested only limited investigations in almost every case as a means of ascertaining sufficient facts upon which to base a determination to go forward or to close out each complaint."

This exchange of memoranda between you and the Director, which took place prior to the Kansas City matter, points up the very problem we have always encountered with complaints of election violations under the Civil Rights Statutes. During every general election year, this Section is flooded with letters, wires, and telephone calls from disappointed candidates or friends of candidates beseeching the Department to institute FBI investigations of election frauds. When these complaints charge on their face a possible civil rights violation and the complainants appear to be substantial people, as distinguished from "crackpot" complaints which we often get, we have no other recourse but to order a preliminary investigation. From the facts obtained during a preliminary investigation, which usually consists of interviewing the complainants, we can then make some intelligent determination as to the course of any later investigation which it seems should be made. It is for these reasons, therefore, that in the great majority of election complaints we only request a preliminary investigation.

Such was the course followed in the Kansas City election frauds case at the outset for the very specific reason that our information in September and October, 1946, from the complainants did not at all make it clear that a Federal candidate was involved in the frauds complained of. It was in order to establish the basis for a full investigation that we asked the Bureau to interview the complainants and get all the facts. When we found, as a

115

result of this preliminary investigation, that the overwhelming proportion of the election frauds consisted of violations of state laws at the most, we concluded to abandon a full investigation at that time. When later knowledge came to our attention indicating new facts which resulted from the State Grand Jury's investigation and which pointed to a possible miscount of the ballots in the Congressional race, you, as Attorney General, immediately ordered a full investigation.

As I have stated to you in a previous memorandum, my connection with the Civil Rights Section did not begin until the year 1943. Since the policy of authorizing FBI investigations was instituted prior to that year, I have made a number of inquiries of members of this Section who were associated with it from the beginning in 1939, as to the considerations involved in establishing such a policy. Among my informants are Justice Henry Schweinhaut, the first Chief of the Section, Victor Rotnem, the second Chief of the Section and whom I succeeded; Sylvester Myers; Eleanor Bontecou; and also Hugh Fisher, whose connection with the Criminal Division dates back some 25 or thirty years. They have informed me that prior to 1939, civil rights and election complaints did not receive special treatment and were handled as any other general crime. Often the United States Attorney would be actually in the middle of a prosecution of a civil rights case or election case before the matter would come to the official attention of the Department. This identical thing occurred in 1936 in the Kansas City fraud case. The United States Attorney acted on his own motion.

The Kansas City cases were taken on appeal by the defendants to the Circuit Court of Appeals and also petition for certiorari was made to the Supreme Court. Therefore, it was along about 1938 or 1939 before these convictions stuck. Due to the widespread publicity these cases received because of the prominence of the individuals involved as well as the number of people prosecuted, it was just about the time that the Civil Rights Section was set up that the Department began to be flooded with other complaints of election violations throughout the country. This has continued since that time. These old members of the Section with whom I talked have stated to me that it is their firm recollection that it was because of this sudden out-cropping of election complaints that the Director and other officials in the Bureau discussed with the Department the plan of clearing these complaints with the Department before formally acting upon such complaints. I am told that the Bureau stated they were overwhelmed with such matters in election years; that many of the complaints resulted in useless loss of manpower by the Bureau, and that it was felt by all who participated in these conferences that it would be in the best public interest to have a screening of these complaints by specialized attorneys in the civil rights and election fields before embarking upon a formal investigation. Experience with the screening process

-4-

demonstrated that many of the complaints could not be brushed off without some preliminary investigation, and thus the practice arose of conducting preliminary investigations in the first instance by interviews of those persons who were claiming to have knowlege of Federal violations in the civil rights election field.

This identical procedure was followed in the Kansas City case and conforms exactly to our handling of dozens of other election complaints. When the results of a preliminary investigation have been obtained and we are satisfied that our informant's knowledge has been exhausted and there is no substantial indication of a civil rights crime, we invariably make the judgment that a full-scale, expensive, and time-consuming investigation is not warranted.

Attachment

144-03
July 18, 1947

The Director, FBI   TLC:WJH:BC

The Attorney General   Orig. to McGregor 7-22-47
                                               with AG's note: "Doug -
Departmental Clearance for   Do you think we should
Civil Rights Investigations   extend to all 51 and 52
                                               cases next fall"

    Reference is made to your memorandum of June 12, 1947,
captioned as above, requesting further instruction if you are
wrong in your assumption that my memorandum of April 22 which
authorizes the Bureau to conduct preliminary investigations of
any Civil Rights complaints or incidents upon its own motion
without the necessity of first clearing the matter with the Department, does not extend to complaints involving the denial of
the right to vote and election frauds in general.

    My memorandum of April 22 expressed a changed policy for
the handling of Civil Rights cases because the former practice of
clearing complaints with the Department necessarily involved delay
which might result in the destruction of valuable evidence or the
hindering of susequent investigation. These considerations which
may be compelling in the usual Civil Rights cases, such as those
involving brutality or mistreatment of persons by local police
officers, are not ordinarily present in cases involving denial
of the right to vote and election frauds generally.

    You are therefore advised that you correctly assumed that
my memorandum of April 22 and Department Circular 3356, Supplement 4, issued in connection therewith, do not extend to
complaints and incidents involving the right to vote and the
integrity of the ballot within the scope of the Civil Rights
Statutes, and that such complaints or incidents will continue
to require the prior authorization of the Department before
investigation.

ADMINISTRATIVE ORDER NO. 38

December 12, 1947

CRIMINAL DIVISION

Effective December 15, 1947, Mr. A. Abbot Rosen

is designated chief of the Civil Rights Section of the

Criminal Division.

T. VINCENT QUINN

Assistant Attorney General

119

December 23, 1948

The Director, Federal Bureau of Investigation

Peyton Ford, The Assistant to the Attorney General

Policy of Prior Clearance As to Certain Offenses

Recently I caused a review to be made of all types of offenses in which the Bureau has been instructed by the Department to obtain prior clearance before instituting an investigation of complaints involving such offenses. I have found that in many of such cases there is no longer any reason for continuing this policy. Accordingly, effective immediately, the Bureau is authorized to handle complaints concerning the following alleged violations in line with the customary practice pursued by the Bureau in other cases under its investigative jurisdiction:

(1) <u>Bribery</u> --all cases, including those in which officials of the Government are charged with bribery.
(2) <u>Federal Escape Act.</u>
(3) <u>Federal Regulation of Lobbying Act.</u>
(4) <u>Fraud against the Government.</u>
(5) <u>Illegal Wearing og the Gold Star Button.</u>
(6) <u>Alleged Criminal Offenses by Highly Placed Government or Public Officials.</u>

With respect to complaints involving the Federal Corrupt Practices Act, the Hatch Act, and other election offenses within the meaning of the Civil Rights statutes, the Bureau is authorized hereafter to conduct preliminary investigations upon its own motion, without the necessity of first clearing the matter with the Department, Prior Departmental clearance, however, will still be required before a full-scale investigation is conducted. This instruction brings election law complaints under the same policy enunciated by the Attorney General in hismemorandum to you, dated April 22, 1947, with regard to civil rights investigations generally.

* * * * *

The Bureau may interview complainants in any case under its investigative jurisdiction, independently of whether or not the policy of prior Departmental clearance is applicable to the type of offense involved. And, in addition, during the course of any investigation the Bureau is conducting, including preliminary investigations authorized by the Department, the Bureau should follow all leads and interview all persons, no matter who they may be. A letter from the Department authorizing such interviews is not only not necessary but should not be requested of the Department, except in the unusual case where the person interviewed insists on not talking to the Bureau without the production of a written authorization from the Department for conducting the interview.

The instructions contained in the present memorandum are to supersede and countermand any and all circulars or memoranda heretofore existing to the contrary.

(Study referred to in Mr.
Ford's memo to the FBI
dated December 23, 1948)

CLEARANCE BY
DEPARTMENT OF JUSTICE   44-03-2 Sec. 5
OF
CERTAIN F.B.I. INVESTIGATIONS

The Federal Bureau of Investigation of the Department of

Justice is charged with investigating all offenses against the

laws of the United States, with the exception of those where

investigative jurisdiction is placed in the Treasury Department

or some other governmental agency.

In the case of most crimes where investigative jurisdiction

resides in the F.B.I., that Bureau itself passes upon all complaints

of alleged violations and makes the investigation on its own

initiative. There are several types of offenses, however, where

the Department of Jusitce has determined that, because of special

considerations or circumstances, complaints must be referred to it

for its decision whether an F. B. I. investigation should be

conducted.

The reason for this special treatment is that a uniform

prosecutive policy is essential in some types of Federal offenses

because of their novel nature, e.g., newly enacted legislation,

or because of their unusual importance to the Government and to

the public, e.g., civil rights, internal security and antitrust

cases. The Department long ago realized that uniformity throughout

the ninety odd Federal judicial districts could not be achieved

without channeling such cases through a central agency.

Thus, there early developed two categories of cases receiving

special treatment from the Department; first, those where an

122

investigation cannot be commenced until the Department so orders, and, second, those where the investigation is left to the discretion of the investigative agency but no prosecution may be instituted without departmental authorization.

An example of the first category is found in antitrust cases, where the Department prior to 1915 adopted a policy of clearance before investigation. An example of the second category, which originated in 1918 in internal security matters, was the policy in cases under the Securities Act of 1933 and the Securities Exchange Act of 1934, where the Department required clearance in advance of the institution of grand jury proceedings when these statutes were new,[1] but revoked such requirement when enough judicial decisions had been rendered to clear up uncertainties of construction.[2]

A survey of the first category, which is the only one with which this memorandum is concerned, discloses that departmental authorization prior to investigation is or was required in the following types of cases which are within the investigative jurisdiction of the F.B.I.;

   1. Anti-Racketeering.

                    * * * * * * *

_____

[1]   Department Circular No. 2886 dated July 24, 1936, and No.
      3083 dated February 17, 1938.

[2]   Department Circular No. 3850, Supplement 2, dated February
      12, 1944.

8. <u>Federal Corrupt Practices Act</u>. By Circular No. 3416
dated September 5, 1940 [4/] Attorney General Robert H. Jackson
ordered that, because of the newness of the legislation and
the necessity of correct and uniform interpretation of its
provisions before prosecutive action was taken, all complaints
of violations of the Hatch Act should be cleared through the
Department. The order stated that the same instructions applied
to complaints under the Federal Corrupt Practices Act, the
Emergency Relief Appropriation Acts of 1939 and 1941, and
sections 208-213, Title 18, U.S.C.

* * * * &

22. <u>Civil Rights and Domestic Violence; Election Laws.</u>
After the creation of the Civil Rights Section in the Criminal
Division in 1939, a definite policy was created for civil rights
cases. Circular No. 3356, Supplement No. 1, dated May 21, 1940,
stated, in part, that "Because of the importance of unified and
consistent legal theory and prosecution plicy in this field, it
is requested that no indictments under 18 U.S.C. Secs. 51 and 52
be prosecuted without clearance from the Department." Circular
No. 3356, Supplement No. 2, dated April 4, 1942, stated, in part,
that "In the interest of consistency and uniformity in the
conduct of investigations, the policy of directing all original
complaints to the Civil Rights Section of the Criminal Division
for clearance and instruction before embarking on a full
investigation will be continued. No investigation or prosecution

---

4/ While this Circular, as well as other similar ones, was
    directed "To All United States Attorneys", such circulars
    are also applicable to the F.B.I.

124

of these cases should be commenced through the offices of the United States Attorneys without Departmental sanction and because of the importance of maintaining consistent legal theory in these cases, it is requested that proposed indictments be submitted to the Department for consideration before undertaking prosecutive action."

In practice, the policy was, generally, for the civil rights section: (1) to screen all complaints since the great majority show no federal jurisdiction on their face; (2) as to those which show some likelihood of such jurisdiction, to request the F.B.I. to conduct a preliminary investigation for the purpose of ascertaining whether there is sufficient indication of a possible federal crime to justify the making of a full investigation; and (3) to request a full investigation only when the preliminary investigation justifies such action.

This policy was discussed in the following exchange of correspondence between the Director of the F.B.I. and the Attorney General:

On September 12, 1946, the Director of the F.B.I. advised the Attorney General by memorandum that:

"I believe that at the present time the Bureau is expending a considerable amount of man power investigating murders, lynchings and assaults, particularly in the Southern States, in which there cannot conceivably be any violation of a federal statute. Generally, as a result of the aggressiveness of pressure groups or as a result of newspaper stories appearing prominently in newspapers, the Bureau is requested to initiate an investigation into a case for the purpose of determining whether there has been a violation of the civil liberties statutes.

125

The improbability of such a violation existing
is manifested by the large number of cases in
which investigation is and has been conducted
and the virtually non-existent prosecution in
the Federal courts. Nevertheless, the Bureau
and the Department of Justice are publicized
as entering these cases and are thereafter
charged in the public mind and in the press with
the responsibility for the solution of the cases.
The vast majority of the public and the majority
of the newspapermen do not understand the legal
distinction (between facts which would justify
state prosecution and not Federal prosecution).

"Regardless of whether we like it, it is a
fact that the Federal statutes penalizing violations of civil liberties are an inadequate weapon
for efficient enforcement by the Department and
I think, consequently, that it is a mistake for the
Department to accept for investigation so many of
these cases in which, as I have indicated, there is
no probability of Federal prosecutive action...."=

The Attorney General replied on
September 24, 1946, that:

"There is no question but that a large percentange
of the investigations initiated in this field prove
in the end to be fruitless, but in each case the
complaint made is indicative of the possibility of
a violation and if we do not investigate we are
placed in the position of having received a complaint
of a violation and of having failed to satisfy ourselves that it is or is not a violation. I know of
no way to avoid at least a preliminary inquiry into
the facts of a complaint which alleges a civil
rights offense. It is my understanding that the
Civil Rights Section has, as a matter of policy,
requested only limited investigations in almost
every case as a means of ascertaining sufficient
facts upon which to base a determination to go
forward or to close out each complaint."=

With repsect to civil rights violations generally,

i.e., lynching, police brutality, etc., this policy has

been modified by the Attorney General's memorandum to the

F.B.I., dated April 22, 1947, and Circular 3356, Supple-

ment No. 4, dated the following day. Under these new

126

instructions, the F.B.I. is authorized to conduct preliminary investigations on its own initiative, Departmental clearance still being required for full scale investigations or prosecutive action. This modification in policy, however, does not apply to election cases under the civil rights statutes. [6] This appears from the memorandum of the F.B.I. to the Attorney General, dated June 12, 1947, and the Attorney General's reply thereto, dated July 18, 1947.

* * * * * *

Departmental policy in the twenty-two types of cases, supra, is, of course, reviewed from time to time and, when circumstances warrant it, is subject to change.

---

[6] It should be noted that election cases involving violations of the Corrupt Practices Act are subject to different instructions. See paragraph 8, supra.

127

File #44-03-2-Sec5,

January 10, 1949

TO: The Attorney General

From: Director, FBI

SUBJECT: POLICY OF PRIOR CLEARANCE AS TO CERTAIN OFFENSES

Reference is made to Mr. Ford's memorandum of December 23, 1948, outlining the policy, which is to be pursued in connection with the handling of certain offenses within the Bureau's jurisdiction and the procedure to be followed in connection with instituting investigations thereof.

Your attention is directed to the instruction indicating that the Bureau should follow all leads and interview all persons no matter who they may be, in the event the Bureau is conducting an investigation, even though such investigation is of a preliminary type.

This would seem to be inconsistent with instructions previously outlined in Mr. Ford's memorandum, which are to the effect that certain investigations would be authorized by the Department, and that Departmental clearance would still be required before a full scale investigation is conducted. It would seem that some clarification in this respect is desired in that the restriction is completely removed, if during the course of a preliminary investigation, the Bureau would be authorized to conduct all leads and interview all persons no matter who they may be.

In view of this apparent inconsistency it is assumed that the Department did not intend that the Bureau would conduct an investigation in those classifications which are restricted. I would appreciate your views in this matter before any instructions are issued to our field offices.

[No restrictions on any investigations - Prior clearance from Department on antitrust and labor cases only -]
(Notation in Attorney General Clark's own handwriting).

128

The Attorney General   January 14, 1949

Director, FBI

POLICY OF PRIOR CLEARANCE AS
TO CERTAIN OFFENSES

Reference is made to the memorandum of Mr. Peyton Ford of
December 23, 1948, in the above entitled matter. It is noted
that you have approved the policy outlined by Mr. Ford in view of
which this memorandum is being called to your attention.

My attention has been directed to the instruction indicating
that the Bureau should follow all leads and interview all persons
no matter who they may be when the Bureau is conducting an investigation, even though such investigation is of a preliminary
type. In this connection you will recall my memorandum of
January 10, 1949 to you indicated that it would seem that the
position enunciated is inconsistent with instructions previously
outlined in Mr. Ford's memorandu, which are to the effect that
certain investigation will be authorized by the Department, and
that Departmental clearance would still be required before a
full-scale investigation is conducted. Some clarification in this
respect was desired in that the restrictive language of Mr. Ford's
memorandym seemed to be completely removed, if during the course
of a preliminary investigation, the Bureau would be authorized to
conduct all leads and interview all persons no matter who they
may be.

In addition to the above referenced memorandum pointing out the
apparent inconsistency, it is felt that there are other matters
of policy which should be called to your attention at this time.
The fact that the instructions in Mr. Ford's memorandum are to
supersede and countermand any and all circulars or memoranda heretofore existing to the contrary, will require the issuance of
entirely new instructions of procedure in handling these matters
in every one of our Divisions throughout the field and at the
Seat of Government. As this change in policy is so widespread it
is our desire to clearly outline the procedure so that the letter
and the spirit of your instructions can be followed.

In connection with Bribery investigations, it is understood
that it has been the practice of the Department for some time in
cases of alleged solicitation or acceptance of bribes by Government officials or employees, for the FBI to initiate investigation only upon a specific authorization of the Criminal Division.
If, after a preliminary report is received from the FBI, it
appears that a full investigation is warranted, a memorandum is
written by the Assistant Attorney General in charge of the

129

-2-

Criminal Division to the Bureau requesting an investigation.
It is understood that such memorandum is routed through the
office of the Assistant to the Attorney General for his approval
and that this is done only where the investigation into the acts
constituting the alleged bribery are committed by officers or
employees of the U.S. Government. The Bureau has heretofore
been advised that the theory behind this procedure seems to be
that the office of the Assistant to the Attorney General has the
responsibility for maintaining proper working relations with
other departments and has therefore been kept informed of, and
should approve, investigation into the affairs of those departments. The Department will not be able to follow the above
policy under the procedure outlined by Mr. Ford.

In connection with the Federal Regulation of Lobbying Act,
this historically is a new regulation. Considerable discussion
has been had publicly concerning the act and these discussions
have been directed to the relationship which exists between the
Government on the one hand and those individuals who may or may
not come within the purview of the regulation. The law according
to public comment is at least by some considered controversial
and no Court decision has as yet been handed down as a guide.
Until a policy can be outlined covering many of the situations
which will necessarily arise in the future you may wish to have
brought to your attention each situation as it arises. The
Department would then be in a position to properly analyze and
evaluate this important field of legislation.

The Federal Escape Act involving negligence of custodians
became effective June 21, 1947. The Amendment extended the
jurisdiction of the Federal Government to provide for punishment
of persons who through negligence allow the escape of a Federal
prisoner. This legislation has been brought to the attention of
the Criminal Division and an opinion has been sought concerning
the Bureau's jurisdiction under the legislation, since July, 1947.
No answer has been received and it would seem desirable that a
determination be reached by the Criminal Division as to whether
the Bureau had jurisdiction and if it would have jurisdiction the
extent thereof, before the Bureau engaged in any investigations
coming within the purview of the act. Of added significance is
the fact that persons within the purview of the act appear to be
officers of other agencies of the Government and other Divisions
of the Department of Justice.

It has long been the policy of this Bureau in cases of
frauds against the Government and all types of criminal cases
involving highly placed Government or public officials to refer
such complaints to the Department and to conduct no investigation
pending Departmental instructions and advice. This procedure
was approved by you in your memorandum of November 24, 1947.
You will recall that the Department's policy was established

130

-3-

because the Department and this Bureau would be saved possible embarrassment and would be assured of better cooperation from officials of other agencies if the facts were made known to the Department and the agency concerned before investigation was initiated. It is believed that the purpose has been well served and you may desire to again consider these factors at this time.

This memorandum is not inclusive of all the details which you may wish to consider in connection with the procedures outlined in Mr. Ford's memorandum. I do feel that the apparent difficulties which could reasonably be expected to arise in connection with the actual operations of the Bureau in pursuance of the policy outlined, should be called to your attention at this time. The change will involve the issuance of suitable instructions which necessarily ential a program of instruction throughout our service. These policies deal with types of cases which have heretofore been the subject of detailed analysis and procedures which I do not desire to have changed unless these instructions could be clearly and unequivocally disseminated throughout the service. I have indicated before and I wish to restate that this memorandum is written for the purpose of bringing these matters to your attention in that it is our desire to not only comply with the letter of the instructions contained therein but with the spirit thereof.

44-03-2 Sec. 5

February 3, 1949

The Attorney General

Director, FBI

POLICY OF PRIOR CLEARANCE AS
TO CERTAIN OFFENSES

Reference is made to my memorandum of January 14, 1949, with respect to certain phases of the change in policy outlined in Mr. Peyton Ford's memorandum of December 23, 1948. Inasmuch as it would be undesirable to have new instructions issued in these matters before having the benefit of your personal observations, it would be appreciated if your views could be made available to the Bureau at an early date.

cc - Mr. Peyton Ford
    The Assistant to the
     Attorney General

A.G.
Mr. Ford
Al Rosen

I suggest you set up conference with Ford's office, FBI and myself on this. (Note: In the handwriting of Attorney General Tom Clark)

February 18, 1949

Memorandum for the Director
Federal Bureau of Investigation

I have your memoranda of January 10th and 14th, 1949,
requesting clarification of the instructions to you contained in the
memorandum of Peyton Ford, The Assistant to the Attorney General,
dated December 23rd, 1948, relative to the Policy of Prior Clearance
as to Certain Offenses.

The memorandum of December 23rd, was the result of a review
which I asked to be undertaken of the Departmental policy as to
prior clearance. The review indicates that there is no further
necessity for the present policy except in cases involving antitrust
matters, the Federal Corrupt Practice Act, the Hatch Act, and other
election and civil rights problems.

With respect to antirtrust cases: The Department desires the
Bureau to interview the complainant only if he appears personally
before the Bureau or one of its field offices, and to refer the
information thereby obtained to the Department for instructions as
to whether the Bureau should proceed, and if so, in what manner.
Whenever the Bureau is requested to conduct an investigation in
antitrust matters, all necessary letters will be furnished by the
Antitrust Division.

With respect to cases involving the Federal Corrupt
Practices Act, the Hatch Act, and other election offenses within the
meaning of the civil rights statutes, as well as civil rights investigations generally: The Bureau is directed to conduct a preliminary
investigation and to consult the Department before proceeding to a
full and complete investigation. (In the preliminary investigation,
however, the complainants and any other witnesses whose testimony
appears to be relevant, or where necessity exists that testimony
be immediately recorded, should be interviewed and pertinent initial
leads followed where thought advisable.)

With respect to the following class of cases:

(1) Bribery -- all cases, including those in which
             officials of the Government are charged
             with bribery.
(2) Federal Escape Act.
(3) Federal Regulation of Lobbying Act.
(4) Fraud against the Government.
(5) Illegal Wearing of the Gold Star Button.
(6) Alleged Criminal Offenses by Highly Placed
    Government or Public Officials.
(7) Anti-Racketeering.
(8) Eight-Hour Day Law.
(9) Extortion -- all cases involving the mailing
    of threatening communications arising out

133

-2-

of labor idsputes. (Insofar as cases of extortion involving the mailing of threatening communications arising out of racial disputes are concerned, such cases are to be handled in the same manner as civil rights cases.)

(10) Interstate Transportation of Strike Breakers.
(11) Kickback Racket Act.
(12) Labor Management Relations Act of 1947.
(13) Railway Labor Act.

The Department authorizes and directs the Bureau to conduct full and complete investigations without prior consultation with the Department. The latitude thus provided is complete. It includes not only interviewing the complainants but all other pertinent witnesses as well, and following all leads to their logical conclusion.

The foregoing remarks apply only to complaints received in the first instance by the Bureau, since appropriate instructions as to investigation are issued by the Department regarding all complaints which it refers directly to the Bureau.

Insofar as Bribery, Frauds Against the Government and Alleged Criminal Offenses by Highly Placed Government or Public Officials are concerned, I am fully aware of the reasons, outlined in your memorandum, for our former policy of prior clearance with the Department. In these categories, as well as others, it may be necessary for you to set up techniques within the Bureau so as to secure maximum coverage of complaints without a corresponding wast of manpower.

As regards to Federal Regulation of Lobbying Act and the Federal Escape Act, I realize that questions of interpretation do arise from time to time since the exact limits of the law, particularly the Federal Regulation of Lobbying Act, are not yet entirely clear. The purpose of the Department's memorandum of December 23rd, was to advise the Bureau to proceed without clearance from us with respect to undertaking investigations in these fields. That memorandum was addressed only to your power to investigate. Interpretation of the law remains, as always, for the Department. Where it is necessary to obtain such advice your field offices may secure it from the United States Attorneys or from the Department through the Bureau here.

This memorandum and the earlier one of December 23rd, are not meant to prevent or discourage the Bureau from making pertinent inquiries of the Department relative to the procedure, policy or method of investigations. The Department, as you know, is always available to assist the Bureau in whatever way it can. I have issued these instructions since I believe they are conducive to a more efficient operation of the Department in the investigative functions it pursues through the Bureau.

-3-

If you have any further questions about the December 23rd memorandum, please communicate with me.

Attorney General

44-03-2
Sec. 5

The Attorney General   February 23, 1949

Director, FBI

POLICY OF PRIOR CLEARANCE
AS TO CERTAIN OFFENSES

Reference is made to the attached memorandum dated February 18, 1949, outlining the policy of prior clearance as to certain offenses. In accordance with your wishes, this memorandum is being returned to you, together with the Bureau's memorandum to you dated January 14, 1949, which was also attached. If it is your desire that the policy as outlined by you be established, appropriate instructions will be issued to our field offices upon receipt of your request.

33-3-11-3-1 Sec. 3

March 11, 1949

AMC:FES:IJP

Director, Federal Bureau of Investigation

The Attorney General

Policy of Prior Clearance as to Certain Offenses

I have your memorandum of February 23, 1949, regarding the above policy, which was the subject of the Department's memoranda to you under dates of December 23, 1948, and February 18, 1949.

You are advised that it is my desire that the policy as outlined in these memoranda be immediately established, and you are requested to issue appropriate instructions to your field offices.

My memorandum of February 18, 1949, is returned merewith.

Director, Federal Bureau of Investigation   December 21, 1951

Attorney General   JMM:rh

                                                                      44-03-2

     It has recently been brought to my attention that over the course of years a practice has developed of obtaining prior authority from the several divisions of the Department before certain investigations within the primary investigative jurisdiction of the Bureau are initiated.

     In order to clarify the situation and do away with any confusion which might result from this situation, I wish to make it clear that the Bureau can in the first instance originate, initiate, and carry through to a conclusion any investigation within its jursidiction. Any prior memorandum or instruction to the contrary may be disregarded.

     I realize, of course, that there will be occasions when consultation will be necessary before and during the investigative process, but the need for such consultation should not be confused with the necessity for a Department authorization.

     It is my view that this memorandum should apply to all cases and situations with the possible exceptions of (1) requests to check grand jurors and petit jurors in major cases, and (2) the institution of antitrust investigations.

44-3-11-3-1

DEPARTMENT OF JUSTICE

FEDERAL BUREAU OF INVESTIGATION

WASHINGTON 25, D.C.

June 5, 1952

MEMORANDUM FOR THE DEPUTY ATTORNEY GENERAL

I am listing below a number of matters which have been pending in the Department and upon which the Bureau has been awaiting
action. These matters are quite important to the operations of
this Bureau and I would appreciate it if it might be possible
for you to effect expeditious action upon them:

* * * * *

IV.

Prior to 1948, on the casis of instructions received from
the Department in connection with individual violations, the
policy was established of securing Departmental authorization
before conducting investigations in certain types of cases. In
1948, the instructions were changed to the effect that the Bureau
was to secure Departmental authority before conducting any investigation in cases involving: (1) Jury Panel Investigations, and (2)
Antitrust Matters.

It was further indicated that the Bureau was to conduct
preliminary investigations only and then obtain Departmental
authority before a full and complete investigation was initiated
in: (1) Election Law cases, (2) Civil Rights and Involuntary
Servitude and Slavery matters, and (3) Extortion cases arising
out of racial disputes.

By memorandum dated December 21, 1951, the former Attorney
General McGrath instructed that the Bureau could "originate,
initiate and carry through to a conclusion any investigation within its jurisdiction," except Jury Panel investigations and
Antitrust matters. Since the change in procedure, considerable
difficulty has been experienced by the Bureau, particularly in
those instances where no specific allegations of the violations
of Federal statutes have been received.

It was believed by the Bureau that the new instructions of
December 21, 1951, were intended to authorize this Bureau to conduct investigations where allegations were made that a criminal
statute had been violated and that investigation was to be
logically directed to secure evidence to establish whether or not
the alleged criminal violation took place.

139

However, since the initiation of this new policy, some requests for investigations have been received from the Criminal Division phrased in such broad, general terms that the nature of the information desired could not be definitely determined. These requests have been all-ecompassing in nature and have gone far beyond the allegations made or beyond any reasonable basis upon which a criminal violation might be predicated.

An example of the above is reflected in the case of the Senator Butler election matter in Maryland. In the case of the former Senator, a sixteen page memorandum was received from the Criminal Division requesting an investigation and outlining the information desired regarding the Election Law violations on the part of individuals associated with the campaign of Senator Butler. This matter had been specifically referred to the Department by the Committee of Senator Hayden in August of last year.

Subsequent to the request received from the Criminal Division, the Bureau was advised that the Criminal Division interpreted its request to mean that an investigation was to be conducted into the activities of both of the individuals involved in this election, although the Senate Subcommittee report on which the Department's request was based contained no such allegations. We were consequently then required to make a similar investigation into the activities of individuals associated with the campaign of former U.S. Senator Tydings.

It would seem from the cases which have been sent to the Bureau since the change in policy in December, that there has been a tendency on the part of the Criminal Division to phrase its requests for investigations in such all-encompassing language as to cover any eventuality which might arise, even though there are no specific allegations worthy of investigation. This places the Bureau in the position of conducting broad, general surveys in order to determine if there are in existence allegations worthy of investigation. This oges far beyond our statutory authority and if continued could result in severe criticism of the policies of the Department. I have previously requested that the Department take steps, as may be deemed appropriate, to restrict requests from the Criminal Division to reasonable lines of inquiry and logical defined scope of investigation. To accomplish this, I believe, as I have previously indicated in memoranda to the Department, there should be a reversion to the policy which existed prior to December 21, 1951.

* * * * * *

Typed 10-7-52

CBM:FES:jw
44-03-2 Sec. 6

Director, Federal Bureau of Investigation

Attorney General

Advance Departmental Authorization
Before Conducting FBI Investigations
in Certain Types of Cases

Reference is made to the memorandum of my predecessor dated December 19, 1951, directing the Bureau to conduct investigations without advance authorization from the Department except in the case of antitrust matters and jury panel checks.

After considering the reasons advanced in your memoranda of June 5 and August 20, 1952, why this policy should be changed, I have decided to rescind the December 19, 1951, memorandum. The policy with respect to advance authorization of FBI investigations in certain types of cases will accordingly revert to that which was in effect prior to the date of that memorandum or, in other words, the policy will be as outlined in the Department's memoranda of December 23, 1948, and February 18, 1949, on this subject.

Director, Federal Bureau of Investigation

Attorney General

Advance Departmental Authorization
Before Conducting FBI Investigations
in Certain Types of Cases

Reference is made to the memorandum of my predecessor dated December 19, 1951, directing the Bureau to conduct investigations without advance authorization from the Department except in the case of antitrust matters and jury panel checks.

After considering the reasons advanced in your memoranda of June 5 and August 20, 1952, why this policy should be changed, I have decided to rescind the December 19, 1951, memorandum. The policy with respect to advance authorization of FBI investigations in certain types of cases will accordingly revert to that which was in effect prior to the date of that memorandum or, in other words, the policy will be as outlined in the Department's memoranda of December 23, 1948, and February 18, 1949, on this subject.

October 10, 1952

Attorney General

CBM:FES:jw

Charles B. Murray, Assistant Attorney General,
        Criminal Division

44-03-2 Sec. 6

Advance Departmental Authorization of FBI
Investigations in Certain Types of Cases.

By a series of memoranda dated December 23, 1948,
February 18, 1949, and March 11, 1949, the Department advised
the Federal Bureau of Investigation in detail respecting the
policy to be followed in connection with advance authorization
from the Department as a condition precedent to the initiation
of investigation by the FBI in certain types of cases. Prior
to this time there were some sixteen broad categories of
cases in which advance departmental authorization was required
as a matter of policy, and the memorandum of February 18
abolished such requirement in thirteen of these categories,
i.e., in all except antitrust cases, jury panel checks and
civil rights cases, including election law matters. In
civil rights cases the Bureau was directed to conduct a
preliminary investigation on its own initiative and to
consult the Department before proceeding to a full and
complete investigation.

The foregoing policy was in effect until December 19,
1951, when your predecessor directed to the Bureau a memorandum,
prepared in the Criminal Division, stating that "I wish to make
it clear that the Bureau can in the first instance originate,
initiate and carry through to a conclusion any investigation
within its jurisdiction" except antitrust investigations and
jury panel checks. A copy of this memorandum, as well as
copies of those referred to in the preceding paragraph, will
be found in Department file number 44-03-2.

According to the Bureau, the change in policy made by
the December 19, 1951, memorandum has imposed a serious burden
upon it because it places the Bureau in the position of having
to conduct a broad general survey eacy time a complaint is
made in order to determine if it is worthy of investigation.
Hence the Bureau has urgently requested that the December 19,
1951, instructions be rescinded, and that the Department
revert to the policy in effect prior to that time.

I am in accord with the Bureau's views in this respect
and am willing to see a return to former departmental policy.
I have accordingly prepared the attached memorandum to the
Bureau for your signature and, if you agree, this will dispose
of the matter to the Bureau's satisfaction.

Attorney General   October 10, 1952

Charles B. Murray, Assistant Attorney General,   CBM:FES:jw
              Criminal Division   44-03-2

Advance Departmental Authorization of FBI
Investigations in Certain Types of Cases.

          By a series of memoranda dated December 23, 1948,
February 18, 1949, and March 11, 1949, the Department advised
the Federal Bureau of Investigation in detail respecting the
policy to be followed in connection with advance authorization
from the Department as a condition precedent to the initiation
of investigation by the FBI in certain types of cases. Prior
to this time there were some sixteen broad categories of cases
in which advance departmental authorization was required as a
matter of policy, and the memorandum of February 18 abolished
such requirement in thirteen of these categories, i.e., in all
except antitrust cases, jury panel checks and civil rights
cases, including election law matters. In civil rights cases
the Bureau was directed to conduct a preliminary investigation
on its own initiative and to consult the Department before proceeding to a full and complete investigation.

          The foregoing policy was in effect until December 19,
1951, when your predecessor directed to the Bureau a memorandum,
prepared in the Criminal Division, stating that "I wish to make
it clear that the Bureau can in the first instance originate,
initiate and carry through to a conclusion any investigation
within its jurisdiction" except antitrust investigations and
jury panel checks. A copy of this memorandum, as well as copies
of those referred to in the preceding paragraph, will be found
in Department file number 44-03-2.

          According to the Bureau, the change in policy made by
the December 19, 1951, memorandum has imposed a serious burden
upon it because it places the Bureau in the position of having to
conduct a broad general survey each time a complaint is made in
order to determine if it is worthy of investigation. Hence the
Bureau has urgently requested that the December 19, 1951, instruc-
tionsbe rescinded, and that the Department revert to the policy
in effect prior to that time.

I am in accord with the Bureau's views in this respect and am willing to see a return to former departmental policy. I have accordingly prepared the attached memorandum to the Bureau for your signature and, if you agree, this will dispose of the matter to the Bureau's satisfaction.

- 2 -

144-012 Sec. 7

TO: Assistant Attorney General
        Warren Olney III   March 17, 1953

FROM: Director, FBI

SUBJECT: PRELIMINARY INVESTIGATIONS
         IN CIVIL RIGHTS MATTERS

During the course of a preliminary investigation in Civil Rights cases, it has been the policy in the past to thoroughly interview the complainant, the original source of information, the victim and all available pertinent witnesses in order to round out the facts surrounding the allegation. In many instances, due to varying circumstances, the subject law enforcement officers have not been interviewed, unless the Department specifically requested same at a later date.

In order to arrive at uniformity, instructions have been issued to all of our field divisions to immediately include interviews with the subject law enforcement officers during the course of the preliminary investigations. It is contemplated that the interviews will be conducted in the absence of the subject's superiors, and in the event the subject declines to be interviewed except in the presence of his superiors, or if permission is denied to him except in the presence of his superiors, efforts to conduct such interview will be immediately discontinued and the facts brought to the attention of the appropriate United States Attorney.

The above is being furnished merely for your information and confirms information orally furnished to Mr. A. B. Caldwell, Chief, Civil Rights Section, Criminal Division, by a representative of this Bureau.

144-012 Sec. 7

March 25, 1953

Director, Federal Bureau of Investigation

Warren Olney III, Assistant Attorney General
Criminal Division

Interview of Police Witnesses in
Civil Rights Cases

     Receipt is acknowledged of your memorandum of March 17, 1953, referring to the telephone conversation of March 13, 1953, between Mr. Richard Held of your Bureau and Mr. Arthur B. Caldwell, Chief, Civil Rights Section, Criminal Division , regarding the policy to be followed in interviewing police officers for information in police brutality cases.

     The new policy, calling for the interview of police officers during the preliminary investigation of a case, whereas previously such persons were interrogated only in the course of a full investigation, is agreeable to the Criminal Division.

     In addition to confirming this understanding, the Division wishes to caution against the employment of the new procedure where its use would jeopardize the success of prosecution or further investigative action, as where the subject is in a position to intimidate prospective informants or destroy evidence. We believe, however, that the Bureau should proceed in accordance with its own discretion in carrying out this policy.

144-021 Sec. 7

TO: Assistant Attorney General   March 27, 1953
         Warren Olney III

FROM: Director, FBI

SUBJECT: PRELIMINARY INVESTIGATIONS IN
         CIVIL RIGHTS MATTERS
         (Your reference 144-012, 144-51-65, JXK)

Reference is made to your memorandum dated March 25, 1953, and entitled, "Interview of Police Witnesses in Civil Rights Cases" wherein you cautioned against the employment of the new procedure outlined in our memorandum of March 17, 1953, where its use would jeopardize the success of prosecution or further investigative action.

For your information, instructions issued to all of our field divisions were such as to cover the above-mentioned situations. As was indicated in this Bureau's memorandum of March 17, 1953, instructions were issued to the effect that the interviews with the subject law enforcement officers were to be conducted in the absence of the subject's superiors and in the event the subject declined to be interviewed except in the presence of his superiors, or if permission was denied him except in the presence of his superiors, efforts to conduct such interviews would be immediately discontinued and the facts brought to the attention of the appropriate United States Attorney.

In addition to the above, our field offices were advised that if any reason existed as to why such individuals should not be interviewed, the reason, therefore, was to be set forth in the initial report. It was also pointed out that whenever difficulty was experienced in connection with an interview with a subject law enforcement officer, this Bureau was to be immediately informed. This instruction was to apply to those instances wherein the subject's superiors refused to permit the interview or for any other reason whatsoever.

In view of the above, it is felt that the existing instructions as issued to our field offices are adequate to cover situations such as are mentioned in your memorandum of March 25, 1953, and in the absence of instructions to the contrary, such policy will be continued in the future.

148

144-012 Sec. 7

April 22, 1953

TO: Assistant Attorney General
         Warren Olney III

FROM: Director, FBI

SUBJECT: CIVIL RIGHTS INVESTIGATIONS

      Reference is made to this Bureau's memorandum dated March 17, 1953, which indicated that in order to arrive at <u>uniformity</u> instructions had been issued to our various field divisions to immediately include interviews with the subject law enforcement officers in all preliminary investigations.

      To further expedite the handling of such matters instructions have also been issued to obtain and report the prosecutive opinion of the appropriate United States Attorney <u>prior to the completion of a Civil Rights investigation.</u> It is not meant that such action will in any way alter the established policy of obtaining the Department's opinion prior to closing a case or initiating porsecutive action. It is felt, however, that such action will be of assistance to the Department in that it will have the benefit of the United States Attorney's opinion prior to reaching its own decision.

      The above is merely for your information.

144-012 Sec. 7

TO: The Attorney General   April 29, 1953

FROM: Director, FBI

SUBJECT: CIVIL RIGHTS MATTERS

In accordance with our conversation yesterday, I thought you would be interested in the following account of our investigations in civil rights matters.

During my tenure since 1924 as Director of the FBI, every civil rights case reported to the FBI has been vigorously investigated. One of the earliest such cases which occurred more than a quarter century ago involved the brutal night-time flogging of a public health officer who was horsewhipped because he denied a city milk permit to one of his attackers. Overwhelming evidence collected by the FBI implicated nine men, but only two of them were brought to trial. Community feeling was high in favor of the defense and they were speedily acquitted. This pattern has been repeated time and time again in cases of this type. Convictions are most difficult to obtain even when the facts clearly establish a violation.

Despite the efforts made, justice does not always triumph in civil rights cases as Federal jurisdiction is limited and the investigators are frequently handicapped by a hostility which arises from local prejudice. In August, 1946, six white men took two Negroes out of the Minden, Louisiana, jail. One of the victims was beaten to death and the other left unconscious. Investigation identified the six white men and produced proof of their guilt. The individuals were indicted and brought to trial, but the jury acquitted all six of them. Their principal defense was an appeal to local prejudices--remarks by the defense attorney about "Federal intervention" and newspaper articles alleging "Northern meddling" in local affairs, and so forth.

From 1924 through 1937, there was not a single conviction for violation of civil rights recorded in the Federal courts. Since that time, however, due to the continued emphasis we have placed on these investigations, a total of seventy-nine convictions have been recorded. Of that number, all but eight have been reported during the past ten years. Only seven cases were investigated by the FBI involving violations of civil rights during the year 1939, when a special civil rights unit was first established, both in the Department of Justice as well as within the FBI, to afford special handling to these cases. The number of such investigations has steadily increased, reaching an all-time high during the fiscal year of 1952 when we handled one thousand eight

150

-2-

hundred forty-one investigative matters in the civil rights
field. During the first nine months of the current fiscal year,
1953, there have already been one thousand five hundred seventy-
nine investigative matters in civil rights cases handled by the
FBI. To date, the FBI has accumulated evidence in a total of
five thousand eight hundred seventy-two cases involving possible
or actual violations of the Civil Rights Statute.

It is interesting to note an apparent correlation between
our achievements in the civil rights field and the decline in the
number of lynchings in the United States, which in part may be
due to our activities. According to the Tuskegee Institute, a
total of four thousand seven hundred twenty-six persons were put
to death by mobs during the period from 1882 through 1952. The
peak year was in 1892 when two hundred thirty-one persons were
victims of this mob violence. Lynch killings during the past
decase, however, have shown a gradual decline. During the past
ten years, a total of twenty-seven lynchings occurred, compared
to one hundred five lunchings during the preceding ten years. In
1952 there was not a single lynching in the United States for the
first time since 1882, when figures were first recorded, according
to the Tuskegee Institute. It is apparent, therefore, that substantial arogress is being made in this field.

In the past several years, due to our educational program
for local law enforcement officers and to the wide-spread publicity
afforded civil rights cases, the public and local police officials
have become cognizant of the rights of the individual. Many
police departments are taking disciplinary action against their
own personnel and in some cases, at conferences between the local
prosecutor and the United States Attorney, it has been agreed that
prosecution would be handled in State Court. Illustrative of
this was a case in an eastern city jail in which two men were
placed in a seldom-used cell and given no food or water for nearly
four days. The police officers responsible for this act were
disciplined locally and the FBI's investigation was terminated
when no violation of a Federal statute was appelled out. In
another case sufficient evidence was collected by the FBI to
indicate a violation by an arresting officer of a civil liberties
guarantee. At a conference of the United States Attorney, the
Governor of the State, and the State Attorney General, it was
agreed that State rather than Federal action could more effectively
curb the activities of the offender. In a more recent case in
Chicago in which the FBI conducted a complete civil rights investigation, the arresting officers were indicted by the Cook County
Grand Jury for compelling the confession of an individual and for
aggravated assault.

Regardless of the station in life occupied by the individuals responsible for such violations or their position in law enforcement, the FBI conducts complete and thorough investigations. An example of such a case handled in the recent past is the one entitled "Roy Best, et al, Charles W. Garton, et al - Victims." At the request of the Department, an investigation was instituted into the alleged beating of six inmates of the Colorado State Penitentiary, Canon City, Colorado, subsequent to an escape attempt on July 16, 1951. After the escape attempt had failed, the victims were beaten by the subject, who was Warden of the institution, and other penitentiary officials. In addition to being Warden of the penitentiary, Best was active, politically, in the State of Colorado, and was a past official of a national association of prison wardens.

After an extensive investigation, which was handled by a hand-picked squad of Agents who had received specialized training in such matters, a Federal Grand Jury returned an indictment charging Warden Best and eight others with a violation of the Civil Rights statutes. On July 3, 1952, a jury in Federal Court, Denver, Colorado, returned a verdict of not guilty as to all defendants. Although convictions were not secured, it is to be noted that the Colorado State Civil Service Commission on July 30, 1952, voted unanimously to suspend Warden Best from his position as Warden for a period of two years.

Another case of this type involved the physical mistreatment of victim Wesley Eugene Byrd, a colored veteran of World War II, by then Sheriff Alfonso L. Apocaca of Dona Ana County, New Mexico, Hubert W. Beasley, then Chief of the New Mexico State Police, and other law enforcement officers. Byrd was tortured for the purpose of extorting a confession from him for the rape-murder of a Las Cruces, New Mexico, waitress by the name of Ovida (Cricket) Coogler. As a result of an extensive investigation conducted by this Bureau, Sheriff Apodaca, Chief Beasley, and one of the other officers were all found guilty of a violation of Byrd's civil rights.

A United States District Court jury returned a verdict of guilty as to Beasley and Apodaca for having participated in the torture of victim Byrd, and a verdict of guilty as to Apodaca and one of the Deputy Sheriffs for having conspired to deny the victim the rights guaranteed him under the United States Constitution was also returned. Chief Beasley was sentenced to a term of one year in the custody of the Attorney General, and Sheriff Apodaca was sentenced to one year on each of two counts of his conviction, the sentences to run concurrently.

-4-

Civil Rights matters in New York City recently had public attention focused on them as a result of an agreement which was entered into on July 11, 1952, between officials of the New York City Police Department and James M. McInerney, who was then the Assistant Attorney General in charge of the Criminal Division of the Department of Justice. This agreement, which was unknown to the FBI, in effect permitted the New York City Police Department to conduct its own investigations into alleged civil rights violations concerning New York City Police Department officers, and delayed our investigations during this period. Our New York Office discovered this agreement during the course of an investigation in a civil rights case involving New York City police officers on January 9, 1953, and I immediately called the existence of this agreement to the attention of then Attorney General James P. McGranery. By memorandum dated January 14, 1953, we were advised by the Department that this agreement had been revoked by the Attorney General. It is interesting to note that from July 11, 1952, through January 14, 1953, while this agreement was in effect, the New York Office of the FBI received three complaints involving alleged civil rights violations on the part of members of the New York City Police Department, but since the revocation of the agreement on January 14, 1953, up until April 28, 1953, eighty-seven civil rights complaints involving alleged violations on the part of members of the New York City Police Department have been received by our New York Office.

Members of the Ku Klux Klan have been involved in numerous floggings and cases of brutality throughout the South. During 1951, the Association of Carolina Klans of the Ku Klux Klan formed a Klavern at Fair Bluff, North Carolina, and in October of 1951, klansmen attired in their white robes and hoods, the Ku Klux Klan regalia, took two victims from their homes in the vicinity of Fair Bluff, North Carolina, placed them in an automobile, and drove across the state line into South Carolina to a secluded spot. At this point both victims, a man and a woman, were flogged and seriously injured. As a result of the FBI investigation, ten subjects were identified and later tried in Federal Court at Wilmington, North Carolina. On May 13, 1952, all ten subjects in this case were convicted and received sentences for violation of the Federal Kidnaping Statute. As a result of the investigation in this case, three other cases involving members of the Ku Klux Klan who had taken victims from their homes on what the Klan members considered as their extra-legal right to lecture and flog, were developed. On January 19, 1953, nineteen subjects in one of these cases were indicted in the United States District Court for the Eastern District of North Carolina for carrying a victim from his home in South Carolina to a point in Fair Bluff, North Carolina, known as

153

"lovers lane" where the victim was held to a tree and lashed fifteen or twenty times. Investigation in the other two cases is still being conducted.

On April 2, 1949, members of the Ku Klux Klan intimidated several white persons and flogged seven Negroes in the small community of Hooker, Georgia, which is located near the Tennessee border. After thorough investigation by the FBI, the Sheriff of Dade County, Georgia, the three Deputy Sheriffs, and six other individuals were charged with violating the Civil Rights Statutes. Eight of the defendants were acquitted but the Sheriff of Dade County and a Deputy Sheriff were convicted in Federal Court for the Northern District of Georgia on March 9, 1950. Each was sentenced to imprisonment for one year and fined $1,000. These convictions were unanimously affirmed by the Court of Appeals for the Fifth Circuit and the Supreme Court of the United States denied a petition for review.

There have been no limitations placed on the time or expense involved in the investigation of civil rights cases. Investigations are conducted by as many men with as much equipment as is needed to do a complete, thorough, impartial, fair and expeditious investigation. Carefully selected Special Agents who are trained in the investigation of civil rights matters are often ordered from one Field Division to another to help conduct investigations in a particular area. In a current case in Kentucky, twenty-seven men from approximately ten offices were brought into Kentucky to assist in the investigation of a civil rights case in that area. A total of fifty-two Agents were assigned exclusively to this particular investigation. This included personnel of the Louisville Division, together with those brought in from other offices. In the Miami bombing cases, which necessitated four simultaneious investigations, nearly the entire force of the Miami Office was engaged in the investigations relative to these bombings. Numerous men were used in the investigation which has extended over a period of many months, and it is estimated that approximately $330,996 had been expended in this investigation as of February 1, 1953. The Cicero bombing case in Chicago necessitated considerable investigative time and expense with as many as forty-four Agents from our Chicago Office being used on this case. The investigation resulted in the conviction in United States District Court of three Cicero police officers.

Constant and close supervision is given to all civil rights cases, both in the Field and at the Seat of Government. In the investigation of the civil rights case in Detroit in which Walter Reuther was the victim, supervision was given at the scene of the crime by the Assistant Director who had had many years of investigative experience. It is interesting to note that during the first two years of this investigation, a total of four thousand seven hundred four Agent days were expended, and that a total of over one thousand seven hundred hours of voluntary overtime were put in by the Agents assigned to the case.

Before being assigned to field investigative work, a new Special Agent is given an intensive sixteen-week period of training. He receives, among other rhings, instruction in Constitutional law and the Bill of Rights. He studies Federal criminal procedure, and is carefully instructed on searches and seizures, interviews and confessions, and the need at all times for the protection of the rights of an individual. The rules of evidence are thoroughly explained and the statutes over which the Bureau has jurisdiction analyzed. Intensive instruction is afforded on the investigation of civil rights cases. The Bureau's training program in every respect is aimed toward teaching Special Agents their obligations as officers of the law.

Agents are periodically brought back to the Seat of Government and afforded a refresher course to bring them up to date as to methods of investigations and current policies. This course also includes instruction in the handling of civil rights investigations. In addition, the Bureau holds specialized training shcools for personnel on a selective basis. This training is designed to give the men selected intensice, individual training in the handling of investigations of civil rights violations. Another of these special schools in the handling of civil rights investigations is scheduled to be held during the month of June, 1953.

It has been determined that effective training of law enforcement officers aids in civil rights. Officers of local agencies attending the FBI National Academy receive training courses designed to promote knowledge and respect for civil rights. For instance, instruction is given on such topics as "Law Enforcement as a Profession," "Ethics in Law Enforcement," "Laws of Arrests, Searches and Seizures," "Rules of Evidence," and "The Constitution and the Bill of Rights." In addition, throughout the period of training, the officers are constantly reminded of their obligations, legal and moral, to respect the rights of every individual. These National Academy courses give the local officer a basic understanding that law enforcement is a profession of honor, legality, and that successful crime detection can only arise from a scrupulous regard for civil rights.

This matter has been brought to the attention of all law enforcement officers at different times. The September, 1952, issue of the FBI Law Enforcement Bulletin contained a statement on civil rights. The article reminded officers that the complete protection of civil rights should be a primary concern of every

-7-

law enforcement officer. Bureau officials have discussed the matter of civil rights in training schools conducted by various police departments throughout the United States. This training is designed to acquaint the police officers with the Federal statutes, to advise them of their duties as members of the law enforcement profession, and to stress the necessity of safeguarding the rights of individuals.

Over a period of time, we have received numerous compliments from prominent individuals and organizations for our efforts in the field of civil rights investigations. The most recent involved the case entitled "Unknown Subjects, Jack Gaesar - Victim, Civil Rights."

In this instance the victim's home, located in Houston, Texas, was severely damaged on April 17, 1953, as a result of a dynamite explosion. The victim, a colored cattle buyer who resided in an all-white neighborhood, was unable to furnish a specific reason for the incident. He stated to the press, "I don't think this was an attempt on my life. I think it was intended as a warning for other Negroes not to buy in this area."

An investigation was immediately initiated by the FBI, resulting in our determining that one Carl Dewey Davis had actually set off the dynamite. It was reportedly done at the request of one George Howell, a neighbor of the victim.

The facts surrounding this incident were presented to the local United States Attorney who advised that it was his opinion that this was a matter better handled by State prosecution than Federal. In this instance both Davis and Howell were charged by the local authorities with "arson by explosion."

Shortly after information regarding this matter reached the press, Mr. Walter White, Executive Secretary for the National Association for the Advancement of Colored People, communicated with the Department complimenting the Bureau and the Department for taking such aggressive action.

On December 11, 1952, shortly after the Federal Grand Jury hearing the Florida bombing incidents recessed, Walter White telegraphed us stating, "May we offer our congratulations in ferreting out some of those responsible for the Miami bombings. We believe the work of the FBI and the Department of Justice will serve as a salutary deterrent to other law breakers who may be tempted to express their prejudices and ignorance through mob action."

156

On February 26, 1953, during the course of the hearings before the Heating Committee regarding civil rights complaints involving members of the New York City Police Department, Mr. Walter White issued a press release. He stated that there were numerous indications that should New York or any other political subdivision be permitted to exclude the FBI and the Department of Justice from acting on violations of civil rights, every Southern community would then demand the same privilege. He continued that the results would be disastrous, and that about the only effective action in such matters had been that affored by the FBI.

Mr. White stated:

"Nothing whatever was done by state or local authorities against the Ku Klux Klan in South Carolina and North Carolina until the FBI intervened and pulled the cover off a long series of brutal beatings and killings. It was federal, not local, officials who broke up the bombings of Synagugues, Catholic churches and a Negro housing project in Miami. It was the FBI which secured the evidence and arrested Vernon Minnick who shot and killed a Negro at Homestead, Fla. last Christmas Day. Minnick had been a police officer in Washington and only recently had been indicted by a Federal grand jury there on charges that he beat up a Negro prisoner in the District of Columbia jail a year ago. He had gone to Florida and obtained a job as a member of the police force to continue his brutality against Negroes."

Mr. White commented to some extent regarding the agreement which existed between the Criminal Division of the Department of Justice and the New York City Police Department and concluded with the statement that "Any impairment of the efficiency or effectiveness of federal police authorities would be disastrous."

By letter dated January 2, 1952, Walter White advised that he was turning over material which he had gathered in reference to the case in which Harry T. Moore was a victim, and stated that he believed that the FBI would do a better job on the investigation of this matter than anyone else.

At the March 26, 1953, meeting of the Miami Branch of the National Association for the Advancement of Colored People, a resolution was passed regarding action taken by the Federal Government with respect to acts of violence and intimidations which had been committed against representatives of that society and citizens of the State of Florida by organizations and persons unknown. The resolution commended the efforts of the Grand Jury, the Federal judge, the Attorney General, the Special Assistants to the Attorney General, and the FBI for their diligent, forthright, and careful endeavors in gathering evidence, hearing testimony, and the preparation of the interim report which exposed the sources of violence and bigotry to the public and state officials.

In the case in Cairo, Illinois, in which Dr. U. F. Bass, a member of the National Association for the Advancement of Colored People, was the victim of a civil rights case, Mr. Thurgood Marshall telephoned a Bureau official and stated that he had been to Cairo where he had seen four of the Bureau's Agents and that they were doing an excellent job.

The Associated Press under a Chicago dateline for December 31, 1952, reported that "The Chicago Defender," a weekly Negro newspaper, on that date named nine persons and three organizations to its Honor Roll of Democracy for 1952. The Federal Bureau of Investigation was commended "for its diligent efforts in rounding up the Ku Klux Klan leadership of the Carolinas, and for its efforts in seeking out the perpetrator of the Florida Bombings."

I have always fought for the rights of the individual citizen and I shall continue to demand that investigations in civil rights matters be conducted in a thorough, impartial and efficient manner.

May 20, 1953

TO: Warren Olney III,
         Assistant Attorney General, ABC:LM:mrh
         Criminal Division

FROM: A. B. Caldwell, Chief,   144-012 Sec. 7
         Civil Rights Section

SUBJECT: <u>Civil Rights Investigations</u>

Reference is made to the attached memorandum dated April 22, 1953, from the Federal Bureau of Investigation to you, captioned Civil Rights Investigations.

The procedure of the Bureau referred to in the first paragraph of the memorandum, whereby interviews with subject law enforcement officers are held during preliminary investigations, having first been cleared with our Division, is now in effect.

The second aspect of the Bureau's memorandum, namely, the practice of obtaining and reporting to the Department the prosecutive opinion of the United States Attorneys in all civil rights investigations, has not been discussed or cleared with the Division, and appears already to have been put into effect.

This new procedure gives the Civil Rights Section more than a little concern. The Bureau predicates the change upon its desire "to further expedite the handling" of civil rights matters. Our experience shows us that the proposed procedure will contribute to delay rather than expedition.

I recognize that in most other types of cases the Bureau does ascertain and report the prosecutive views of the United States Attorney, but I think you will agree that the handling of civil rights cases are, and necessarily must be, so far removed from the handling of ordinary run-of-the-mine Federal offenses as not to lend itself to the uniformity of treatment accorded offenses generally.

The wisdom of the Bureau's asking the opinion of the United States Attorneys as to prosecution in <u>all</u> civil rights cases is doubtful. The chances are too great that prior to giving such an opinion, the United States Attorneys would not have the opportunity or may not take the time to go over the reports carefully and read the necessary reported cases in connection therewith (as we do in our Section). In such instances, what we would get would be snap judgments which might lead to unnecessary confusion later on. Such judgments could be avoided only by a careful study of the investigative reports, many of which tend to be lengthy. Therefore, delay in getting later reports to us would be inevitable.

159

If, as is true in most cases, we here decide to close a case without prosecution, it will have been a waste of valuable time on the part of the United States Attorney to have reviewed an investigation in order to render a prosecutive opinion to the Bureau. Moreover, we cannot fail to recognize that in some sections of the country, the mores of the community are such that some United States Attorneys are less than enthusiastic about civil rights prosecutions. This is bound to be reflected in delay while the Bureau seeks to obtain their prosecutive opinions.

By the procedure heretofore followed in the Department since the Section was set up fourteen years ago, the Criminal Division generally holds the initiative in expressing prosecutive views and urges and directs the United States Attorneys to prosecute only in cases worthy of such action. By this procedure, there are avoided (1) unnecessary review by the United States Attorney of the investigative reports in the overwhelming proportion of cases which are closed in any event, (2) possible hardening of expressed views of United States Attorneys, either for or against prosecution, arrived at without the benefit of a resort to available citations, large numbers of which are not to be found in the annotations of the civil rights statutes, and the accompanying need to argue them out of their expressed views.

Since preparation of the foregoing, it has been noted that a letter dated May 12, 1953, from J. Edward Lumbard, the United States Attorney for the Southern District of New York (accompanying this memorandum), discloses Bureau instructions to agents that the United States Attorney's prosecutive opinion "should be obtained and set forth in the preliminary report," (emphasis supplied) rather than as set out in the Bureau's memorandum to us "prior to the completion of a civil rights investigation." This practice would but further complicate the problems inherent in applying the Bureau's plan as originally set out in its memorandum to us. There is attached a self-explanatory interim reply to Mr. Lumbard's letter.

It might, for the foregoing reasons, be better if the Bureau confined itself to ascertaining the United States Attorney's desire relative to further investigation and to reporting, as it occasionally has, anything the United States Attorney might say in connection therewith regarding prosecution.

It is therefore recommended that the Bureau be informed that we prefer that in civil rights cases requests for prosecutive opinions be directed to the Criminal Division rather than to United States Attorneys as it is our constant aim, through discussion and correspondence with the United States Attorneys, to arrive at concurring prosecutive views - and due to importance of a uniform policy.

WO:MWH:efr
144-012 Sec. 7   May 27, 1953

AIR MAIL

Harley A. Miller, Esquire
United States Attorney
San Juan, Puerto Rico

          Re: Civil Rights Violations

Dear Mr. Miller:

        This will further refer to your letter of April 27,
1953, concerning your conferences with the Governor and the
Secretary of Justice of Puerto Rico relative to the handling
in Puerto Rico of violations of the civil rights statutes. We
note that the Governor is, apparently, opposed to the prosecution of civil rights cases by the United States and that the
Secretary of Justice has advised that if violations are referred
to his department, prompt investitation will be undertaken and
violators punished. We note, also, your recommendation that
complaints received by your office be turned over to local
authorities and to the FBI for preliminary investigation and
that Federal prosecution be undertaken unless the local authorities act within a reasonable time.

        The recent adoption and ratification of the Puerto Rican
Constitution have, of course, altered the governmental structure
of Puerto Rico and provided for the people of that commonwealth
a much greater measure of self-government. We can, therefore,
readily understand and appreciate the attitude of the Governor
and the Secretary of Justice as set forth in your letter. However, Public Law 600, Eighty-first Congress (64 Stats. 319),"adopted in the nature of a compact," expressly continued in force
and effect certain provisions of the act approved March 2, 1971,
as amended (39 Stats. 951, 48 U.S.C. 731, et seq.). Among these
provisions are Section 7 (48 U.S.C. 737, Supp. V) and Section 9
(48 U.S.C. 734). Section 7 provides that "The rights, privileges,
and immunities of citizens of the United States shall be respected
in Puerto Rico to the same extent as though Puerto Rico were a
State of the Union and subject to the provisions of paragraph 1
of Section 2 of Article IV of the Constitution of the United
States." Section 9 provides that "The statutory laws of the
United States not locally inapplicable, except as hereinbefore
or hereinafter otherwise provided, shall have the same force and
effect in Puerto Rico as in the United States. . ." In view of
these statutory provisions, it would seem to be the duty of this
Department to see that the Federal civil rights statutes are
enforced. We, therefore, do not feel that we can defer to the
wishes of the Governor and adopt a policy of declining to prosecute
in appropriate cases.

Concerning your recommendation, it is our opinion, after careful consideration, that complaints of alleged civil rights violations arising in Puerto Rico should be handled just as they are handled in the States and in the territories and possessions of the United States. At the present time, it is the Department's policy to investigate and prosecute violations of the statutes immediately and vigorously, as stated in the Criminal Division Bulletin of March 2, 1953. We do, however, cooperate with local authorities whenever possible by withholding prosecution and, in some instances, deferring investigation if it appears that bona fide, appropriate action has been taken or is being taken by the local authorities. Any such local action usually originates because of information obtained by local authorities from their own sources or from the F.B.I., which, whenever it is conducting an investigation, informs the local authorities of that fact. Of course, there would be no objection to your office informally discussing reported violations with local officials in order to encourage them to initiate and conduct whatever proceedings may be necessary or appropriate. We are afraid, however, that the practice of making formal referrals, such as you suggest, might create a tendency on the part of such officials not to act at all unless and until such referrals are made.

After you have considered our views, as stated above, we should appreciate receiving the benefit of any further suggestions which you may have. Meanwhile, we agree that your office should continue to refer complaints received by you to the F. B. I. for preliminary investigation.

Respectfully,

For the Attorney General

WARREN OLNEY III
Assistant Attorney General

C O P Y   June 4, 1953

                                     WO:LM:mrh

                                     144-012 Sec. 7

Director, Federal Bureau of Investigation

Warren Olney III, Assistant Attorney General
              Criminal Division

Civil Rights Investigations

        Reference is made to that aspect of your memorandum of
April 22, 1953, on the above subject, dealing with instructions
to agents to obtain and report the prosecutive opinion of the
appropriate United States Attorney in the course of a civil rights
investigation.

        We recognize that on occasion complaints have been
pending decision as to further investigation when time might be
of some importance. However, the Civil Rights Section of the
Criminal Division, which devotes its full time to these matters,
strives constantly, through discussion and correspondence with
United States Attorney, to arrive at concurring prosecutive
views. This makes both for uniformity of policy in the handling
of these cases and generally reduces the element of delay in
arriving at prosecutive conclusions.

        Accordingly, we prefer that in civil rights cases,
requests for prosecutive opinions be directed to the Criminal
Division rather than to United States Attorneys, and that agents
ascertain the United States Attorneys' desires relative to further
investigation, and that they continue to report, as they occasionally
do, anything a United States Attorney might say in connection
therewith regarding prosecution.

June 11, 1953

To: Assistant Attorney General
          Warren Olney III

From: Director, FBI   144-012 Sec. 8

Subject: CIVIL RIGHTS INVESTIGATIONS
          (Your reference 144-012, LM)

Reference is made to this Bureau's memorandum dated
April 22, 1953, and the Department's reply dated June 4, 1953,
regarding contact with the United States Attorneys at the completion of a Civil Rights investigation for their opinions relative
to the merits of a particular case.

As you are aware difficulties have been experienced in the
past as the result of delays on the part of United States Attorneys
to promptly initiate action with respect to specific cases resulting
in undue criticism being directed at both the Department and the
Bureau. Classic examples are, of course, the incidents involving
Paul Vernon Minnick who is the subject of two different cases. It
will be recalled that while a member of the Metropolitan Police
Department in the District, Minnick was involved in a Civil Rights
incident. Delays were experienced with respect to prosecutive
action and subsequent to leaving Washington, D.C., and securing
employment as an officer in Homestead, Florida, Minnick was
involved in the shooting and killing of one Emmett Jefferson. The
second incident occurred some months after the one in Washington,
D.C., and prior to any decision being rendered with respect to it.

In addition to the above, it has been noted that other
delays are being experienced which if eliminated would hasten the
completion of the investigation. This is reflected in those
instances where, upon completion of the investigation, the Department finds it necessary to communicate directly with the United
States Attorney for his opinion regarding the merits of a complaint;
for his suggestions as to the value of further inquiry, and such.
As a result further action with respect to the individual case
is at a standstill awaiting the United States Attorney's reply.

In the interest of efficiency and expediency, both from
the standpoint of the Department and the Bureau, instructions
were directed to our field offices on April 28, 1953, based upon
the action set forth in our memorandum to the Department dated
April 22, 1953. It will be noted that our memorandum to the
Department points out that the opinions of the United States
Attorneys would be obtained at the completion of an investigation
and that such action would in no way alter the established procedure of obtaining the Department's opinion prior to closing a
case or initiating prosecutive action. To further stress this
point our field offices were also instructed that such action
would not change existing regulations of not permitting arrests
to be made or complaints filed by FBI personnel in Civil Rights
cases without first obtaining Department approval through the
Bureau.

164

The above procedure has been instituted pursuant to and in accordance with our memorandum of April 22, 1953, which was prepared subsequent to being discussed with various representatives of the Civil Rights Section in the Department. It is noted that your memorandum of June 4, 1953, stated that you would prefer that requests for prosecutive opinions be directed to the Criminal Division rather than to the United States Attorneys. It is also noted that Agents are to ascertain the United States Attorney's desires relative to further investigation and that they, the Agents, are to continue to report anything the United States Attorny might say regarding prosecution.

Such instructions appear somewhat contradictory in that our Agents are not to request prosecutive opinions from the United States Attorneys but by the same token are to ascertain the United States Attorneys' desires as to the necessity for further inquiry and report any statements made by him regarding prosecution.

Inasmuch as the policy presented in our memorandum of April 22, 1953, was primarily initiated to serve as an aid to the Department in arriving at an opinion, advice is requested as to whether or not it is desired that this policy be continued.

Director, Federal Bureau of Investigation

Warren Olney III, Assistant Attorney General
                Criminal Division

Typed: 6-24-53)

June 25, 1953
WO:ABC:mrh

144-012 Sec. 8

Civil Rights Investigations

Reference is made to your memorandum of June 11, 1953, concerning the above subject. You refer therein to your memorandum, dated April 22, 1953, and the Department's reply, dated June 4, 1953.

The Department has no objection to obtaining the United States Attorney's opinion relative to the merits of a particular case at the completion of the investigation, or to the immediate handling of any logical investigation the United States Attorney might request.

The Criminal Division's concern about the change of procedures suggested in your memorandum of April 22, 1953, was based solely on the belief that any attempt to secure the prosecutive opinion of the appropriate United States Attorney might very well result in delay rather than expedition in the handling of civil rights cases. In this connection, your attention is invited to your memorandum to the Attorney General, dated January 6, 1953, subject: Civil Rights Cases in the District of Columbia, in which you point out the delay in the Minnick and other cases and state on page 4, last paragraph, as follows: "The aforementioned cases have very briefly been outlined for your ready reference. It appears they indicate unwarranted delays on the part of the United States Attorney's office in reaching a decision as to whether an investigation should be instituted and also whether prosecution is to be entertained." It was just such delay as occurred in the Minnick case we wished to avoid by our suggestion that the Bureau contact the Criminal Division for our prosecutive opinion rather than hold up the completion of the investigation until the prosecutive opinion of the appropriate United States Attorney could be obtained.

144-012 Sec. 8

Director, FBI   July 2, 1953

William P. Rogers
Deputy Attorney General
Handling of Civil Rights
Cases in the District of Puerto Rico

    Attached is a copy of a memorandum addressed to me by
Mr. Olney, Assistant Attorney General for the Criminal Division,
and a copy of his letter to Mr. Harley Miller, United States
Attorney for the District of Puerto Rico, both having to do
with the handling of Civil Rights cases in the District of
Puerto Rico.

    I am in accord with Mr. Olney's letter to Mr. Miller.
I would call your attention to the last paragraph of the
memorandum to me, which suggests that notice that an investigation of a Civil Rights violation be given to the Attorney
General of Puerto Rico at the time such investigation is
initiated.

    I would appreciate your comments on this suggestion.

144-012 Sec. 8

July 3, 1953

Assistant Attorney General
Warren Olney III

Director, FBI

CIVIL RIGHTS INVESTIGATIONS
(Your Reference 144-012-ABC)

Reference is made to previous correspondence concerning Civil Rights investigations involving the question of interviewing United States Attorneys relative to the obtaining of an opinion as to the merits of a particular case.

As you know, oral discussions were had prior to the time the Bureau instituted this procedure of obtaining United States Attorneys' opinions, if readily available, in order to submit them along with facts developed for consideration and study by the Criminal Division.

You will recall that the Minnick case was specifically called to the attention of the Criminal Division as a classic example of delay. Because of the Minnick case wherein the United States Attorney failed to give an opinion over a period of many months although the Criminal Division had requested it on several occasions, these discussions were held and the procedure put in force of contacting the United States Attorney in order that a similar delay on the part of a United States Attorney would not occur.

It has been our understanding that the United States Attorney's opinion is not the final determination as to the disposition of a case and that this determination rests with the Criminal Division of the Department of Justice. However, the Department has, in the past, sought the opinion of the United States Attorney in numerous cases and as has been indicated it was thought that this policy would streamline and assist the Civil Rights Section of the Department in the handling of Civil Rights cases.

From your memorandum of June 25, 1953, we understand that you approve of the present procedure and the Bureau will keep this policy in effect unless advised to the contrary.

168

144-012 Sec. 8

TO: Mr. William P. Rogers
           Deputy Attorney General

July 10, 1953

FROM: Director, FBI

SUBJECT: HANDLING OF CIVIL RIGHTS CASES
         IN THE DISTRICT OF PUERTO RICO

Reference is made to your memorandum of July 2, 1953, requesting comments as to whether or not the Attorney General in Puerto Rico should be advised when a Civil Rights investigation is initiated.

Further reference is made to the memorandum of Mr. Olney, Assistant Attorney General for the Criminal Division, addressed to you under date of June 16, 1953, recommending that this Bureau advise the Puerto Rican Attorney General of the institution of investigations in Civil Rights cases. This notification was to be in addition to that given to local authorities. It is observed that the Attorney Generals of the various states of the United States, as well as the corresponding officials of county and municipal governments in the United States, are not formally advised when an investigation is initiated by this Bureau regarding an alleged violation of the Civil Rights Statutes. It is not believed advisable to establish a policy of notifying the Attorney General of a particular area when an investigation is being initiated by this Bureau. Such a practice might well establish a precedent and result in similar requests being made by state, county and municipal authorities throughout the entire United States. It is not believed that special notification should be given to the Attorney General of Puerto Rico that a Civil Rights investigation is being initiated by this Bureau.

As was pointed out in Mr. Olney's letter to United States Attorney Miller of Puerto Rico, under date of May 27, 1953, the practice of making formal referrals to local officials might create a tendency on the part of such officials not to act at all unless a formal referral to them had been made. As you know this Bureau, in conducting investigations of an alleged violation of Civil Rights, contacts the head of the law enforcement agency to verify that the subject is a duly accredited officer. During this interview the head of the law enforcement agency is advised an allegation has been made against an officer and that this Bureau, in discharging its duties, is conducting an investigation to obtain the facts of the incident so that a determination may be made by the Criminal Division as to whether or not there has been a violation of the Civil Rights Statutes. Thus the head of the law enforcement agency is aware of the fact that an investigation is being conducted by this Bureau and may, if he desires, advise the pertinent officials of his branch of the government, or institute local action.

169

144-012 Sec. 8

July 20, 1953

Mr. J. Edgar Hoover
Director, Federal Bureau of Investigation

William P. Rogers
Deputy Attorney General

HANDLING OF CIVIL RIGHTS CASES
IN THE DISTRICT OF PUERTO RICO

Reference is made to your memorandum of July 10, 1953, regarding the above subject.

I have read the memorandum, and I concur with your view that it would be unwise to establish the practice of advising the Attorney General of Puerto Rico when an investigation is initiated by the Federal Bureau of Investigation with respect to violations of Civil Rights by bona fide officers of that area.

I am referring a copy of your memorandum of July 10, together with a copy of this memorandum to Mr. Warren Olney, Assistant Attorney General, Criminal Division

WO:MWH:efr

144-012

August 4, 1953

144-012 Sec. 8

C. M. Raemer, Esquire
United States Attorney
East St. Louis, Illinois

Re: Policy Relative to the Investigation of
Civil Rights Cases

Dear Mr. Raemer:

This will acknowledge your letter of July 20, 1953. We
note that you refer to the great number of insubstantial complaints regarding alleged deprivations of civil rights by police
officers and request instructions regarding the policy of this
Department regarding such matters.

We recognize that civil rights complaints will sometimes
increase following an incident or incidents which call attention
to the activity of the Federal Government in this field. We
know, also, that most of such complaints are not likely to reflect violations of the civil rights statutes and that the
persons making them are apt to be motivated by a desire to
escape the consequences of whatever acts which caused their
arrest or alleged trouble with law enforcement authorities. It
is true, also, that most people do not understand the limitations
on Federal jurisdiction and, therefore, make complaints which
should be addressed to the state authorities.

Our policy in handling complaints is as follows:

1. If it is apparent that the facts, as stated by him,
do not involve violations of the civil rights statutes, the
complainant is so informed and the matter is closed without
investigation.

2. Where the information given by the complainant, if
true, would indicate a violation of the civil rights statutes,
either a preliminary or a full investigation is requested. If
such information is given to a United States Attorney, he should
request a preliminary investigation and, after it is completed,
a determination is made by him and the Civil Rights Section as
to whether a full investigation is warranted.

To this, we might add that, whenever you are in doubt as
to whether a particular matter warrants investigation, the
information can be referred to the Civil Rights Section for its
consideration and decision. Of course, we do not want to spend

171

-2-

unnecessary time investigating and considering matters which
are either devoid of substance or without our jurisdiction.
On the other hand, it is important that meritorious cases are
not overlooked.

We shall be glad to attempt to resolve any further
questions you may have with respect to the above if you feel
that it is not clear or if there are suggestions you care to
make.

In connection with the case involving Joseph Bonner
(Everett Farrow - Victim), we note from the report of Special
Agent Kermit F. Johnson, dated July 8, 1953, that it may be
tried in the State court at the fall session in September.
After the State case has been concluded, please let us have your
opinion as to prosecution under the Federal civil rights statutes.
If the defendant is acquitted in the State case, decision will
have to be made as to whether, under all the circumstances, a
trial in the Federal courts is warranted for the alleged violation of the civil rights statutes.

Respectfully,

For the Attorney General

WARREN OLNEY III
Assistant Attorney General

WO:LM:aik
144-012 - Sec. 8   August 4, 1953

(Typed: 7-30-53)

William M. Steger, Esquire
United States Attorney
Tyler, Texas

Dear Mr. Steger:

This is to acknowledge your letter of July 24, 1953 to Mr. Arthur B. Caldwell, Chief of our Civil Rights Section.

United States Attorneys are authorized, when requested, to render opinions to the Federabl Bureau of Investigation as to the feasibility of continued investigation of criminal matters generally and to inform it whether their investigation justified prosecution in most types of cases. However, in Civil Rights cases, following completion of the investigation (preliminary or full, as the case may be), the Bureau Field Agent may, if he so desires, informally review the case with the United States Attorney or his Assistant to obtain his general reactions, but not to obtain his final prosecutive opinion. The United States Attorney and the Criminal Division will mutually determine the disposition of the case in accordance with the practice which has previously obtained.

Guided by the foregoing policy, it would seem that as a practical matter, when on the basis of information in the Bureau's possession, an Agent (prior to submission of any written report) seeks the United States Attorney's prosecutive views or his reactions as to the feasibility of investigation, the United States Attorney may disclose his views even though he indicates that the facts as reported appear to him to be lacking in merit, but he should not authorize the Federal Bureau of Investigation to close the case until after receipt of its written report and the concurrence of the Criminal Division.

We trust that the foregoing clarifies the matter. We are in addition enclosing a copy of an address delivered by Mr. Caldwell on July 16, 1953 dealing with the activities of the Civil Rights Section for such assistance as it may be to you.

                    Respectfully,

                    For the Attorney General

                    WARREN OLNEY III
                    Assistant Attorney General

Enclosure No. 95718

144-012 Sec. 8

August 6, 1953

Honorable John S. Fine
The Governor of Pennsylvania
Harrisburg, Pennsylvania

My dear Governor Fine:

In reading newspaper accounts of the recent Governors'
Conference, I noted certain remarks which were attributed to you
concerning the Federal Bureau of Investigations's handling of
Civil Rights matters and I want to send this letter to you to
furnish you my views. The news article attributed to you a
statement to the effect that investigations into mental and penal
institutions in the State of Pennsylvania might lead to the
establishment of a new area of encroachment of the Federal
Government upon the rights of the states. It further reported
that the Federal Bureau of Investigation had insisted upon
conducting its own investigation despite the fact that an investigation had been conducted by state and local authorities. The
article also referred to the Robert H. Byers case as a specific
case in point.

In fulfilling our obligation, the Federal Bureau of Investigation, which is a fact-finding organization and the investigative
arm of the Department of Justice, obtains the original facts and
furnishes them to the Department of Justice for its opinion. The
Federal Bureau of Investigation conducts a complete investigation
into an alleged Civil Rights violation only at the direction of
the Attorney General of the United States. When such investigation
is ordered by the Attorney General, it is our duty to promptly
investigate and obtain all facts concerning the alleged violation.

Attorney General Herbert Brownell, by letter dated April 15,
1953, directed to the Honorable Robert E. Woodside, the Attorney
General for the Commonwealth of Pennsylvania, concerning the
Byers case, advised Attorney General Woodside of the statutes
under which that investigation was conducted and the reason that
investigation by the Federal Bureau of Investigation was requested
by the Department of Justice.

The thought occurred to me that this information might be of
interest to you.

With kind personal regards,

Sincerely yours,

174

144-012 Sec. 8

August 6, 1953

Honorable Thomas E. Dewey
The Governor of New York
Albany, New York

My dear Governor Dewey:

I wanted to take this opportunity to write you concerning the comments which Governor Fine of Pennsylvania made at the Governors' Conference in Seattle, Washington, which comments appeared in the press. The press indicated that you agreed with Governor Fine in his complaint concerning this Bureau's alleged interference in the operation of state penal and mental institutions.

There appears to be some question or misunderstanding as to the role of this Bureau in the investigation of Civil Rights cases. This Bureau, as you are aware, is a fact-finding service organization designed to investigate alleged violations of Federal laws. Certain of these laws have been specifically assigned to this Bureau by the Congress and others by the Department of Justice for enforcement. Among these laws or statutes are the Federal Civil Rights Statutes.

The duty of the Federal Bureau of Investigation is to investigate and to investigate thoroughly, without bias or prejudice, all alleged violations of Federal laws. To that end, I have and will continue to direct the Federal Bureau of Investigation. I am sure you realize that the execution of this duty is the only goal which investigating Agents have in the investigation of Civil Rights cases or other allegations of violations of Federal laws. It never has been or will be the intention of this Bureau to interfere with or dictate in any manner, the internal operations of state penal or mental institutions. In the investigation of Civil Rights cases, preliminary facts are gathered by the Federal Bureau of Investigation and transmitted to the Criminal Division of the Department of Justice where a decision is made as to further investigation or prosecution.

It is noted that you were quoted by the newspapers as saying that the State of New York would "swarm" with Federal Bureau of Investigation Agents if the Federal Government decided to investigate every complaint of an alleged Civil Rights violation by inmates of these state institutions. The decision of whether or not the Federal Government should investigate allegations made by inmates of state penal and mental institutions against state officials is one which is made by the Criminal Division of the Department of Justice only after a careful study indicates that the allegations appeared to be substantial and to

175

indicate a violation of the Federal Civil Rights Statute. After that decision is made, this Bureau is merely carrying out its duty and responsibility in conducting an investigation into such allegations.

It is not the intention of the Federal Bureau of Investigation to investigate every complaint made by inmates of these institutions against state officials. However, it is this Bureau's duty to investigate where the allegations are of a substantial nature indicating a violation of the Civil Rights Statute.

I did want to write you in this matter in order to apprise you of the position of the Federal Bureau of Investigation in carrying out its responsibility in Civil Rights matters.

With kind personal regards,

Sincerely yours,

144-012 Sec. 8

August 6, 1953

Honorable John S. Battle
The Governor of Virginia
Richmond, Virginia

My dear Governor Battle:

I have noted recent news comments in which it was stated
you had supported Governor John S. Fine of Pennsylvania in his
assertions concerning the Federal Bureau of Investigation's
handling of Civil Rights cases. This article reported that
you indicated the Federal Bureau of Investigation had investigated a complaint in a Virginia penal institution after the
state had tried and convicted those guilty. The article further
indicated that you believed the Federal Bureau of Investigation
might, if it investigated every incident in a state mental
or penal institution, interfere with the orderly operation of
the state governments.

In this regard, I did want to point out to you the FBI's
responsibilities in connection with its investigations of
alleged civil-rights violations. The Civil Rights Statutes
are part of the enacted law of the United States and, as such,
create a responsibility in the Federal Bureau of Investigation
to investigate violations thereof. However, in every instance
where a complaint is received alleging a civil-rights violation,
the facts as originally obtained are furnished to the Department of Justice for its consideration. Thereafter, the
Criminal Division of the Department of Justice, after due study,
instructs whether or not a complete investigation shall or shall
not be conducted by the FBI.

As you can see, the FBI functions as a service agency
and performs these investigations under the direction of the
Attorney General. You may rest assured, however, that in
fulfilling our obligations there is no intention on the part
of this Bureau to interfere with the orderly operation of state
government.

In this same regard, you will undoubtedly recall the
letter from Attorney General Brownell to you, dated June 9,
1953. Therein it was stated that the FBI had been instructed
by the Department of Justice to conduct investigations into
alleged violations which had occurred in a Virginia penal
institution after the Department of Justice had made a thorough
review of the facts available, including the results of local
action and prosecution.

177

In view of the comments in the press and in view of the responsibilities which the FBI must discharge, I wanted to give you the benefit of the foregoing comments.

With kind personal regards,

Sincerely yours,

144-012 Sec. 9

October 23, 1953

MEMORANDUM FOR THE ATTORNEY GENERAL

I am attaching hereto a copy of an article which appeared in the Jackson, Michigan "Citizen Patriot" for October 20, 1953. I call particular attention to the statement issued by Attorney General Frank G. Millard of Michigan, who states that the next time the FBI probes a state government agency, the Governor and the Attorney General will be let in on the secret. Mr. Millard states that this assurance had been given to a Committee of the Attorneys General Association by the Department of Justice.

This article further goes on to point out that Mr. Millard stated that the Association had complained to you about the secret movement of FBI Agents into state agencies. He specifically refers to the fact that the FBI probed civil rights violations in a Southern Michigan Prison this year without advising the state authorities in advance.

I bring this article to your attention because I have not been advised of any complaint filed by the Attorneys General Association concerning the conduct of the FBI in making inquiries into alleged violations of civil rights. Neither have I been advised that there has been a change agreed to in the procedure which the FBI has followed in the past and is following at the present time.

As you are aware, this Bureau never initiates an investigation of a state institution without first advising the head of that particular institution. In the instance cited by Mr. Millard, to the effect that we had investigated a Southern Michigan Prison without telling state officials in advance, he is absolutely incorrect. Warden William H. Bannan of the State Prison of Southern Michigan was personally advised by the Agent in Charge of our Detroit Office before the investigation was initiated and, in addition, was personally contacted by the two Special Agents of the Detroit Office who were assigned to the investigation prior to the actual conducting of the investigation. We did not contact the Governor of Michigan nor the Attorney General of Michigan but we did contact the State official in charge of the institution, namely Warden Bannan. That has always been our practice and is our practice at the present time. It would seem to me that in informing the head of a state institution we are proposing to initiate an investigation that we have met the requirements of protocol and courtesy and it is then the responsibility of the head of that particular state agency to notify his superiors if he desires to do so.

I strongly resent the continued intimation that the FBI moves secretly into states to conduct investigations of alleged violations of the civil rights statutes.

179

I also note from the attached article that the preliminary investigation to be conducted by the FBI will be made to determine if a team of Agents should be moved in. If so, at that point the states will be informed of Federal plans. Again, this is not the procedure we have followed in the past, nor are following at the present time, and I have received no instructions to the contrary.

At the present time the Bureau conducts a preliminary inquiry but before initiating that we inform the head of the state agency in which, or of which, the inquiry is to be made. It is not a question of moving a team of Agents into the situation because sometimes the investigation can be conducted by one Agent and again it may require several, whether it be in the preliminary or in the full investigation.

Since this Bureau and myself have been the butt of practically all the attacks made by Governors and Attorneys General of states, I would certainly appreciate being informed as to whether the procedures which we have followed up to the present time are unsatisfactory and, further, as to whether those procedures have been changed because I have not been advised to that effect. It is impossible to properly meet the duties and responsibilities which face this Bureau unless I am advised of dissatisfaction upon the part of the Department of the Bureau's procedures or informed of changes that have been effected or are to be effected.

Respectfully,

John Edgar Hoover
Director

144-012 Sec. 9

December 1, 1953

TO: Assistant Attorney General
          Warren Olney III

FROM: Director, FBI

SUBJECT: CIVIL RIGHTS INVESTIGATIONS

From time to time an allegation of a civil rights violation is received by one of our field offices wherein a question arises as to whether or not a violation actually exists warranting consideration as to whether a preliminary investigation should be instituted. In some instances in these questionable situations, the field has presented the facts to the United States Attorney for an opinion prior to initiating any preliminary investigation. In those cases wherein it was determined from the United States Attorney that, in his opinion, a violation of the statutes did not exist, the original allegation together with the United States Attorney's opinion, has been referred on to the Civil Rights Section of the Criminal Division for a final determination.

Your memorandum of June 25, 1953, (your reference 144-012, ABC), authorizes the Bureau to obtain the United States Attorney's opinion relative to the merits of the particular case at the completion of the investigation. It will be noted, however, that this situation only covers those instances wherein an investigation has been completed, and it will be appreciated if you will advise whether the procedure outlined in the first paragraph should be continued.

December 4, 1953

TO: Assistant Attorney General
          Warren Olney III

FROM: Director, FBI

SUBJECT: CIVIL RIGHTS INVESTIGATIONS

The Bureau and its various offices are receiving at the present time a number of letters from persons who are incarcerated in State penal institutions. These letters usually allege a violation of the prisoners' civil rights and in most instances there is not enough detail in the letters to enable one to determine whether a violation of the Federal Civil Rights Statutes exists.

It has been the policy of this Bureau in those instances where there is not enough information to enable one to determine whether or not a violation exists to interview the alleged victim. If the information supplied by the victim then indicates a violation a preliminary investigation is immediately instituted, after which the results are sent to you for an opinion as to further investigation or contemplated prosecutive action; if the information given by the victim does not indicate a violation, the facts are forwarded to you for an opinion and your information.

If there are sufficient details in the letter which indicate a possible violation, the victim is immediately interviewed, as signed statement obtained and a preliminary investigation instituted.

Your advice is requested as to whether or not a preliminary investigation should be instituted immediately after the interview of the victim if the facts supplied by him indicate a possible violation or whether this information supplied by him should be referred to you for an opinion before instituting a preliminary investigation.

Director
Federal Bureau of Investigation

Warren Olney III, Assistant Attorney
General, Criminal Division

WO:LM:fmm

144-012

December 17, 1953

Civil Rights Investigations

Reference is made to your memorandum of December 1, 1953, on the captioned subject.

It is felt that the procedure outlined in the first paragraph of your memorandum serves a highly useful purpose in helping both the Bureau and the Department to eliminate at an early stage large numbers of frivolous, insubstantial and legally unfounded complaints. We approve its continuance.

January 18, 1954

TO: Assistant Attorney General
           Warren Olney III

FROM: Director, FBI

SUBJECT: Civil Rights Investigations

        Reference is made to my memorandum dated December 4,
1953, in which your advice was requested as to whether or not
a preliminary investigation should be instituted immediately
after interview of a victim who is incarcerated in a state
penal institution if the facts supplied by him indicate a
possible violation or whether this information supplied by the
victim should be referred to you for an opinion before
instituting a preliminary investigation.

        It is requested that you advise as soon as possible
of your decision in this matter.

The Director

Warren Olney III, Assistant Attorney
General, Criminal Division

Civil Rights Investigations

WO:LM:rmm
144-012   Sec. 9
February 15, 1954

     Reference is made to your memorandum of December 4,
1953 relative to preliminary investigations of alleged violations of the civil rights of prisoners in state penal institutions.

     The policy and procedure now being followed by the
Bureau, as described in the first three paragraphs of your
memorandum of December 4, have proved to be satisfactory and
no change is considered necessary. If unusual examples arise
in which the Bureau is in doubt as to the advisability of
conducting a preliminary investigation, the complaint may be
referred to the Criminal Division for an opinion.

UNITED STATES DEPARTMENT OF JUSTICE

OFFICE OF THE ATTORNEY GENERAL

WASHINGTON, D. C.

February 9, 1954

ORDER NO. 40-54

TO ALL UNITED STATES ATTORNEYS, THE FEDERAL BUREAU OF INVESTIGATION, AND ATTORNEYS OF THE CRIMINAL DIVISION:

Subject: Civil Rights and Peonage, Slavery and Involuntary Servitude Statutes (18 U.S.C. 241, 242, 243, 1581, 1583, 1584)

It is the policy of the Department to be alert to and to act promptly and vigorously in all matters involving possible violations of the civil rights statutes (18 U.S.C. 241, 242, 243) or the peonage, slavery, or involuntary servitude statutes (18 U.S.C. 1581, 1583, 1584) without regard to the district in which the offense may have been committed. Any information and all complaints concerning such matters possibly within the jurisdiction of the Department will be given immediate attention and appropriate action.

The investigation of all complaints and the prosecution and handling of all cases involving possible violations of 18 U.S.C., Section 242 - willful deprivations of federal rights of inhabitants under color of law (Screws v. United States, 325 U.S. 91 (1945)); Williams v. United States, 341 U.S. 97 (1951)), Section 241 - conspiring to injure citizens in exercise of federal rights (United States v. Williams, 341 U.S. 70 (1951)), other than in election and labor cases*, and Section 243 - exclusion of jurors on account of race or color; and the investigation of all complaints and the prosecution and handling of all cases involving possible violations of 18 U.S.C., Section 1581 (peonage, arrest with intent to place in peonage), Section 1583 (carrying persons to be sold into involuntary servitude or held as a slave), and Section 1584 (involuntary servitude), are subject to the following instructions:

1. The Federal Bureau of Investigation is authorized to conduct preliminary investigations into all complaints involving possible violations of any of the above statutes, without the necessity of prior authorization of the Criminal Division. Whenever a complaint involving a possible violation of any of these statutes comes to the

─────────────────────────

* Separate Orders will cover election matters and labor matters involving Section 241.

186

attention of the United States Attorney, or any other official or employee of the Department, he shall immediately refer it to the Federal Bureau of Investigation and advise the Criminal Division of such referral.

2. Upon completion of the preliminary investigation and receipt of the Bureau's reports, the United States Attorney for the District having jurisdiction will promptly review such reports and forward to the Criminal Division his recommendations concerning the need for further investigation or whether the matter should be closed, giving his reasons therefor. (In unusual cases where it clearly appears that violations have been committed and where time is of the essence, the Federal Bureau of Investigation may be instructed to complete the investigation in cooperation with the United States Attorney without obtaining clearance from the Criminal Division.)

3. In no case is prosecution under the civil rights statutes, or under the peonage, slavery or involuntary servitude statutes, including presentation of the case to a grand jury for investigation or indictment, to be instituted without prior approval of the Criminal Division.

4. The Criminal Division should be notified immediately of any court decision or order in any civil rights, peonage, slavery or involuntary servitude case. While no appeal should be prosecuted on behalf of the Government in these cases without prior authorization, the United States Attorney may, where the statute provides a basis for appeal by the Government and time is short, file a protective appeal. When such appeal is noted, or any similar action is taken to protect the interests of the Government, the Criminal Division should be promptly notified.

5. It is the policy of the Department, insofar as consistent with Departmental regulations prohibiting disclosure of confidential documents or information, to lend all possible aid to State prosecutive action, where appropriate. When it appears that prompt and vigorous action is taken in good faith by the State to prosecute persons who have violated State law as well as the federal statutes covered by this Order, federal prosecution may be deferred pending disposition of the State charges. However, such State prosecutions must be closely followed and the Criminal Division kept currently advised of all developments in order to protect the interests of the Government and prevent the running of the federal statute of limitations. Final disposition of the federal offense will be determined following the receipt of recommendations by the United States Attorney, whose views will be fully considered.

This Order supersedes Circular No. 3356 and Supplements 1, 2, 3 and 4, and Circular No. 3591.

/Signed/
HERBERT BROWNELL, JR.
Attorney General

UNITED STATES DEPARTMENT OF JUSTICE

OFFICE OF THE ATTORNEY GENERAL

Washington 25, D. C.

February 9, 1954

ORDER NO. 41 - 54.

TO ALL UNITED STATES ATTORNEYS, THE FEDERAL BUREAU OF INVESTIGATION,
AND ATTORNEYS OF THE CRIMINAL DIVISION:

Subject: Elections, Election Campaigns and Political Activity

The investigation of all complaints and the handling and
prosecution of all cases involving possible violations of the statutes
designated below as "election laws" shall be conducted in accordance
with the following instructions:

1. The Federal Bureau of Investigation is authorized to
conduct preliminary investigations into all complaints involving possible
violations of any of the election laws, without the necessity of prior
authorization of the Criminal Division. Whenever a complaint involving
a possible violation of any of these statutes comes to the attention of
the United States Attorney, he shall immediately refer it to the Federal
Bureau of Investigation and advise the Criminal Division of such referral.

2. Upon completion of the preliminary investigation and receipt
of the Bureau's reports, the United States Attorney for the District having
jurisdiction will promptly review such reports and forward to the Criminal
Division his recommendations concerning the need for further investigation
and the advisability of prosecutive action, giving his reasons therefor.
In unusual cases where it clearly appears that violations have been committed and where time is of the essence, the Federal Bureau of Investigation
may be instructed to complete the investigation in cooperation with the
United States Attorney without obtaining clearance from the Criminal
Division.

3. In no case is prosecution under the election laws, including
the presentation of the case to a grand jury for investigation or indictment, to be instituted without prior approval of the Criminal Division.
However, where it appears that tangible evidence such as ballots, ballot
books and tally sheets will be destroyed in accordance with state law
after a certain date, and time is short, the United States Attorney may
petition the court for an order impounding such paraphernalia without
prior authorization of the Criminal Division.

188

4. The Criminal Division should be notified immediately of any court decision or order in any election law case. While no appeal should be prosecuted on behalf of the Government in these cases without prior authorization, the United States Attorney may, where the statute provides a basis for appeal by the Government and time is short, file a protective appeal. When such appeal is noted, or any similar action is taken to protect the interests of the Government, the Criminal Division should be promptly notified.

The following Sections of Title 18, U.S.C., are considered "election laws" for the purpose of this Circular:

Section 241 - conspiracies to injure federal rights. (See United States v. Classic, 313 U.S. 299).

Section 242 - deprivation of constitutional rights under color of law (See United States v. Classic, supra, and Screws v. United States, 325 U.S. 91).

Section 591 - (Corrupt Practice Act, Section 302) - definitions.

Section 592 - troops at polls prohibited.

Section 593 - interference by armed forces with elections.

Section 594 - (Hatch Act, Section 1) - intimidation of voters in a federal election.

Section 595 - (Hatch Act, Section 2) - use of official authority to affect elections.

Section 596 - polling armed forces

Section 597 - (Corrupt Practice Act, Section 311) - bribery of voters. (See United States v. Blanton, 77 F. Supp. 812).

Section 598 - (Hatch Act, Sections 7 & 8) - use of relief appropriations to coerce voters.

Section 599 - (Corrupt Practice Act, Section 310) - promise of appointment by candidate.

Section 600 - (Hatch Act, Section 3) - promise of employment in consideration for political activity.

- 3 -

Section 601 - (Hatch Act, Section 4) - deprivation of
employment for political activity.

Section 602 - (Corrupt Practice Act, Section 312) -
solicitation of political contributions from
Government employees. (See United States v.
Wurzback, 280 U.S. 396).

Section 603 - solicitation of political contributions on
Government property. (See United States v.
Thayer, 209 U.S. 39, United States v. Smith,
163 F. 926).

Section 604 - (Hatch Act, Section 5) - solicitation of
political contributions from persons on relief.

Section 605 - (Hatch Act, Section 6) - disclosure for
political purposes of names of persons on relief.

Section 606 - intimidation to secure political contributions.

Section 607 - political contributions solicited by and from
Government employees.

Section 608 - (Hatch Act, Section 13) - $5,000 limitation on
certain political contributions.

Section 609 - (Corrupt Practice Act, Section 314) - Maximum
contributions and expenditures.

Section 610 - (Corrupt Practice Act, Section 313) - contributions or expenditures by national banks,
corporations or labor organizations.

Section 611 - (Hatch Act, Section 20) - contributions by
firms or individuals contracting with the
United States.

Section 612 - publication or distribution of anonymous political
literature.

In addition to the above listed criminal election laws certain
other statutes having to do with the subject appear in Title 2, Sections 241
to 248 and 252. The pertinent provisions of Title 2 (originally Sections 303
to 309 of the Corrupt Practices Act) require the filing of financial statements by political committees, condidates for the House and Senate and individual contributions with the Clerk of the House of Representatives or the
Secretary of the Senate. Although the filing provisions of Title 2 carry a
criminal penalty, they are, nevertheless, primarily administrative in nature.

It is, therefore, the Department's policy not to institute investigations into possible violations of the laws in question in the absence of a request from the Clerk of the United States House of Representatives or the Secretary of the United States Senate, whose interest in the administration of these laws is considered paramount to that of the Department of Justice. The Federal Bureau of Investigation and the United States Attorneys should, therefore, refer all complaints involving possible failure to comply with the filing provisions of these statutes directly to the Criminal Division of the Department and should take no further action in the absence of express instructions.

Title 5, Section 118 (i - o) (originally Sections 9, 12 and 14 to 19 of the Hatch Act) also pertains to the subject of elections and political activity. The provisions of this section limit the political activity of federal employees under penalty of dismissal or suspension from the service. Being wholly administrative in character they are within the exclusive jurisdiction of the Civil Service Commission.

This Order supersedes Circulars No. 2882, 3220, 3285, 3298, 3301, 3302, 3338, 3354, 3404, 3416 and 3510.

(Signed) Herbert Brownell, Jr.

HERBERT BROWNELL, JR.
Attorney General

Office Memorandum   ABC:IC

To: The Attorneys of the   February 12, 1954
         Civil Rights Section
From: A. B. Caldwell, Chief,
         Civil Rights Section
Subject; Investigations of Civil Rights
         Violations based on Unconstitu-
         tional Searches

        Reference is made to the opinion of the Supreme Court in
United States v. Irvine, handed down on Monday, February 8,
and the request by two members of the Court that the Department of Justice investigate the facts to determine whether a
violation of the civil rights statute occurred.

        Following a conference between Mr, Olney and Mr. J.
Edgar Hoover, it was decided that the Bureau would not conduct
investigations on complaints based entirely on illegal or unconstitutional searches until after such complaint had been referred to the Criminal Division and the Criminal Division
specifically authorizes an investigation. In this connection,
all such complaints must be thoroughly and carefully examined,
and before any request for investigation is made to the Bureau
it must be cleared through the front office.

        Please initial the original of this memorandum and
retain the copy makred for you.

TO: Assistant Attorney General   10, 1954
        Warren Olney III
                                            144-012 Sec. 9

FROM: Director, FBI

SUBJECT: CIVIL RIGHTS AND INVOLUNTARY
         SERVITUDE AND SLAVERY MATTERS

        Reference is made to Department Order #40-54, dated
February 9, 1954, and directed to all United States Attorneys,
the Federal Bureau of Investigation, and Attorneys of the
Criminal Division, regarding Civil Rights and Peonage and
Involuntary Servitude and Slavery Statutes.

        This order states that the investigation of all complaints
and the prosecution and handling of all cases involving
possible violations of the Civil Rights and Involuntary Servitude and Slavery Statutes are subject to certain instructions.
The last sentence in Instruction #2 states "...in unusual cases
where it clearly appears that violations have been committed
and where time is of the essence, the Federal Bureau of Investigation may be instructed to complete the investigation in cooperation with the United States Attorney without obtaining clearance
from the Criminal Division...."

        This matter was discussed on February 26, 1954, with Mr.
A. B. Caldwell, Chief, Civil Rights Section, Criminal Division,
by a representative of this Bureau, at which time it was pointed
out that we were presently following the procedure outlined in
the Department's memorandum of October 10, 1952, which states
that in Civil Rights and Involuntary Servitude and Slavery
investigations no full and complete inquiry is to be conducted
unless authorized by the Department.

        Mr. Caldwell stated that he felt the Bureau should
continued to follow the original instruction and in the event
a situation should ever arise wherein a United States Attorney
requests that a full investigation be conducted, little or no
time would be lost in holding up on such action until clearance
had been obtained from the Department. However, this would not
be in strict accordance with the recent Department Order
#40-54. Please advise whether this Bureau is to follow the
policy previously followed, or change its procedure in accordance with the most recent Department pronouncement.

72-02   Sec. 3

March 11, 1954

Assistant Attorney General
Warren Olney III

Director, FBI

Election Laws Investigations

Reference is made to Department Order #41-54 directed to all United States Attorneys, the Federal Bureau of Investigation and attorneys of the Criminal Division regarding elections, election campaigns, and political activity.

This Order states that the investigation of all complaints and the handling and prosecution of all cases involving possible violations of the statutes designated as Election Laws are to be conducted in accordance with certain instructions. The last sentence of Instruction #2 states "...in unusual cases where it clearly appears that violations have been committed and where time is of the essence, the Federal Bureau of Investigation may be instructed to complete the investigation in cooperation with the United States Attorney without obtaining clearance from the Criminal Division...."

This matter was discussed on February 26, 1954, with Mr. A. B. Caldwell, Chief, Civil Rights Section, Criminal Division, by a representative of this Bureau at which time it was pointed out that we are presently following the procedure outlined in the Department's memorandum of October 10, 1952, which states that the Bureau is to revert to the policy in existence prior to December 21, 1951. This policy as originally established by the Department by memorandum dated December 23, 1948, states that the Bureau may conduct preliminary investigations without obtaining Departmental clearance but that such authorization is necessary before instituting a full scale investigation.

Mr. Caldwell stated that he felt the Bureau should continue to follow the original instruction and in the event a situation should ever arise wherein a United States Attorney requests that a full investigation be conducted, little or no time would be lost in holding up on such action until clearance had been obtained from the Department. However, this would not be in strict accordance with the recent Department Order #41-54. Please advise whether this Bureau is to follow the policy previously followed, or change its procedure in accordance with the most recent Department pronouncement.

194

March 19, 1954
WO:ABC:FIH
144-012 Sec. 9

TO: The Director, Federal Bureau of
         Investigation
FROM: Warren Olney III, Assistant Attorney
         General, Criminal Division

SUBJECT: Civil Rights and Involuntary Servitude
         and Slavery Matters

This refers to your memorandum of March 10, 1954, concerning investigations pursuant to Departmental Order No. 40-54,
signed by the Attorney General on February 9, 1954. The Bureau
and the Criminal Division are, of course, bound by the terms of
this Order. It supersedes all previous directives, memoranda,
etc., on the subject, and the procedures are to be followed as
outlined therein. No person under the Attorney General has any
authority to issue instruction contrary to his orders.

With respect to the problem discussed with Mr. Caldwell,
the second sentence of instruction #2 controls. Thus, in unusual
cases where (1) it clearly appears that violations may have been
committed, and (2) where time is of the essence, a full investigation may be undertaken as stated. Mr. Caldwell advises me that he
did not state that the memorandum of October 10, 1952, to which
you refer, or any previous instructions or memoranda, should be
followed. (Rather, he stated that the Bureau, as a practical matter,
could, if it desires, comply with the provisions of the earlier
instructions, as well as the new Order #40-54, because in any case
where quick action is indicated notice to the Department could be
made in a matter of a few hours, or if necessary by teletype or
phone within a few minutes, and no delay in the conduct of any
investigation, whether it be full or preliminary, would be
encountered. Thus, during the first stages of the preliminary
investigation, there would be ample time to notify the Department
of the United States Attorney's request for a full investigation.)

If for some reason the Department decides that such
investigation would not be warranted or desirable in the particular
case, the few steps taken during the short interim of time before
the Division has been advised of the request of the United States
Attorney would not appear to be a serious factor, since in the
conduct of investigation of Civil Rights violations the prospective
defendants are almost always persons who are of some prominence
in the community and not likely to flee the jurisdiction.

Subsequent to the receipt of your memorandum of March
10, 1954, referred to above, we have received your memorandum of
March 11, 1954,--Subject, Election Laws Investigations, in which
reference is made to similar language in Departmental Order
#41-54.

While Mr. Caldwell does not recall that this problem was
discussed with the representative of the Bureau in connection with
investigations of violations of election laws, it is admitted
that the wording of Order #41-54 is similar in this respect to

195

Order #40-54, and, therefore , our answer set out above concerning Order #40-54 is equally applicable to your memorandum of March 11, 1954.

TO: Assistant Attorney General   March 30, 1954
        Warren Olney III

                                         144-012 Sec. 9
FROM: Director, FBI

SUBJECT: Civil Rights and Involuntary Servitude
          and Slavery Matters

        Reference is made to your memorandum of March 19, 1954
(your references WO:ABC:FIH 144-012; 50-012; 72-02), concerning
investigations of civil rights and involuntary servitude and
slavery matters, pursuant to Departmental Order No. 40-54, signed
by the Attorney General on February 9, 1954. Your memorandum also
encompasses Departmental Order No. 51-54, concerning election laws
investigations, which contains language similar to Order No. 40-54.

        Predicated upon your memorandum, the Bureau is advising
the field offices of the FBI as to the contents of Departmental
Orders Nos. 40-54 and 41-54, and instructing compliance therewith.
We are further advising them that the afore-mentioned Departmental
Orders Nos. 40-54 and 41-54, dated February 9, 1954, supersede the
Department's instructions of October 10, 1952, which required the
Bureau to secure clearance clearance from the Department before
conducting a full-scale inquiry.

        With regard to the discussions with Mr. Caldwell alluded
to in your memorandum, the Bureau has no desires concerning the
question as to whether clearance should or could be obtained from
the Department in advance of compliance with an instruction from
the United States Attorney to the field office for a full-scale
inquiry. It is assumed that if the United States Attorney has
any doubts concerning the propriety of ordering a full-scale inquiry,
he will communicate said doubts to the Department, and the Bureau
will not initiate any clearance with the Department prior to comply-
ing with the request of the United States Attorney for such full-
scale investigation.

```
Director                                      WO:LM:rmm
Federal Bureau of Investigation               144-012
                                              Sec. 10
Warren Olney III, Assistant Attorney
General, Criminal Division                    July 20, 1954
```

Chelsie L. Bailes, was, et al.;
George Lee Acree, et al. - Victims
Civil Rights;
Obstruction of Justice;
Federal Train Wreck Statute;
Obstruction of United States Mail

     Reference is made to your memorandum of June 16, 1954, on the captioned subject. No further investigation is desired on the Civil Rights aspect of the matter.

     In consequence of the decision of the Solicitor General declining to authorize an appeal to the Supreme Court from the dismissal of the Civil Rights indictment against the subjects, the Department will discontinue to use 18 U.S.C. 241 as a means of enforcing the rights secured by 29 U.S.C. 157. Consequently, complaints alleging a violation of the latter section in conjunction with 18 U.S.C. 241 should no longer be investigated by the Bureau.

     Should, however, the need for additional investigation arise in connection with the pending case of U.S. v. Farmer Allen, et al., Crim. No. 8182 Lexington in the Eastern District of Kentucky, such investigation should be conducted.

144-012 Sec. 10

April 1, 1955

James L. Guilmartin, Esquire
United States Attorney
Miami, Florida

Re: Civil Rights Violations
Your Ref: JLG:ppg

Dear Mr. Guilmartin:

This refers to your letter of March 1, 1955 in which
you present two legal questions raised by local police
officials. The first relates to the possible criminal
liability of police officers who arrest persons "on
suspicion" and hold them incommunicado for seventy-two
hours; and the second concerns the liability of police
officers accompanying shore patrol or military police who
arrest AWOL servicemen in private homes or establishments.

Generally, we are reluctant to furnish legal opinions
for the benefit of persons outside the Government. Formally
and officially we never furnish legal advice or opinions to
non-governmental personnel, since it is as you know the
consistent policy of the Department (Attorney General) to
furnish such information only to the President and the heads
of the several executive establishments. Even informally
we hesitate to give legal advice, particularly in constitutional law, in view of our dependence upon the Supreme Court
for precise interpretation of the rights covered by our civil
rights statutes. In addition, we should always try to avoid
the possibility of being embarrassed at some future date by
a defense in a civil rights prosecution based upon "clearance"
from the Department.

Being fully sympathetic to the difficult positions in
which police officers anxious to enforce the law often find
themselves, however, we would have no objection to your informally discussing the two questions with them in the light
of your experience and legal knowledge and the comments set
forth below. It may be suggested, however, that the police
officials confer with the appropriate state and local attorneys
for guidance and advice with respect to specific cases and
problems. In many instances, even though police actions may
not violate federal criminal law, they may violate state law
and leave the police open to civil suits if not criminal
prosectuion. The common-law right of action in tort and
the cause of action provided by the federal civil rights
statutes in Title 42, U.S.C., can cause almost as much grief
as our limited misdemeanor statute, 18 U.S.C. 242.

199

With respect to both questions raised by the police, it should be noted that no violation of the civil rights statute is committed unless the conduct or action in question was <u>wilful</u>, i.e. with the specific intent to deprive another of his federal rights. The <u>Screws</u> case, pages 101-107, 325 U.S., sets forth practically all the law on this point, insofar as here material. We would stress the paragraph beginning on page 104, since good faith may not be enough where the officer's action "flies in the teeth of decisions" of the courts. Thus, if a federal court were specifically to hold that "arrests for suspicion" unsupported by a warrant violate the right not to be deprived of liberty without due process of law, custom, reasonableness, etc., may be inadequate to support the officer's conduct. Thus wilfully does not necessarily mean with bad faith or evil intent; "reckless disregard" of another's rights may be sufficient.

The question which next presents itself is, whether a person has a federal right not to be arrested except with a warrant, or while actually committing an offense, or as otherwise provided by state law and common law. We do believe that there is such a federal right, and the cases would appear to sustain it. To be arrested for, or on, suspicion and held three days incommunicado is a substantial deprivation of liberty in our view, and if not supported by facts justifying such action may very well be a deprivation without due process. As you note, however, we would ordinarily not prosecute such a case because the officers usually are acting in good faith and on a real suspicion- i.e. without wilfulness. In addition, as noted above, the problem is not resolved with any degree of finaility and we understand it is the subject of much discussion and debate in many police departments, legal groups, and prosecuting attorneys' offices. We would hesitate to settle such a matter by criminal proceedings; however, if an appellate court were to rule specifically that such actions violate the 14th Amendment, we would endeavor to enforce the guaranteed rights. This view ties in with the mentioned paragraph in the <u>Screws</u> opinion.

We would invite the interested police officers to read "Philadelphia Police Practice and the Law of Arrest," 100 Penn. Law Rev. 1182-1216 (June 1952), which would indicate to them not only that the law is far from clear in many respects, but also that they always face a real danger when they make arrests except as provided by statute or common law. Perhaps, as previously stated, the police would be best advised to seek and obtain the legal counsel of the appropriate law officers, since if the police act pursuant to legal advice it would be doubtful that they acted wilfully -- at least in the absence of a clear judicial pronouncement contradicting such legal advice.

As to the second question, Article S of the Uniform Code of Military Justice, 50 U.S.C. 562, authorizes "any civil officer having authority to apprehend offenders under the laws of the United States or of any State," summarily to apprehend a deserter from the Armed Forces and to deliver him to proper custody. The Code does not distinguish between desertion and absence without leave (see Sections 679 and 680, 50 U.S.C.; Articles 85 and 86), but for the purpose of arresting ("apprehending") a serviceman who is absent from his place of service, it would seem that it can be assumed that he is a deserter.)At his trial he of course can try to prove that he did not intend to remain away permanently or to do any of the things that would make him a deserter within Section 679.) Accordingly, a peace officer who accompanies armed service police to a private home or establishment either to witness or assist in the arrest, would not in our opinion be in violation of Section 242 of Title 18, U.S.C. It should be noted, of course, that we cannot furnish to the police a general legal opinion concerning the rights and duties and liabilities of a civilian peace officer in cases of this kind; we can indicate only our views as to the applicability of the civil rights statute.

If you are not in accord with these liews, please do not hestitate to advise us. In any event, any comments you may care to make will be appreciated.

Sincerely,

WARREN OLNEY III
Assistant Attorney General
Criminal Division

By:

ARTHUR B. CALDWELL
Chief, Civil Rights Section

typed on Dec. 14, 1955

NOTICE TO UNITED STATES ATTORNEYS
CIVIL RIGHTS

<u>Exclusion of Citizens from Grand and Petit Juries on
the Basis of Race of Color</u>. The United States Supreme Court
has again affirmed the rule that valid jury selection, state
or federal, is a federally-protected right under the Fourteenth
Amendment, and that the indictment of a defendant by a grand
jury from which members of his race have been systematically
excluded is a denial of his right to the equal protection of
the laws, <u>Reece</u> v. <u>Georgia</u>, December 5, 1955. See also
<u>Michel</u> v. <u>Louisiana,</u> decided the same day. In addition, it
is a crime for state or federal officers to disqualify
citizens from grand or petit jury service on account of race
or color, 18 U.S.C. 243.

United States Attorneys have been requested to inform the
Criminal Division of all allegations or reports of such racial
discrimination, in order that the law may be properly enforced
and that the Department may be saved the embarrassment of
first learning of such practices when a case reaches the Supreme
Court after many months of publicly known litigation. See the
old Criminal Division Bulletin, issues of July 17, 1950 (Vol.
9, No. 14) and June 8, 1953 (Vol. 12, No. 9). As mentioned in
the latter item, the late Justice Jackson, in his dissenting
opinion in <u>Cassell</u> v. <u>Texas</u>, 339 U.S. 282, 298 (1950), observed
that Congress had provided by Section 243 direct and effective

means to enforce the right of Negroes and other citizens to participate in grand jury service, but that the Government had neglected the available criminal remedies. (See also the dissenting opinion of Justice Black in Michel v. Louisiana, December 5, 1955.) The Criminal Division nevertheless has not received one report or reference concerning a possible violation of Section 243. It is therefore again requested that all United States Attorneys promptly inform the Division of any situation involving a possible violation of the statute.

Comments and suggestions in this problem are invited.

BULLETIN

CRIMINAL DIVISION   DEPARTMENT OF JUSTICE

Vol. 12	June 8, 1953	No. 9

NOTICE TO UNITED STATES ATTORNEYS

Exclusion of Citizens from Grand and Petit Juries on the Basis of Race. In Avery v. Georgia, 21 U.S.L.W. 4395, the Supreme Court has again reaffirmed the rule that exclusion of jurors on the basis of race may deprive the accused of equal protection of the law guaranteed by the Fourteenth Amendment. The Court held that the method of placing the names of Negroes on colored slips in the jury box to distinguish them from the names of white jurors, which were placed on white slips, presented a prima facie case of racial discrimination.

The attention of United States Attorneys is directed to the fact that deliberate exclusion or failure to summon citizens as jurors because of their race constitutes a violation of 18 U.S.C. 243. Despite the prior notice given United States Attorneys in the July 17, 1950 issue of the Criminal Division Bulletin (Vol. 9, No. 14, p. 1) and despite the apparent continuing practice of racial discrimination in selecting juries, evidenced by the crude method of exclusion in the Avery case, no case of this type of alleged violation has been reported to the Criminal Division by United States Attorneys since the Bulletin's request for such information. It is requested again that United States Attorneys promptly inform the Criminal Division of any allegations of such racial discrimination in the selection of juries which may be brought to their attention, in order that the Department may be saved the embarrassment of first learning of such practices when a case reaches the Supreme Court.

SUBVERSIVE ACTIVITIES

Petitions Filed with Subversive Activities Control Board to Require Registration of Communist-Front Organizations. On April 22, 1953, the Attorney General filed petitions under Section 13(a) of the Internal Security Act of 1950 with the Subversive Activities Control Board against twelve alleged Communist-front organizations seeking an order directing these organizations to register with the Attorney General as provided in Section 7 of the Act. Such registration requires said organizations to reveal the identity of their officers and give an accounting of all moneys received and expended.

144-012-21

September 27, 1955

Honorable Herbert Brownell, Jr.
Attorney General of the United States
Washington, D. C.

Dear Mr. Brownell:

There is enclosed for your information a copy of a
Resolution adopted by the Board of Directors of the South Carolina
Penitentiary at its September meeting.

I also have established the following rules governing
the admission of federal agents to our penal institutions:

1. No federal agent will be permitted to enter any
penal institution of South Carolina for investigative purposes
without the written consent of the Governor.

2. Each request for such permission must be accompanied
by written statement showing that no complaints leading up to the
request have been sent from the penal institution in violation of
prison rules.

3. Each request for such permission must also be
accompanied by copies of all papers and reports on which the request
is based, except in the case of a proposed investigation within
the federal jurisdiction not involving the institution or its
officials and in that event the request must be accompanied by a
supporting written statement as to the purpose of the investigation.

4. When investigations are made by federal agents,
they shall be conducted in the presence of an official of the
penal institution.

It has been the practice of our penal institutions to
forward all letters, petitions or complaints by prisoners addressed
to the Department of Justice, to Federal and State Courts, to
lawyers, or to other legitimate persons, and that rule will
continue to prevail.

It has been and will continue to be the policy of this
State to cooperate with the federal authorities in the meritorious
investigation of crime.

It has come to my attention that, in the past, the
Justice Department has ordered numerous and fruitless investigations that were based on complaints made by prisoners and
smuggled out of the institution in violation of well-known prison
rules. These investigations have encouraged a spirit of rebellion
among the prisoners and disrespect for penal officials and penal
regulations. Despite this, South Carolina has been fortunate in

205

not having been plagued by prison riots. So long as the State has the responsibility for the safe keeping of its prisoners, it will not be a party to any unwarranted interference in the discharge of that responsibility. It is for that reason, that it has become necessary to adopt the above rules concerning future penal investigations.

Yours very truly,

George Bell Timmerman, Jr.

144-012-21

TO: The Attorney General   September 28, 1955

FROM: Director, FBI

SUBJECT: South Carolina State
         Penitentiary
         Columbia, South Carolina

     I want to advise you that the Board of Directors of
the South Carolina Penitentiary at a September meeting adopted
a resolution to the effect that (1) no Federal agents, including
the FBI, be permitted to enter the South Carolina Penitentiary
for investigative purposes without the consent of the Governor;
(2) the Governor be requested to refuse permission for such
entry unless copies of all papers and reports on which investigation based are submitted with the request and unless it is
plainly shown that such papers and reports have not been sent
from the prison except through regular channels; (3) when investigation is made under the Governor's authority such investigation
shall be in the presence of an official of the penitentiary.

     During April 1955 this Bureau conducted investigation
in two civil rights cases entitled "Sergeant N.O Shealy; Roy
(Scoope) Garrett, et al - Victims, Civil Rights," (your reference
144-67-150) and "Guy V. Whetstone, et al; Joseph Gilliard, et al -
Victims, Civil Rights" (your reference 144-67-153). During these
investigations it was ascertained that prisoners are strapped and
whipped in the presence of South Carolina Penitentiary officials
as a disciplinary measure for violation of prison rules.

     Colonel Wyndham W. Manning, Superintendent of the South
Carolina Penitentiary, advised Agents of our Savannah office that
whippings were authorized by him and he considered whippings of
prisoners an effective means of punishment and would continue such
whippings as disciplinary measures whenever he deemed them appropriate.

     At the request of the Criminal Division, United States
Attorney Morrisette of the Eastern District of South Carolina
arranged a conference with Colonel Manning in August of 1955 in
which Colonel Manning was told that the Federal Government would
forego prosecution in the two afore-mentioned cases but the Department of Justice would feel obligated to prosecute should the facts
warrant if recourse is made to illegal disciplinary whippings in
the future. It should be noted that United States Attorney
Morrisette has advised the Criminal Division that the South Carolina
Constitution prohibits corporal punishment and it is the opinion
of the office of the Attorney General of South Carolina that
whippings are illegal.

     At this conference Colonel Manning would not promise not
to order any more whippings but did state that he would resort

to whippings as seldom as possible but he considers them a very effective means of punishment and the whippings would be given only at the penitentiary and not at the camps throughout the state. Colonel Manning also indicated that he might explore the possibility of having the legislature pass a statute giving him authority to administer such whippings.

On September 23, 1955, an Agent of our Savannah Office attempted to interview several inmates of the South Carolina Penitentiary on matters not pertaining to civil rights. The Agent was referred to Colonel Manning who told him of the resolution and stated that while he had no animosity toward this Bureau he did feel that the Department of Justice was to blame for his difficulties by injecting itself into the administrative operations of the penitentiary. The Agent also contacted Governor Timmerman of South Carolina who verified the action of the Board of Directors of the penitentiary. A copy of the resolution adopted by the Board of Directors is enclosed for your information. Copies of the resolution are also enclosed for Mr. Rogers and Mr. Olney.

The Special Agent in Charge of our Savannah Office has been instructed to contact Governor Timmerman and discuss this matter further with him. You will be advised of the results of this contact.

144-012-21

Oct. 3, 1955

To: The Attorney General

From: Director, FBI

Subject: SOUTH CAROLINA STATE PENITENTIARY
          COLUMBIA, SOUTH CAROLINA

Mr. John V. Lindsay, your Executive Assistant, furnished the letter dated September 27, 1955, from the Governor of South Carolina, setting forth rules governing the admission of Federal Agents to penal institutions in South Carolina, and stated that you desired my views in this matter.

In my memorandum of September 28, 1955, I pointed out that the Special Agent in Charge of our Savannah Office had been instructed to contact Governor Timmerman in this matter. Mr. Lopez met with Governor Timmerman xxxthixxmxxtxxx on September 29, 1955, and I wish to advise you of the results of their meeting.

Governor Timmerman advised that the main complaint of the officials of the penitentiary was the smuggling of letters and communications out of the penitentiary by inmates which, in many instances, resulted in investigations being conducted under the Civil Rights Statute. As the smuggling of such communications was in violation of penitentiary rules, the officials wanted to be fully advised of all such instances of smuggled letters. Governor Timmerman advised that neither he nor other state officials felt any resentment toward this Bureau in the handling of such matters and he felt that the fault lies with the Department of Justice in Washington, D. C.

Governor Timmerman stated that with regard to record and personnel file checks at the pentitentiary, there would not be any change in the procedure. Agents of this Bureau will continue to have free access to penitentiary files without the requirement of any clearance.

The Governor advised that it would be necessary to obtain permission from his office before interviewing any inmate regardless of the purpose of the interview. The request could be made orally, he stated, but it would be necessary in each instance for a written statement to be furnished to his office concerning the objective of each interview desired with inmates.

If the interview concerned a criminal matter other than a civil rights case, it would not be necessary to set forth the ix details of the case, but the statement to the Governor should clearly indicate that the interview would not in any way relate to a civil rights investigation involving an official or employee of the penitentiary.

2

If the proposed interview involved a civil rights matter pertaining to officials or employees of the penitentiary, such fact should be stated in writing. If the case was based on a communication smuggled out of the penitentiary through other than prescribed channels, a copy of such communication must be furnished with xkx the statement.

With regard to the requirement that an official of the penitentiary be present during any authorized interview, Governor Timmerman stated that if the interview pertained to a civil rights investigation involving penitentiary officials or employees, it would be necessary that the penitentiary representative sit in and listen to the interview. In instances not involving civil rights investigations of personnel of the penitentiary, the prison represenative would not desire to listen to the interview, but would be stationed nearby to insure the physical security of the inmate.

It was learnedfxm from Governor Timmerman that in emergency cases he would not insist that the written statement be provided before authorizing the interview. He stated that he would authorize such interview upon oral assurance that the written statement would be submitted later.

Governor Timmerman stated that the regulations would apply not only in connection with interviews at the main penitentiary, but also at its several branches as well as interviews with inmates in the various juvenile and industrial schools in South Carolina.

The conditions imposed by the Governor of South Carolina are a hindrance to the efficient handling of investigations at the institutions in that state. The presence of prison personnel during an interview will undoubtedly limit the information which may be developed by the interviewing Agents. This Bureau, however, will endeavor to fulfill its responsibilities as fully and as promptly as possible in spite of the regulations.

Whenever a complaint is received concerning a possible violation of civil rights by an official or employee of the prison system in South Carolina, this Bureau will not institute an investigation under the conditions set up by the South Carolina authorities. The information received will be furnished to the Criminal Division so that a determination may be made in each instance as to the procedure to be followed. It is noted that the prison authorities in Georgia and Florida do not permit inmates to be interviewed in private in civil rights investigations and a similar procedure is followed so that a determination may be made as to whether to proceed by an investigation by this Bureau or by inquiry by a Federal grand jury.

I am enclosing the letter from Gov. Timmerman to you dated September 27, 1955, together with its enclosure.

210

144-012-21
November 7, 1955

Honorable George Bell Timmerman, Jr.
Governor of the State of South Carolina
Columbia, South Carolina

My dear Governor:

This acknowledges your letter of September 27, 1955, enclosing a copy of a resolution adopted by the Board of Directors of the South Carolina Penitentiary at its September meeting, concerning the establishment of a new procedure for interviews by Federal agents with prisoners in South Carolina penal institutions. Federal agents henceforth may conduct such interviews only in the presence of a prison official after you have given your written consent, which will be issued only upon the basis of a written application showing that the complaint being investigated has not been made in violation of prison rules.

In the two investigations which presumably led to adoption of this new procedure it was conceded that disciplinary whippings of prisons had occurred at the South Carolina Penitentiary and the Boykin Prison Farm, a subsidiary institution, despite the provisions of the South Carolina Constitution (Art. 1, Sec. 19) proscribing corporal punishment. Such whippings constituted illegal summary punishment in violation of 18 U.S.C. 242 if wilfully inflicted within the meaning of that statute.

I assure you that Federal agents do not solicit or facilitate the making of unauthorized complaints. The complaints in these two cases, as is often true, did not come to us in letters smuggled out of prison. On those infrequent occasions when such letters alleging violations of Federal rights are received, however, we still are required by the Federal laws to investigate. A prisoner, for example, might smuggle out a letter giving information about a Dyer Act or Mann Act violation. We could not ignore the information even though the prisoner might not have observed prison regulations in sending out the complaint. The same considerations would apply in a civil rights case or in the case of other claimed Federal violations.

You state that this Department has ordered "numerous and fruitless" investigations based upon prisoners' complaints smuggled out of the institution in violation of well-known prison rules and that the investigations have encouraged a spirit of rebellion among the prisoners.

In accordance with our obligations to investigate alleged violations of Federal law, it has been necessary to interview prisoners in State and local institutions, including those in South Carolina. It is my impression that such investigations in your State have not been especially numerous. I am sure you

211

understand our responsibilities to investigate when xx a violation of Federal law is claimed, in the absence of clear evidence that no offense occurred.

Nor can such investigations in my view be fairly characterized as "fruitless." In the case of alleged civil rights violations in South Carolina penal institutions, investigations have resulted in at least two indictments and one convictions. In still some other instances brutality to inmates by custodial personnel was disclosed by such investigations. To what extent these institutions were part of the prison system covered by the resolution, I am unable to say.

Complaints of prison brutality may originate with prisoners, former prisoners, or other sources. Allegations which come from law violators, while subject to far greater scrutiny than would otherwise be the case, cannot just be disregarded because of their source. In this connection I am mindful of the following comments of the Missouri State Penal Institutions Survey Committee in its report to the Governor of December 28, 1954:

<blockquote>While it is true that prisoners, living as they do within a compressed area, are likely to feel the effects of imaginary wrongs, tell untruths, exaggerate, and sometimes enlarge, distort, or misinterpret situations, it further holds that they are not all always guilty of these weaknesses and sometimes do speak the truth and have just reason for complaint. Therefore, any testimony from prisoners must be accepted with some reservation, but at the same time, balanced with other observations and impressions.</blockquote>

We are not officially concerned with grievances of State prisoners which are confined to internal conditions, but only with the reported denial of rights secured by the Federal Constitution. That the alleged victim may be a State prisoner does not mean that he has lost his right to be free from punishment otherwise than is authorized by law or that he has lost other rights which are secured to him by the Federal Constitution.

As stated by the Court of Appeals for the Fifth Circuit in United States v. Jones, 207 F. 2d 785, 786-87 (C.A. 5, 1953):

<blockquote>...The Government concedes that the state has the power to manage the affairs of its penal institutions and to enforce discipline among its prisoners; and we hold that the federal government has no power to control or regulate the internal discipline of the penal institutions of its constituent states. All such powers are reserved to the states,</blockquote>

and the 14th Amendment does not authorize
Congress to legislate upon such matters.
[Cases.]

Nevertheless, federal laws may be violated
within prison walls, and federal crimes
committed therein, as well as elsewhere within
the territorial limits of a state; and the fact
that state officers are violating state as well
as federal laws does not exonerate them from
penalties under the latter. Facts are stubborn
things when proven or admitted in the disposition
of a case; and, paradoxical as it may seem, the
defendant was whipping these prisoners under color
of law although doing it in violation of law....

See also, United States v. Walker, 216 F. 2d 683 (C.A. 5, 1954).

I regret that it has been deemed necessary to establish
a procedure which will make it more difficult to investigate
reported Federal violations, including the disproof of unwarranted
charges, in South Carolina. Since it remains our duty, however,
to enforce laws which the Congress has charged us with enforcing,
we must continue in South Carolina and elsewhere to investigate
Federal violations which are reported to have been committed.

Sincerely,

HERBERT BROWNELL, JR.
Attorney General

144-012-21

STATE OF SOUTH CAROLINA

EXECUTIVE OFFICE

COLUMBIA   November 19, 1955

Mr. J. M. Lopez
Special Agent in Charge
Federal Bureau of Investigation
P.O. Box 948
Savannah, Georgia

Dear Mr. Lopez:

I have your letter concerning a private interview with Guy E. Key. Under the resolution of the Board of Directors of the South Carolina Penitentiary, interviews with prisoners are required to be conducted in the presence of an official of the penal institution. The rule is stated in paragraph 4 of my letter of September 29, and since then there has been no change in it.

There was and is no intention under the new procedure to make it apply only to a civil rights investigation. It applies to all interviews. The State of South Carolina is equally interested in law enforcement and it has the sole responsibility for the safe keeping of its prisoners and the orderly administration of its penal system. The rule, I am told, is quite similar to the procedure used in the federal prison system.

In our discussion, I had in mind, although I may not have expressed it in appropriate language, that you needed an exception to the rule in a security type of investigation in which the Federal Bureau of Investigation has exclusive jurisdiction and in which the national security would require a private interview. I had intended bringing this to the attention of the Board for appropriate action and will do so at its next meeting. For that reason, I am sending a copy of this letter to the Superintendent so that he may call it to my attention at the next meeting.

With reference to Guy E. Key, there seems to be no reason at present to deviate from the established policy. Should it develop from your interview with him that he has information that he wishes to give pertaining to a security type of investigation, then an exception, if necessary, I feel sure could be arranged that would not violate security.

Trusting that this will clarify the matter, I am

George Bell Timmerman, Jr.

214

TO: Assistant Attorney General   November 9, 1955
         Warren Olney III

FROM: Director, FBI

SUBJECT: Racial Segregation in Public
         Parks and recreation areas
         Civil Rights

This is to confirm a conversation between Mr. A. B. Caldwell, Chief, Civil Rights Section, and a representative of this Bureau on November 8, 1955.

On November 7, 1955, the United States Supreme Court handed down two decisions declaring unconstitutional racial segregation in public parks and recreation areas.

Mr. Caldwell advised that the Department would consider complaints concerning racial segregation in public parks and recreation areas in the same manner as complaints involving racial segregation in public schools. Mr. Caldwell advised that (upon the receipt of a complaint the Bureau should obtain full details from the individual making the complaint and without conducting investigation refer the matter to the Criminal Division so that the alleged facts in each case could be reviewed prior to the institution of any investigation. As in the case of racial segregation in public schools, no investigation will be instituted by the Bureau unless requested by ~~your office~~.)

144-012- Sec. 10

November 16, 1955

From: Mr. Caldwell

To: Mr. Olney

Re: FBI memorandum dated Nov. 9, 1955, re Racial Segrega-
        tion in Public Parks and Recreation Areas.

The attached memorandum from the Bureau confirms a
telephone conversation between Clem McGowan, of the FBI
Civil Rights Section, and myself.

When asked by the Bureau what our policy would be, in
view of the recent Supreme Court decision, with regard to
investigating complaints of alleged violations of Section 242
in public parks and recreational areas, I informed them that
we would follow the same cautious procedure governing complaints
arising out of school segregation matters. I did so because of
the similarity of the legal problems, as well as procedures,
inherent in the school cases and possible public park incidents.
I recommend that this be the procedure followed and unless you
feel differently about the matter, it will be so followed by
the Bureau.

                        A.B.C.

144-012 Sec. 11

February 10, 1956

TO: Assistant Attorney General
Warren Olney III

FROM: Director, FBI

SUBJECT: CIVIL RIGHTS MATTERS

This is to confirm a conversation between Mr. A. B. Caldwell, Chief of the Civil Rights Section, and a representative of this Bureau on February 9, 1956.

It was pointed out to Mr. Caldwell that instances had arisen in which law enforcement officers who were subjects in civil rights cases had declined to be interviewed unless their superior officer was present during the interview, and in a few cases the superior officer had declined to permit the law enforcement officer who was the subject in a civil rights matter to be interviewed unless the superior officer was present. Mr. Caldwell was asked as to what action was desired in the future in such situations.

Mr. Caldwell stated that the procedure which had been in effect is very satisfactory and recommended that this procedure be continued. He stated that in the event an interview with a law enforcement officer who is the subject of a civil rights investigation cannot be conducted unless a superior officer is present the attempt to conduct such an interview should be discontinued and the United States Attorney and the Department should be advised.

Mr. Caldwell pointed out that in some instances it might be possible for the Department to make a determination without the necessity of an interview being conducted with the subject, and in other instances it might be desirable to have an interview conducted in the presence of his superior officer. In the latter case, the Department could request such an interview. He further pointed out that it might, in some instances, be preferable to proceed by grand jury inquiry and permit the subject to make any statement he might desire before a grand jury. Mr. Caldwell stated that this procedure would enable the Department to review the matter on an individual case basis and make a determination as to the best procedure to be followed.

In view of Mr. Caldwell's recommendation, this Bureau will not interview law enforcement officers who are subjects in civil rights matters in the presence of their superior officers but will bring such situations to the attention of the appropriate United States Attorney and the Criminal Division so that a final determination may be made in each case.

217

144-012   Sec. 11

March 1, 1956

TO: The Attorney General

FROM: Director, FBI

Subject: UNKNOWN SUBJECTS:
           Clarence Mitchell and
           Reverend Horace Sharper - VICTIMS
           CIVIL RIGHTS

I want to refer to the situation which developed on
Tuesday afternoon, February 28, 1956, as a result of the arrest
of Mr. Clarence Mitchell, the Washington representative of the
National Association for the Advancement of Colored People, in
Florence, South Carolina, when he refused to use the entrance
of the railroad station set aside for the use of Negroes.

The Bureau was requested to have agents attend the hearings
in Florence, South Carolina, in which Mr. Mitchell was arraigned.
We in the Bureau felt very strongly that it would be improper for
the Bureau to undertake this assignment and ultimately the
coverage of the hearings was handled in line with the very
excellent suggestion of Mr. Rogers to have the National Association for the Advancement of Colored People secure a transcript
of the proceedings.

I am bringing the matter up now since it can be anticipated
there will be similar situations arising in the future. (It is
my considered judgment that certainly the FBI should not be
injected into a situation wherein an inference could be drawn
that the FBI was monitoring a municipal, county or state judicial
proceeding. This would at once cause the state's rights
advocates to charge a meddling into local matters and to heap
vituperation upon the FBI, the Department of Justice and the
Attorney General.

It seems to me that should similar situations arise wherein
the Criminal Division feels it is necessary to know what
transpired in judicial proceedings and, if there is no other way
whereby a full account can be obtained, it would seem preferable
to have this handled by the United States Attorney who would
appear in a legal capacity and not in the capacity of an investigative agency as would be the case if the Bureau undertook
such an assignment. It further seems that a transcript would
be the best record of what did transpire and that wherever
possible, as Mr. Rogers suggested Tuesday afternoon, this would
be the best possible approach to the matter.)

218

I did want to call this to your attention in order that you may be giving some thought to the procedure to be followed by the Bureau in the future should this question arise, as it undoubtedly will.

cc- Mr. William P. Rogers
    Deputy Attorney General

144-012 Sec. 12

November 19, 1956

Mr. William P. Rogers
Deputy Attorney General

Director, FBI

PERSONS VOTING IN THE PRESIDENTIAL
ELECTIONS OF 1952 and 1956;
CIVIL RIGHTS

By memorandum of November 13, 1956, the Criminal
Division requested this Bureau to ascertain the number of white
persons and the number of Negroes who voted in the Presidential
elections of 1952 and 1956 in the states of Alabama, Georgia,
Louisiana, Mississippi, North Carolina, and South Carolina. It
was indicated that perhaps such information could be obtained
from the Secretary of State or some other officer in each of
the named states.

Mr. A. B. Caldwell, Chief of the Civil Rights Section,
advised Special Agent C. L. McGowan, Jr., of this Bureau, on
November 15, 1956, that this information was not desired in
connection with the consideration of the violation of any
Federal statute, but that the information was desired for
consideration in presenting to the next session of Congress
the recommendations of the Department of Justice for enactment
of new statutes concerning civil rights.

This request does not concern a violation of any Federal
statute within our jurisdiction and any effort made to obtain
the desired information might result in comment that we were
conducting inquiries outside of our investigative jurisdiction.
It is respectfully suggested that the information could be more
properly obtained by the United States Attorneys in the various
states.

cc: 1 - Assistant Attorney General
      Warren Olney III

220

144-012 Sec. 13
Feb. 7, 1957

TO: Assistant Attorney General
Warren Olney III

FROM: Director, DBI

SUBJECT: CIVIL RIGHTS MATTERS

Chief Herbert Jenkins of the Atlanta, Georgia, Police Department has presented a hypothetical situation and inquired as to the
desirability in such an instance of using sworn statements obtained
by local officials from the police officer rather than interviewing
the particular officer in a preliminary investigation.

In the case suggested by Chief Jenkins, an individual at the
time of arrest became belligerent and assaulted the officer, making
it necessary for the officer to use force to effect the arrest. If
the individual makes a complaint to the police department, the matter
is investigated and a sworn statement obtained from the officer
involved. If the police board finds there is no basis for the
allegation of misconduct on the part of the officer, the individual
can institute civil action against the officer. Also, he can
institute criminal action by referring the matter to state or county
authorities. In the event the civil action is heard and dismissed
and the state or county authorities find no basis for indicting or
proceeding against the officer, the individual can then make a
complaint to the FBI regarding a violation of his civil rights.

Chief Jenkins pointed out that upon receipt of a complaint the
Bureau would institute a preliminary investigation and in the course
of such an investigation would interview the officer involved. He
suggested that rather than interviewing the police officer in such
a case it might be desirable to use in lieu thereof the sworn statement on file with the Atlanta Police Department. An interview by
Federal officers in such a case would amount to the particular
officer being questioned on four occasions regarding the same set
of facts.

Chief Jenkins stated he realized that if the Department of
Justice had any question concerning the sufficiency of the statement
or the reliability of the officer involved that he would expect the
FBI to come back to interview the officer and take any additional
steps which the Department felt essential in order to get the
complete facts.

It would be appreciated if you would consider this question and
advise the Bureau of your views as to accepting the sworn statement
of an officer on file with the Atlanta Police Department under
circumstances outlined by Chief Jenkins in his hypothetical situation rather than interviewing the officer involved.

221

144-012 Sec. 13
March 12, 1957

TO: The Director, FBI

FROM: Warren Olney III, Assistant Attorney General
Criminal Division

SUBJECT: Civil Rights Matters (Atlanta, Georgia,
Police Brutality Investigations)

This refers to your memoranda of February 7 and February 18,
1957 concerning the desirability of accepting a sworn statement
previously made by a police officer in connection with a local
investigation, in lieu of the Bureau interviewing the officer, in
an alleged police brutaility matter in Atlanta, Georgia, involving
personnel of the Atlanta Police Department.

Although this is primarily a matter of investigative technique
within the province of the Bureau, we would suggest in reply to your
request for our views that it probably would not be desirable to
institute any procedure or pattern in the conduct of investigations
under Section 242 which would result in a different or special
approach to or handling of civil rights matters in any particular
city or area, or with respect to any particular police department.
We would not, therefore, recommend adoption of the suggestion made
by Chief Jenkins as to his police department.

Considering the matter from the over-all basis, however, we
would suggest that in the case of all routine police brutality
preliminary investigations instituted by the Bureau on its own
initiative, you might find that the possible subjects need not be
interviewed. If there are on file copies of statements made by the
officers in connection with a local or state investigation, or made
in purauance of ordinary routine, copies thereof might be obtained
by the Bureau and incorporated in the reports xxpx as part of the
preliminary investigation. This would in fact be routine, since when
the records pertaining to a matter under investigation are examined,
the Bureau Agents ordinarily, in any event, report statements which
are on file pertaining to the case under investigation. However, we
would suggest that the Special Agents should be free to interview
police officers even in a preliminary investigation, where there
may be unusual considerations warranting special handling.

In the ordinary police brutality investigation the Bureau of
course would in the usual manner submit the reports of a the
preliminary investigation to the Criminal Division which would then
determine whether or not further investigation should be conducted.
If a full investigation is requested, the officers (subjects) would
routinely be interviewed as part of the investigation.

As indicated above, although we are pleased to submit these
suggestions and views, this memorandum deals with a matter which is
primarily one of investigative technique within the Bureau's jurisdiction. The Bureau therefore will make the decision in the matter.

222

144-012 Sec. 13

June 14, 1957

Arthur B. Caldwell, Esq.
Chief, Civil Rights Section
Department of Justice
Washington 25, D. C.

Dear Mr. Caldwell:

A matter of procedure in Civil Rights cases has arisen, on which I would appreciate your advice.

I find that when the FBI investigative report reaches our office, in the first instance, it has been the practice here to recommend a further investigation or decline prosecution. It is my further understanding that the Department of Justice in Washington receives a copy of the same report that we do and that this is followed ultimately by a recommendation from Washington.

It is my impression that in all Civil Rights matters the question of whether or not to prosecute is determined in Washington, so that there seems to be some conflict as to what is the correct procedure.

So that there will be no misunderstanding between your office and ours, I would appreciate it if you would formulate for me the best policy to be followed. It is particularly important now because we are receiving a large number of investigative reports dealing with police problems in the City of Philadelphia. The matter has, as you are aware, become one of public interest locally.

Sincerely yours,

HAROLD K, WOOD
United States Attorney

223

July 23, 1957

SJB:ARG

144-012

The Staff

St. John Barrett, Chief, Civil Rights Section

Replies to Prisoner Mail

It has, in the past, been the practice of the Civil Rights Section, when answering letters from prisoners in either state or federal institutions, to address the answer directly to the prisoner. On the other hand, it has been the practice of Messrs. Gottshall and Byerly, in custodial matters, to answer prisoner mail by writing to the Warden of the institution, informing him of the substance of the prisoner's inquiry and advising him of the reply he might pass on to the prisoner.

Henceforth, in answering all prisoner mail, the general practice should be followed of addressing the reply to the Warden of the institution. Messrs. Gottshall and Byerly have a list of state correctional institutions together with the names of the heads of such institutions, which may be consulted. A copy of the letter to the head of the institution may be sent along with the original in order that it can be turned over to the prisoner if the head of the institution so desires.

There may well be many instances in which it is undesirable to write to a Warden rather than to the prisoner. The attorney should use his judgment in each case as to whether an exception should be made to the general rule.

224

144-012- Sec. 13.
August 8, 1957
WO:SJB:bg

Mr. Vernon M. Smith
Lorain County Sheriff
Elyria, Ohio

Dear Mr. Smith:

During your visit to the Department of Justice on July 10,
1957, you and Inspector Carl C. Bare expressed interest in the
policies and procedures of the Department insofar as they relate
to the processing of civil rights complaints against police
officers. At that time you were promised a letter re-stating some
of the matters that were covered in our conference. We regret
that the press of other work has prevented our writing sooner.

Enclosed is a copy of an address prepared by Arthur B.
Caldwell, former Chief of the Civil Rights Section, Department of
Justice. This address relates, generally, to the organization and
functions of the Civil Rights Section as of January 5, 1957. It
includes information regarding the processing of complaints against
local law enforcement officers for the violation of the federal
civil rights statutes.

At the present time the work of the Civil Rights Section relates not only to the enforcement of Section 241 and 242 of
Title 18 of the United States Code, commonly referred to as the
civil rights statutes, but also relates to the use and enforcement
of the Fugitive Felon Act, the criminal provisions of the Universal
Military Training and Service Act, the Lindbergh law (kidnapping),
the Wire-Tapping Act (47 U.S.C. 605) and matters relating to the
custody of federal prisoners. Thus the Civil Rights Section
administers not only statutes relating strictly to the violation of
constitutional rights, but also other statutes relating more
generally to personal liberties.

A considerable portion of the work of the Section, volume-wise,
is devoted to the processing of complaints of the alleged violation
of citizens, constitutional rights by federal and local law enforcement officers. All such complaints eventually come to the attention
of the Civil Rights Section regardless of whether they are initially
made to the Federal Bureau of Investigation, to the Criminal Division
of the Department of Justice, or to a United States Attorney's
office. Many of these complaints on examination are found to be
frivolous. Others, while indicating possible misconduct on the part
of officers, will not fall within the scope of the federal statutes.
A police officer in investigating crime and apprehending criminals
will often have difficult decisions to make in the performance of
his duty. Errors in judgment causing injury to private citizens, even
though they may be gross errors and may involve violation of local
laws and regulations, do not necessarily constitute violations of
federal criminal law. A violation of the civil rights statutes does
occur where a police officer acting under the cloak of his official

225

-2-

authority intentionally deprives a citizen of any rights secured
by the United States Constitution. Such rights include the right
not to be coerced into confessing or giving a statement regarding
an alleged offense, and the right not to be summarily punished
other than in the manner prescribed by law. Thus an officer who
strikes a prisoner for the purpose of compelling the prisoner to
confess or make a statement is violating a federal law. Likewise,
an officer who in the exercise of his authority strikes a citizen
in retaliation for something the citizen has said or done, - in
other words, "punished" the citizen, - is violating federal law.

When the Department receives a complaint the allegations of
which, if true, involve a violation of federal law, we are then
obliged to determine, if possible, the truth of the allegations.
We recognize that many motives can exist for the making of ground-
less, and even malicious complaints against police officers. We
believe that it is as much to the interest of local law enforcement,
as it is a necessity for the protection of federal rights, that
the meritorious complaints be winnowed from those that are ground-
less. This can be done only by investigation. In many cases a
very slight investigation is sufficient to disclose that a complaint
is without any real substance. In others a full and exhaustive
investigation may be necessary to determine whether a violation has
occurred. Such investigations can, of course, be impeded by lack
of cooperation on the part of the local law enforcement agencies.
Happily however, such lack of cooperation is rare.

After notifying the head of the local law enforcement agency
of the ixitiitkimx initiation of an investigation, as is the
usual procedure, it is an exceptional case where the Bureau does
not receive the complete cooperation of the law enforcement agency
whose officers are the object of the investigation. Ordinarily,
no difficulty is encountered in arranging for the officers to
be privately interviewed by Bureau agents and it is in only rare
cases that, because of inability of the Bureau to arrange such
interviews, the United States Attorney is compelled to proceed by
means of a grand jury investigation. After the statements of the
alleged victims, of witnesses, and of the police officers themselves,
have been obtained by the Federal Bureau of Investigation, the
complete reports of the investigation are submitted to the Civil
Rights Section and to the United States Attorney in whose district
the complaint originated. A careful assessment is then made of the
merits of the original complaint. If it appears that certain matters
are still unresolved, further investigation may be requested. Only
after a full and exhaustive investigation and a careful study of the
evidence by both the Civil Rights Section and the United States
Attorney, will any decision be made as to possible prosecutive
action. It might be of interest to you to know the number of
prosecutions throughout the country that have been brought under
Sections 241 and 242 during the past ten years, viz: 1947, 10;
1948, 19; 1949, 22; 1950, 18; 1951, 16; 1952, 15; 1953, 29; 1954,

226

32; 1955, 18 and 1956, 17, or a total of 190 prosecutions filed.
Not all of these cases, of course, involved misconduct by police
officers.

We hope that this information may be of some interest and value
to you. We appreciate very much your having called in person with
Inspector Bare at the Department of Jusitce, and believe that such
direct contact between the Department and local officials can be
of mutual benefit.

Sincerely,

WARREN OLNEY III
Assistant Attorney General
Criminal Division

By:
ST. JOHN BARRETT
Chief, Civil Rights Section

144-012 Sec. 13

WO:SJB:ARG   June 24, 1957

Harold K. Wood, Esquire
United States Attorney
Philadelphia 7, Pennsylvania

Dear Mr. Wood:

In your letter of June 14, 1957, you ask to be advised
regarding the procedure in handling civil rights cases.

You are correct in stating that the Department receives
copies of all investigative reports relating to alleged violations of the civil rights statutes. You state that it has
been the practice of your office, upon receiving a copy of
the FBI investigative report in a civil rights case, to
either request further investigation or decline prosecution.
We assume that you are here referring to the report of a
preliminary, as distinguished from a full investigation. (If,
on examining the report of the preliminary investigation you
desire some further details to be checked out by the
investigating agents it would, of course, be entirely proper
for your office to request such limited additional information. However, as is stated in the United States Attorneys'
Manual, Title II, p. 63, a full investigation in a civil
rights case should not be requested without prior authorization from the Department.)

If, on the other hand, after examining the reports of
the preliminary investigation you determine that neither
further investigation nor prosecution is warranted, it is
proper for you to so advise the investigating agents. In
the ordinary course your views will be relayed to the Department by the FBI. If, after you have declined prosecution
we, from examination of the report of the preliminary
investigation, have any suggestions or questions, we will
communicate with you. In the absence of any communication
from the Department you may assume that we concur in your
decision declining prosecution and closing the case.

When your office received the reports resulting from
a full investigation of an alleged civil rights violation
prosecution should not be instituted by your office without
first obtaining authorization from the Department. The
correct procedure would be for your office to write to
the Department giving your views and asking for authority
to prosecute. If after full investigation you determine
that the evidence does not warrant prosecutive action you
can either state your view to the local FBI, in which case
it will be relayed to the Department, or you can write
directly to the Department. In the absence of any further

-2-

communcation from the Department to your office you may
assume that we concur in your decision declining prosecution.

We trust that we have sufficiently answered your
inquiry.

Sincerely,

WARREN OLNEY III
Assistant Attorney General
Criminal Division

By:
ST. JOHN BARRETT
Chief, Civil Rights Section

144-012 Sec. 13

Assistant Attorney General   October 21, 1957
Criminal Division

Director, FBI

CIVIL RIGHTS INVESTIGATIONS
WASHINGTON, D. C.

As a result of the decision of the United States Court
of Appeals for the District of Columbia, in the case of
Fryer versus United States, 207 F. (2d) 134 (1953), the
Department instructed that if a case is likely to be tried
in the District of Columbia, the statement of a witness,
wherever taken, should not be signed.

Assistant United States Attorney Frederick G. Smithson,
District of Columbia, has recently advised the Washington
Field Office of this Bureau that the United States Attorney's
office for the District of Columbia desires our Agents to
obtain signed statements from all victims in civil rights
cases. He said the purpose of obtaining the statement is
to insure the victim tells the truth.

You are requested to advise whether signed statements
should be taken from victims in civil rights cases as requested
by the United States Attorney's office for the District of
Columbia or whether privous Departmental instructions should
be followed in connection with signed statements taken from
witnesses where the case is likely to be tried in the
District of Columbia.

144-012 Sec. 13

Dec. 13, 1957

TO: Rufus D. McLean, Acting Assistant
         Attorney General, Criminal Division
FROM: W. Wilson White, Assistant Attorney
         General, Civil Rights Division
SUBJECT: Jurisdiction of Civil Rights Division

In operating under the provisions of my memorandum for the Attorney General regarding jurisdiction of the Civil Rights Division, dated December 10, 1957, and approved by the Attorney General, I expect to adopt the following practices as to these matters:

1. <u>Habeas Corpus.</u> Habeas corpus matters relating to federal prisoners will be handled by the Civil Rights Division along with the other federal custodial work.

2. <u>Threatening Communications.</u> In conformity with the statement at the bottom of page 2 of my memorandum of December 10 regarding the right of the Civil Rights Division to utilize additional ancillary and statutory remedies in cases involving civil rights matters, violations of Sections 875 and 876, Title 18 U.S.C. which arise from racial disputes will be handled by the Civil Rights Division. Violation of those sections not arising from racial matters, will, or course, not be handled by the Civil Rights Division.

3. <u>Obstruction of Justice.</u> It will be assumed that violations of 18 U.S.C. 1503 which are committed in connection with a (pending) case over which the Criminal Division has primary jurisdiction will be handled by the Criminal Division and referral to or consultation with the Civil Rights Division will be unnecessary. The Civil Rights Division will handle obstructions of justice that are not related to a criminal case being handled by the Criminal Division.

4. <u>Juveniles and Mental Incompetents.</u> When, in connection with a criminal case being handled by the Criminal Division, queries are received prior to judgment and sentence regarding the mental competency of the accused or the application of non-applications of juvenile proceedings, such queries may be answered by the Criminal Division after consultation with members of the appropriate section or unit in the Civil Rights Division. Such consultation may be on an informal basis. For example, in cases where a United States Attorney has requested authorization of the Attorney General to use adult procedure against a juvenile the Criminal Division, after consulting with the appropriate personnel in the Civil Rights Division and receiving the authorization of the Civil Rights Division, should write the letter to the United States Attorney granting or denying the request for authorization. By such means it should be possible to avoid the necessity of the Civil Rights Division corresponding with the United States Attorneys on pending

231

-2-

cases at any stage of the proceeding prior to judgment and sentence. On the other hand, inquiries received from United States Attorneys relating to matters within the jurisdiction of the Civil Rights Division and receives subsequent to imposition of sentence, will be answered by the Civil Rights Division after informal consultation with such personnel of the Criminal Division as may have handled the case in its prosecutive stage.

144-012 Sec. 13

Rufus D. McLean, Acting Assistant Attorney
   General, Criminal Division   January 15, 1958

W. Wilson White, Assistant Attorney General
   Civil Rights Division

Jurisdiction of Civil Rights Division

   This will confirm our conversation of yesterday regarding the
procedure to be followed hereafter in carrying out the terms of
my memorandum to the Attorney General regarding the jurisdiction of
the Civil Rights Division, dated December 10, 1957. We agreed that
my memorandum of December 13, 1957 to you on this same subject required clarification and that the practice that had been followed
with respect to outgoing correspondence regarding juveniles and
mental defectives should be changed.

   1. Habeas Corpus

   Habeas corpus matters arising from immigration and naturaliza-
tion cases will be handled by the Criminal Division. All other
habeas corpus matters relating to federal prisoners will be handled
by the Civil Rights Division.

   2. Obstruction of Justice

   Violations of 18 U.S.C. 1503 which are committed in connection
with a case over which the Criminal Division has jurisdiction, will
be handled by the Criminal Division and referral to or consultation
with the Civil Rights Division will be unnecessary. The Civil Rights
Division will handled obstructions of justice that are not related to
any case within the subject matter jurisdiction of the Criminal
Division.

   3. Juveniles and Mental Incompetents.

   Inquiries to the Department regarding juveniles and mental
incompetents will be handled by the Civil Rights Division and
answers to such inquiries will be prepared for the signature of the
Assistant Attorney General in charge of the Civil Rights Division.
The practice previously outlined in my memorandum of December 13,
1957, will not be followed. Thus, any request by a United States
Attorney for authorization of the Attorney General to use adult
procedure against a juvenile will be handled by the Civil Rights
Division, and the response will be sent out over the signature of
the Assistant Attorney General in charge of the Civil Rights Division.

FROM

First Assistant

to

the Office indicated below the check mark

MEMORANDUM

August 5, 1958

Executive Assistant   1

Due Process Unit   2

No investigation with reference to
the attached shall be request unless a formal complaint is received.
The Attorney General has specified
as a general function of this Division "requesting and reviewing
investigations arising from reports
or complaints of public officials
or private citizens with respect to
matters affecting civil rights."
Newspaper article standing alone do
not fall within this classification.

Joseph M.R. Ryan, Jr.
First Assistant

November 28, 1958

Messrs. Ryan, Barrett, Bassford, Greene,
 Putzel, Krouse, Gottshall, Hubbard and Caldwell

W. Wilson White, Assistant Attorney General,
 Civil Rights Division

Cooperation with civil rights authorities of states.

In line with our policy of encouraging state action to
investigate and punish civil rights violations occurring
within the states, I have now had discussions with the
authorities of the states of Pennsylvania, New York, and
Massachusetts.

Please advise me of any due process complaints rising
in any of these states so that consideration may be given to
reference to the state authorities before any full investigation
by the FBI.

Department of Justice

FOR RELEASE TO A. M. NEWSPAPERS
MONDAY, APRIL 6, 1959

Ninety four United States Attorneys from as many districts in the

states and territories, will convene here Monday for a two-day conference

with officials of the Department of Justice. They will discuss problems

of Federal law enforcement, with especial reference to the drive on

organized crime and racketeering, and intra-departmental administrative

matters.

The group will be welcomed Monday morning by Attorney General

William P. Rogers and one of the first matters to be presented to them

will be the following statement:

MEMORANDUM TO THE UNITED STATES ATTORNEYS

In two decisions on March 30, 1959, the Supreme Court of the United

States reaffirmed the existence of a power to prosecute a defendant under

both federal and state law for the same act or acts. That power, which the

Court held is inherent in our federal system, has been used sparingly by

the Department of Justice in the past. The purpose of this memorandum

is to insure that in the future we continue that policy. After a state prosecu-

tion there should be no federal trial for the same act or acts unless the

reasons are compelling.

236

In <u>Abbate</u> v. <u>United States</u> and <u>Bartkus</u> v. <u>Illinois</u> the Supreme Court held that there is no violation of the double jeopardy prohibition or of the due process clause of our federal Constitution where there are prosecutions of the defendant, both in the state and in the federal court, based upon the same act or acts.)

This ruling reaffirmed the holding in <u>United States</u> v. <u>Lanza</u>, 260 U.S. 377, decided by the Supreme Court in 1922. In that case Chief Justice Taft, speaking for a unanimous Court, said:

> "We have here two sovereignties, deriving power from different sources, capable of dealing with the same subject matter within the same territory .... Each government in determining what shall be an offense against its peace and dignity is exercising its own sovereignty, not that of the other.
>
> "It follows that an act denounced as a crime by both national and state sovereignties is an offense against the peace and dignity of both and may be punished by each."

(But the mere existence of a power, of course, does not mean that it should necessarily be exercised.) In the <u>Bartkus</u> case the Court said:

> "The men who wrote the Constitution as well as the citizens of the member states of the Confederation were fearful of the power of centralized government and sought to limit its power. Mr. Justice Brandeis has written that separation of powers was adopted in the Constitution 'not to promote efficiency but to preclude the exercise of arbitrary power.' Time has not lessened the concern of the Founders in devising a federal system which would likewise be a safeguard against arbitrary government. The greatest self-restraint is necessary <u>when that federal system yields results with which a court is in little sympathy</u>."
> (Emphasis added)

The Court held then that precedent, experience and reason supported the conclusion of separate federal and state offenses.

It is our duty to observe not only the rulings of the Court but the spirit of the rulings as well. In effect, the Court said that although the rule of the Lanza case is sound law, enforcement officers should use care in applying it.

Applied indiscriminately and with bad judgment it, like most rules of law, could cause considerable hardship. Applied wisely it is a rule that is in the public interest. Consequently - (as the Court clearly indicated - those of us charged with law enforcement responsibilities have a particular duty to act wisely and with self-restraint in this area.

Cooperation between federal and state prosecutive officers is essential if the gears of the federal and state systems are to mesh properly. We should continue to make every effort to cooperate with state and local authorities to the end that the trial occur in the jurisdiction, whether it be state or federal, where the public interest is best served. If this be determined accurately, and is followed by efficient and intelligent cooperation of state and federal law enforcement authorities, then consideration of a second prosecution very seldom should arise.

In such event I doubt that it is wise or practical to attempt to formulate detailed rules to deal with the complex situation which might develop, particularly because a series of related acts are often involved. However, no federal case should be tried when there has already been a state

prosecution for substantially the same act or acts without the United

States Attorney first submitting a recommendation to the appropriate

Assistant Attorney General in the Department.   No such recommendation

should be approved by the Assistant Attorney General in charge of the

Division without having it first brought to my attention.

/s/   William P. Rogers
Attorney General

CIVIL RIGHTS DIVISION MANUAL

This Civil Rights Manual is composed of numerous directives issued by the Department of Justice concerning proceedures to be followed in the Civil Rights Division and by the Federal Bureau of Investigation and the U. S. Attorneys.   Also included are Legislative histories of the Civil Rights Act of 1957 and the Civil Rights Act of 1960.

The memoranda and other material contained herein were assembled by Arthur B. Caldwell for his own use as Chief of the Civil Rights Sec tion from 1952 to 1957,.   When the Section was raised to a Division of the Department , he served as Assistant to the Assistant Attorney General in Charge of Civil Rights.

Since all the documents contained herein are copies of official documents in the Department of Justice, in Washington, D. C.—the use of this material should be restricted to serious researchers and should not be made available to members of the press for publication generally.

Arthur B. Caldwell,
Class of 1929

I. ORGANIZATION

DEPARTMENT OF JUSTICE

OFFICE OF THE ATTORNEY GENERAL

Washington, D. C.

December 9, 1957

ORDER NO. 155-57

ESTABLISHMENT OF THE CIVIL RIGHTS DIVISION IN THE DEPARTMENT
OF JUSTICE

By virtue of the authority vested in me by law, including
particularly section 161 of the Revised Statutes of the United States
(5 U.S.C. 22) and section 2 of Reorganization Plan No. 2 of 1950
(64 Stat. 1261), and as Attorney General of the United States, it is
hereby ordered as follows:

1. There is hereby established in the Department of Justice
a division to be known and designated as the Civil Rights Division, at
the head of which there shall be an Assistant Attorney General.

2. Subject to the general supervision and direction of the
Attorney General, the following-described matters are assigned to, and
shall be conducted, handled, or supervised by, the Assistant Attorney
General in charge of the Civil Rights Division:

(a) Enforcement of all Federal statutes affecting
civil rights, and authorization of such enforcement,
including criminal prosecutions, and civil actions and
proceedings on behalf of the Government; and appellate
proceedings in all such cases.

(b) Requesting, directing and reviewing of investigations arising from reports or complaints of
public officials or private citizens with respect to
matters affecting civil rights.

(c) Conferring with individuals and groups who
call upon the Department in connection with civil-rights
matters, advising such individuals and groups thereon,
and initiating action appropriate thereto.

(d) Coordination within the Department of Justice
of all matters affecting civil rights.

(e) Consultation with and assistance to other
Federal departments and agencies and State and local
agencies on matters affecting civil rights.

(f) Research on civil-rights matters, and the
making of recommendations to the Attorney General as
to proposed policies and legislation therefor.

(g) Upon their request, assisting the Commission
on Civil Rights and other similar Federal bodies in
carrying out research and formulating recommendations.

3. All functions, records, property, positions, and funds
of the Civil Rights Section of the Criminal Division are hereby
transferred to the Civil Rights Division.

/s/ William P. Rogers

William P. Rogers
Attorney General

December 11, 1957

MEMORANDUM TO THE STAFF,

CRIMINAL DIVISION.

There is attached a copy of a memorandum approved by the

Attorney General with respect to jurisdiction of the new Civil Rights

Division, including certain statutes which are to remain in the

Criminal Division.

Section assignments have been inserted in the list of statutes

reverting to the Criminal Division.

Rufus D. McLean,
Acting Assistant Attorney General,
Criminal Division.

CIVIL RIGHTS DIVISION MEMORANDUM NO. 4

Re: Reassignment of personnel.

The following are transferred to and will comprise

the Trial Staff of the Civil Rights Division:

Arthur B. Caldwell
Ben Brooks
Allen J. Krouse
William A. Kehoe
John Ossea

The following clerical personnel are assigned to

the Trial Staff:

Florence Fried
Colleen Wushnak
Vacancy (vice Baker)

Mr. Arthur B. Caldwell is designated Acting Chief

of the Trial Staff.

/s/ Joseph M. F. Ryan, Jr.

JOSEPH M. F. RYAN, JR.
Acting Assistant Attorney General
Civil Rights Division

October 22, 1959

245

CIVIL RIGHTS DIVISION CIRCULAR NO. 5

ORGANIZATION OF DIVISION

1. The Civil Rights Division shall have the following

organization:

Assistant Attorney General

First Assistant

Second Assistant

Executive Assistant

Administrative Section

Appeals and Research Section

General Litigation Section

  Constitutional Rights Unit
  Federal Custody Unit

Trial Staff

Voting and Elections Section

2. This organization supersedes that described in

Civil Rights Division Circular No. 1.

    /s/ Joseph M. F. Ryan, Jr.

    JOSEPH M. F. RYAN, JR.
   Acting Assistant Attorney General
    Civil Rights Division

October 22, 1959

OFFICE OF THE ATTORNEY GENERAL

WASHINGTON, D. C.

February 3, 1939.

ORDER NO. 3204

Effective this date there is established within the Criminal Division of the Department of Justice a unit to be known as the Civil Liberties Unit.

The function and purpose of this unit will be to make a study of the provisions of the Constitution of the United States and Acts of Congress relating to civil rights with reference to present conditions, to make appropriate recommendations in respect thereto, and to direct, supervise and conduct prosecutions of violations of the provisions of the Constitution or Acts of Congress guaranteeing civil rights to individuals.

FRANK MURPHY

Attorney General.

247

Brien McMahon
Assistant Attorney General

DEPARTMENT OF JUSTICE
Washington

February 3, 1939.

ORDER

Pursuant to the Order of the Attorney General
numbered 3204, dated February 3, 1939, establishing
a Civil Liberties Unit within the Criminal Division
of the Department of Justice, Mr. Henry A. Schweinhaut, Special Assistant to the Attorney General, is
hereby designated as Chief of such unit.

Brien McMahon,
Assistant Attorney General.

Henry A. Schweinhaut is 37 years of age and a native of the District of Columbia. He attended the local public schools and was graduated in 1924 from the National University Law School. He was in the general practice in Washington, D. C., from 1924 until 1934 when he was appointed an Assistant United States Attorney. He served in that office until 1936 when he was appointed a Special Assistant to the Attorney General. Since then he has been a member of the Trial Section of the Criminal Division. He is a former Vice President of the D. C. Bar Association and has been on the faculty of the Washington College of Law since 1932.

Mr. Schweinhaut took an important part in the Harlan County prosecution and has also been associated in the presentation of the evidence to the grand jury in the matter of the Jersey City difficulties.

CHIEF OF THE CIVIL RIGHTS SECTION

from

FEBRUARY 3, 1939 to DECEMBER 9, 1957

Henry Schweinhaut	1939-1941
Victor Rotnem	1941-1945
Turner Smith	1945-1947
A. Abbott Rosen	1947-1948
Leo Meltzer (acting chief)	1948-1950
George Friedman	1950-1951
Leo Meltzer (acting chief)	1951-1952
Arthur B. Caldwell	1952-1957
St. John Barrett	5-14-57 - 12-9-57

JURISDICTION

December 10, 1957

MEMORANDUM FOR THE ATTORNEY GENERAL

Re: Jurisdiction of the Civil Rights Division

In accordance with your Orders of yesterday, December 9, 1957, assigning me as head of the Civil Rights Division, and establishing a Civil Rights Division in the Department of Justice, I herewith submit for your approval a list of statutes over which I believe the new division should exercise primary enforcement jurisdiction.

Civil Rights
18 U.S.C. 241 (Conspiracy to injure citizens
242 in the exercise of their civil rights;
depriving persons of civil rights)
243 (Exclusion of jurors on account of race
or color)
244 (Discrimination against person wearing
uniform of armed forces)

Sentence, Judgment and Execution
18 U.S.C. 3566 (Execution of death sentence)
3567 (Death sentence may prescribe
dissection)
3568 (Effective date of sentence)

Hatch Act & Corrupt Practices Act
18 U.S.C. Ch. 29 (Elections & Political activities)

Escape and Rescue
18 U.S.C. 751 (Prisoners in custody of institution or officer)
752 (Instigating or assisting escape)
753 (Rescue to prevent execution)
754 (Rescue of body of executed offender)
755 (Officer permitting escape)
1072 (Concealing escaped prisoner)
42 U.S.C. 261 (Penalties for introduction of narcotics into
hospitals, escaping from, or aiding and
abetting escape from hospitals, etc.)

Fugitive Felon Act
18 U.S.C. 1073

Merchant Seamen
        18 U.S.C. 2191-2193, 2195 (Maltreatment of crew; mutiny,
                                abandonment in foreign port, etc.)
                2196 (Drunkenness or neglect of duty)
        46 U.S.C. 542a, 545-568, 570-571, 575, 643, 652-653, 658,
                660, 662, 667, 672, 701

Obstruction of Justice
        18 U.S.C. 1503

Peonage and Slavery
        18 U.S.C. 1581-1588

Prisons and Prisoners (Legal Matters)
        18 U.S.C. 1791 (Traffic in contraband articles)
                1792 (Mutiny, riot, dangerous instrumentalities
                    prohibited)
                3569 (Discharge of indigent prisoner)
                3651, 3653 (Suspension of sentence and probation)
                4082 (Commitment to Attorney General, transfer)
                4083 (Penitentiary imprisonment; consent)
                4161-4166 (Good time allowances)
                4201-4207 (Parole)
                4241-4248 (Mental defectives)
                5005-5026 (Youth Corrections Act)
                5031-5037 (Juvenile Delinquency)
                Indigent Convicts

Search Warrants
        18 U.S.C. 2234 (Authority exceeded in executing warrant)
                2235 (Search warrant procured maliciously)
                2236 (Searches without warrant)

Shanghaiing Sailors
        18 U.S.C. 2194

The new Civil Rights Act enacted September 1957

        My understanding is that the Division's primary jurisdiction in relation
to these statutes above enumerated will in no way prejudice the right of the
Civil Rights Division to utilize additional and ancillary statutory remedies in any
given case, even though primary jurisdiction of such additional and ancillary
statutes may be within the scope of another Division's responsibility. In any

such instance, of course, you may be assured that the provisions of Section 26, entitled "Jurisdictional Agreements," of the proposed organizational order of the Department of Justice (which order is before you for approval) will be observed.

Heretofore in the Criminal Division the Civil Rights Section was charged with the enforcement of certain statutes which I have listed below.

18 U.S.C. 3146 (Bail jumping) (Section having case)
18 U.S.C. 1791 (Traffic in contraband articles) (Administrative Regulations)

Kidnapping
18 U.S.C. 1201 (Transportation in interstate or foreign commerce; failure to release within 24 hours; conspiracy) (General Crimes)
1202 (Receiving, possessing, or disposing of ransom money) (General Crimes)

Motion attacking sentence (Section having case)
28 U.S.C. 2255

Prison-made goods (Administrative Regulations)
18 U.S.C. 1761 (Transportation or importation)
1762 (Marking packages)

Selective Service (Administrative Regulations)
50 U.S.C. (App.) 462

Soldiers' and Sailors' Civil Relief Act of 1940 (Administrative Regulations)
50 U.S.C. (App.) 520, 530

Strikebreakers, Transporting (Organized Crime)
18 U.S.C. 1231

Wiretapping (Administrative Regulations)
47 U.S.C. 605

I believe primary jurisdiction over these statutes should remain in the Criminal Division.

W. Wilson White
Assistant Attorney General
Civil Rights Division

CIVIL RIGHTS DIVISION MEMORANDUM No. 1

Re: Jurisdiction of sections and units.

1. Until otherwise directed, the jurisdiction of the sections and units of this Division will be as follows:

Administrative Section

This Section handles administrative matters, including the compilation of statistics; the keeping of personnel and other records, dockets and record controls; and the keeping of a complete and accurate record of all cases and investigative matters handled by the Division. The Administrative Section receives all factual data and information and maintains full files and indices.

Appeals and Research Section

This Section is responsible for handling appeals of court cases within the jurisdiction of the Division. It prepares briefs, motions, memoranda, and other pleadings in connection with cases pending before the courts of appeals and is responsible for the oral argument of cases in these courts. In all cases where the government has a right of appeal to an appellate court, the Appeals and Research Section prepares the necessary papers and recommends to the Solicitor General whether such an appeal should be taken. The Section further is charged with responsibility for Civil Rights Division cases in the Supreme Court, in that it prepares memoranda to the Solicitor General recommending for or against certiorari or appeal; and, under the supervision of the Solicitor General, drafts briefs in opposition or in support of petitions for writ of certiorari, briefs on the merits, and other pleadings.

The Section collects information regarding litigation in the field of civil rights in order to be fully apprised of all legal developments in this field.

The Appeals and Research Section has responsibility for studying and analyzing existing and proposed laws relating to matters over which the Civil Rights Division has jurisdiction. It makes recommendations for change and drafts new legislation in accordance with the general responsibility of the Department. The Section maintains permanent files of legal memoranda and is responsible for the maintenance of a law library for the Division.

The Section has general responsibility for drafting and revising such parts of the United States Attorneys' Manual as relate to matters within the jurisdiction of the Division.

The Appeals and Research Section, upon request, assists in the drafting of court pleadings and maintains a permanent file of pleading forms.

General Litigation Section

The General Litigation Section is charged with the responsibility of supervising the enforcement of all federal statutes within the jurisdiction of the Division other than those relating to elections and voting. This

responsibility covers both the investigatory and trial stages. For
operational purposes, the work of the Section is divided among an
Equal Protection Unit, a Federal Custody Unit, and a Due Process Unit.

The Equal Protection Unit handles all complaints and cases involving
a denial of the equal protection of the laws guaranteed by the Fourteenth
Amendment to the Constitution. This unit also supervises the enforcement of the federal obstruction of justice statute (18 U.S.C. §1503); the
Fugitive Felon Act (18 U.S.C. §1073); the exclusion of jurors on account
of race or color (18 U.S.C. §243), and any discrimination against persons
wearing the uniform of the Armed Forces (18 U.S.C. §244).

The Federal Custody Unit deals with legal and administrative questions
arising from the time of arrest of a federal prisoner on criminal charges
to his final discharge from sentence. The Unit is responsibile for preparing
answers to inquiries of United States Attorneys, District Judges, the Bureau
of Prisons, the Board of Parole, and from prisoners or their representatives
regarding such matters as the construction and validity of criminal sentences,
the application and construction of the Probation Act, the parole statutes,
the Juvenile Delinquency Act, and the sentencing provisions of the Youth
Corrections Act. The Unit also has the responsibility of advising United
States Attorneys in habeas corpus matters, of assisting them in the preparation of pleadings to resist non-meritorious petitions by federal prisoners
for writs of habeas corpus, and of handling problems relating to mentally
defective defendants temporarily committed pending recovery. The Unit
supervises the enforcement of the federal criminal statutes regarding the
escape and rescue of prisoners.

The Due Process Unit handles all complaints and cases involving a denial of due process of law under the Fifth and Fourteenth Amendments. Denials of due process may arise from such situations as the infliction of unlawful summary punishment by law enforcement officers, the coercion of confessions from arrested persons by means of force or threats, the unlawful infliction of corporal punishment by jail personnel, the illegal detention of persons under color of law, and the unlawful taking of a person from one State to face criminal charges in another State without following the proper extradition procedure. The Due Process Unit is also charged with supervising the enforcement of federal criminal statutes relating to peonage and slavery (18 U.S.C. §§1581-1588), merchant seamen (18 U.S.C. §§2191 et seq., 46 U.S.C. §§542(a) et seq.), the unlawful use of search warrants (18 U.S.C. §§2234-2236) and the shanghaiing of sailors (18 U.S.C. §2194).

Elections and Voting Section

The Elections and Voting Section is charged with the responsibility of administering the new remedies afforded the Attorney General by the Civil Rights Act of 1957. This Act authorizes the Attorney General to institute in the name of the United States civil actions or other proper proceedings for preventive relief to secure the right of persons to vote free from certain types of unlawful interference. In cases where information regarding such interference comes to the attention of the Division, the Section, when appropriate, requests the Federal Bureau of Investigation to investigate, analyzes the results of the investigation, determines whether court action should be instituted, and participates in such action.

In addition to the performance of duties under the new Civil Rights Act, the Section is charged with the enforcement of federal criminal statutes applicable to election frauds and interference with the right to vote, the Hatch Act, and the Corrupt Practices Act. In all these instances, the Section has responsibility for collecting and analyzing information concerning violations, consulting with United States Attorneys regarding possible court action, and supervising, participating in, or handling any resulting litigation.

2. During the formative period of the Division, each of the operating sections will be called on for a large amount of legal and factual research and assembly of data: The coordination of this research between the Appeals and Research Section and the other operative sections will be handled by the Executive Assistant.

Assistant Attorney General
Civil Rights Division

December 31, 1957

CIVIL RIGHTS DIVISION MEMORANDUM NO. 3

Re: Jurisdiction of sections and units.

1. Until otherwise directed, the jurisdiction of the
sections and units (including the Trial Staff), will be as
follows:

Administrative Section

This Section handles administrative matters, including the
compilation of statistics; the keeping of personnel and other
records, dockets and record controls; and the keeping of a
complete and accurate record of all cases and investigative
matters handled by the Division. The Administrative Section
receives all factual data and information and maintains full
files and indices.

Appeals and Research Section

This Section is responsible for handling appeals of court
cases within the jurisdiction of the Division. It prepares
briefs, motions, memoranda, and other pleadings in connection
with cases pending before the courts of appeals and is responsible for the oral argument of cases in these courts. In
all cases where the government has a right of appeal to an appellate court, the Appeals and Research Section prepares the
necessary papers and recommends to the Solicitor General
whether such an appeal should be taken. The Section further
is charged with responsibility for Civil Rights Division cases

in the Supreme Court, in that it prepares memoranda to the Solicitor General recommending for or against certiorari or appeal; and, under the supervision of the Solicitor General, drafts briefs in opposition or in support of petitions for writ of certiorari, briefs on the merits, and other pleadings.

The Section collects information regarding litigation in the field of civil rights in order to be fully apprised of all legal developments in this field.

The Appeals and Research Section has responsibility for studying and analyzing existing and proposed laws relating to matters over which the Civil Rights Division has jurisdiction. It makes recommendations for change and drafts new legislation in accordance with the general responsibility of the Department. The Section also maintains permanent files of legal memoranda.

The Section has general responsibility for drafting and revising such parts of the United States Attorneys' Manual as relate to matters within the jurisdiction of the Division.

The Appeals and Research Section, upon request, assists in the drafting of court pleadings and maintains a permanent file of pleading forms.

General Litigation Section

The General Litigation Section is charged with the responsibility of supervising the enforcement of all federal statutes within the jurisdiction of the Division other than those relating to elections and voting. This responsibility covers both the investigatory and trial stages (except in those instances in which responsibility is assigned to the Trial Staff). For operational purposes, the work of the Section is divided between a Constitutional Rights Unit and a Federal Custody Unit.

The Constitutional Rights Unit handles all complaints and cases involving a denial of due process of law under the Fifth and Fourteenth Amendments. Denials of due process may arise from such situations as the infliction of unlawful summary punishment by law enforcement officers, the coercion of confessions from arrested persons by means of force or threats, the unlawful infliction of corporal punishment by jail personnel, the illegal detention of persons under color of law, and the unlawful taking of a person from one State to face criminal charges in another State without following the proper extradition procedure. The Unit is also charged with supervising the enforcement of federal criminal statutes relating to peonage and slavery (18 U.S.C. §§1581-1588), merchant seamen (18 U.S.C. §§2191 et seq., 46 U.S.C. §§542(a) et seq.), the unlawful use of search warrants (18 U.S.C. §§2234-2236) and the shanghaiing of sailors (18 U.S.C. §2194).

In addition the Constitutional Rights Unit has cognizance of all complaints and cases involving a denial of the equal

protection of the laws guaranteed by the Fourteenth Amendment
to the Constitution. This Unit also supervises the enforcement
of the federal obstruction of justice statute (18 U.S.C. §1503);
the Fugitive Felon Act (18 U.S.C. §1073); the exclusion of jurors
on account of race or color (18 U.S.C. §243), and any discrimination against persons wearing the uniform of the Armed Forces
(18 U.S.C. §244).

The Federal Custody Unit deals with legal and administrative
questions arising from the time of arrest of a federal prisoner
on criminal charges to his final discharge from sentence. The
Unit is responsible for preparing answers to inquiries of
United States Attorneys, District Judges, the Bureau of Prisons,
the Board of Parole, and from prisoners or their representatives
regarding such matters as the construction and validity of
criminal sentences, the application and construction of the
Probation Act, the parole statutes, the Juvenile Delinquency
Act, and the sentencing provisions of the Youth Corrections
Act. The Unit also has the responsibility of advising United
States Attorneys in habeas corpus matters, of assisting them in
the preparation of pleadings to resist non-meritorious petitions
by federal prisoners for writs of habeas corpus, and of handling
problems relating to mentally defective defendants temporarily
committed pending recovery. The Unit supervises the enforcement
of the federal criminal statutes regarding the escape and rescue
of prisoners.

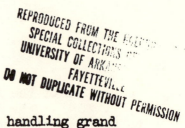

Trial Staff

The Trial Staff shall be responsible for handling grand jury presentations and trials of matters and cases assigned to it from the General Litigation and Voting and Elections Sections, together with such other assignments as may be made. The Chief of the Trial Staff will report directly to the Second Assistant.

Voting and Elections Section

The Voting and Elections Section is charged with the responsibility of administering the new remedies afforded the Attorney General by the Civil Rights Act of 1957. This Act authorizes the Attorney General to institute in the name of the United States civil actions or other proper proceedings for preventive relief to secure the right of persons to vote free from certain types of unlawful interference. In cases where information regarding such interference comes to the attention of the Division, the Section, when appropriate, requests the Federal Bureau of Investigation to investigate, analyzes the results of the investigation, determines whether court action should be instituted, and participates in such action.

In addition to the performance of duties under the new Civil Rights Act, the Section is charged with the enforcement of federal criminal statutes applicable to election frauds and interference with the right to vote, the Hatch Act, and the

Corrupt Practices Act. In all these instances, the Section has responsibility for collecting and analyzing information concerning violations, consulting with the United States Attorneys regarding possible court action, and taking other appropriate action.

2. This memorandum supersedes Civil Rights Division Memorandum No. 1, effective immediately.

/s/ Joseph M. F. Ryan, Jr.

JOSEPH M. F. RYAN, JR.
Acting Assistant Attorney General
Civil Rights Division

PROCEDURE AND POLICY

UNITED STATES DEPARTMENT OF JUSTICE

OFFICE OF THE ATTORNEY GENERAL

WASHINGTON, D. C.

February 9, 1954

ORDER NO. 40-54

TO ALL UNITED STATES ATTORNEYS, THE FEDERAL BUREAU OF INVESTIGATION,
AND ATTORNEYS OF THE CRIMINAL DIVISION:

Subject: Civil Rights and Peonage, Slavery and Involuntary Servitude
Statutes (18 U.S.C. 241, 242, 243, 1581, 1583, 1584)

It is the policy of the Department to be alert to and to act
promptly and vigorously in all matters involving possible violations of
the civil rights statutes (18 U.S.C. 241, 242, 243) or the peonage,
slavery, or involuntary servitude statutes (18 U.S.C. 1581, 1583, 1584)
without regard to the district in which the offense may have been committed. Any information and all complaints concerning such matters
possibly within the jurisdiction of the Department will be given
immediate attention and appropriate action.

The investigation of all complaints and the prosecution and
handling of all cases involving possible violations of 18 U.S.C.,
Section 242 - willful deprivations of federal rights of inhabitants
under color of law (Screws v. United States, 325 U.S. 91 (1945));
Williams v. United States, 341 U.S. 97 (1951)), Section 241 - conspiring to injure citizens in exercise of federal rights (United States v.
Williams, 341 U.S. 70 (1951)), other than in election and labor cases*,
and Section 243 - exclusion of jurors on account of race or color; and
the investigation of all complaints and the prosecution and handling of
all cases involving possible violations of 18 U.S.C., Section 1581
(peonage, arrest with intent to place in peonage), Section 1583
(carrying persons to be sold into involuntary servitude or held as a
slave), and Section 1584 (involuntary servitude), are subject to the
following instructions:

1. The Federal Bureau of Investigation is authorized to
conduct preliminary investigations into all complaints involving
possible violations of any of the above statutes, without the necessity
of prior authorization of the Criminal Division. Whenever a complaint
involving a possible violation of any of these statutes comes to the

---

* Separate Orders will cover election matters and labor matters
involving Section 241.

attention of the United States Attorney, or any other official or employee of the Department, he shall immediately refer it to the Federal Bureau of Investigation and advise the Criminal Division of such referral.

2. Upon completion of the preliminary investigation and receipt of the Bureau's reports, the United States Attorney for the District having jurisdiction will promptly review such reports and forward to the Criminal Division his recommendations concerning the need for further investigation or whether the matter should be closed, giving his reasons therefor. In unusual cases where it clearly appears that violations have been committed and where time is of the essence, the Federal Bureau of Investigation may be instructed to complete the investigation in cooperation with the United States Attorney without obtaining clearance from the Criminal Division.

3. In no case is prosecution under the civil rights statutes, or under the peonage, slavery or involuntary servitude statutes, including presentation of the case to a grand jury for investigation or indictment, to be instituted without prior approval of the Criminal Division.

4. The Criminal Division should be notified immediately of any court decision or order in any civil rights, peonage, slavery or involuntary servitude case. While no appeal should be prosecuted on behalf of the Government in these cases without prior authorization, the United States Attorney may, where the statute provides a basis for appeal by the Government and time is short, file a protective appeal. When such appeal is noted, or any similar action is taken to protect the interests of the Government, the Criminal Division should be promptly notified.

5. It is the policy of the Department, insofar as consistent with Departmental regulations prohibiting disclosure of confidential documents or information, to lend all possible aid to State prosecutive action, where appropriate. When it appears that prompt and vigorous action is taken in good faith by the State to prosecute persons who have violated State law as well as the federal statutes covered by this Order, federal prosecution may be deferred pending disposition of the State charges. However, such State prosecutions must be closely followed and the Criminal Division kept currently advised of all developments in order to protect the interests of the Government and prevent the running of the federal statute of limitations. Final disposition of the federal offense will be determined following the receipt of recommendations by the United States Attorney, whose views will be fully considered.

This Order supersedes Circular No. 3356 and Supplements 1, 2, 3 and 4, and Circular No. 3591.

/Signed/
HERBERT BROWNELL, JR.
Attorney General

UNITED STATES DEPARTMENT OF JUSTICE

OFFICE OF THE ATTORNEY GENERAL

Washington 25, D. C.

February 9, 1954

ORDER NO. 41 - 54.

TO ALL UNITED STATES ATTORNEYS, THE FEDERAL BUREAU OF INVESTIGATION,
AND ATTORNEYS OF THE CRIMINAL DIVISION:

Subject: Elections, Election Campaigns and Political Activity

The investigation of all complaints and the handling and
prosecution of all cases involving possible violations of the statutes
designated below as "election laws" shall be conducted in accordance
with the following instructions:

1. The Federal Bureau of Investigation is authorized to
conduct preliminary investigations into all complaints involving possible
violations of any of the election laws, without the necessity of prior
authorization of the Criminal Division. Whenever a complaint involving
a possible violation of any of these statutes comes to the attention of
the United States Attorney, he shall immediately refer it to the Federal
Bureau of Investigation and advise the Criminal Division of such referral.

2. Upon completion of the preliminary investigation and receipt
of the Bureau's reports, the United States Attorney for the District having
jurisdiction will promptly review such reports and forward to the Criminal
Division his recommendations concerning the need for further investigation
and the advisability of prosecutive action, giving his reasons therefor.
In unusual cases where it clearly appears that violations have been committed and where time is of the essence, the Federal Bureau of Investigation
may be instructed to complete the investigation in cooperation with the
United States Attorney without obtaining clearance from the Criminal
Division.

3. In no case is prosecution under the election laws, including
the presentation of the case to a grand jury for investigation or indictment, to be instituted without prior approval of the Criminal Division.
However, where it appears that tangible evidence such as ballots, ballot
books and tally sheets will be destroyed in accordance with state law
after a certain date, and time is short, the United States Attorney may
petition the court for an order impounding such paraphernalia without
prior authorization of the Criminal Division.

269

4. The Criminal Division should be notified immediately of any court decision or order in any election law case. While no appeal should be prosecuted on behalf of the Government in these cases without prior authorization, the United States Attorney may, where the statute provides a basis for appeal by the Government and time is short, file a protective appeal. When such appeal is noted, or any similar action is taken to protect the interests of the Government, the Criminal Division should be promptly notified.

The following Sections of Title 18, U.S.C., are considered "election laws" for the purpose of this Circular:

Section 241 - conspiracies to injure federal rights. (See United States v. Classic, 313 U.S. 299).

Section 242 - deprivation of constitutional rights under color of law (See United States v. Classic, supra, and Screws v. United States, 325 U.S. 91).

Section 591 - (Corrupt Practice Act, Section 302) - definitions.

Section 592 - troops at polls prohibited.

Section 593 - interference by armed forces with elections.

Section 594 - (Hatch Act, Section 1) - intimidation of voters in a federal election.

Section 595 - (Hatch Act, Section 2) - use of official authority to affect elections.

Section 596 - polling armed forces

Section 597 - (Corrupt Practice Act, Section 311) - bribery of voters. (See United States v. Blanton, 77 F. Supp. 812).

Section 598 - (Hatch Act, Sections 7 & 8) - use of relief appropriations to coerce voters.

Section 599 - (Corrupt Practice Act, Section 310) - promise of appointment by candidate.

Section 600 - (Hatch Act, Section 3) - promise of employment in consideration for political activity.

Section 601 - (Hatch Act, Section 4) - deprivation of employment for political activity.

Section 602 - (Corrupt Practice Act, Section 312) - solicitation of political contributions from Government employees. (See United States v. Wurzback, 280 U.S. 396).

Section 603 - solicitation of political contributions on Government property. (See United States v. Thayer, 209 U.S. 39, United States v. Smith, 163 F. 926).

Section 604 - (Hatch Act, Section 5) - solicitation of political contributions from persons on relief.

Section 605 - (Hatch Act, Section 6) - disclosure for political purposes of names of persons on relief.

Section 606 - intimidation to secure political contributions.

Section 607 - political contributions solicited by and from Government employees.

Section 608 - (Hatch Act, Section 13) - $5,000 limitation on certain political contributions.

Section 609 - (Corrupt Practice Act, Section 314) - Maximum contributions and expenditures.

Section 610 - (Corrupt Practice Act, Section 313) - contributions or expenditures by national banks, corporations or labor organizations.

Section 611 - (Hatch Act, Section 20) - contributions by firms or individuals contracting with the United States.

Section 612 - publication or distribution of anonymous political literature.

In addition to the above listed criminal election laws certain other statutes having to do with the subject appear in Title 2, Sections 241 to 248 and 252. The pertinent provisions of Title 2 (originally Sections 303 to 309 of the Corrupt Practices Act) require the filing of financial statements by political committees, condidates for the House and Senate and individual contributions with the Clerk of the House of Representatives or the Secretary of the Senate. Although the filing provisions of Title 2 carry a criminal penalty, they are, nevertheless, primarily administrative in nature.

It is, therefore, the Department's policy not to institute investigations into possible violations of the laws in question in the absence of a request from the Clerk of the United States House of Representatives or the Secretary of the United States Senate, whose interest in the administration of these laws is considered paramount to that of the Department of Justice. The Federal Bureau of Investigation and the United States Attorneys should, therefore, refer all complaints involving possible failure to comply with the filing provisions of these statutes directly to the Criminal Division of the Department and should take no further action in the absence of express instructions.

Title 5, Section 118 (i - o) (originally Sections 9, 12 and 14 to 19 of the Hatch Act) also pertains to the subject of elections and political activity. The provisions of this section limit the political activity of federal employees under penalty of dismissal or suspension from the service. Being wholly administrative in character they are within the exclusive jurisdiction of the Civil Service Commission.

This Order supersedes Circulars No. 2882, 3220, 3285, 3298, 3301, 3302, 3338, 3354, 3404, 3416 and 3510.

(Signed) Herbert Brownell, Jr.

HERBERT BROWNELL, JR.
Attorney General

Section Chiefs and Unit Heads   August 27, 1965

Joseph M. F. Ryan, Jr., First Assistant

Information concerning the form, format
and substance of Civil Rights Division
Staff Meetings

Time:

The standard time of the Civil Rights Division staff
meeting is 11:00 a.m. every Thursday unless you are otherwise informed. Meetings will be held in the Office of the
First Assistant.

Attendance:

Attendance of all Section Chiefs and Unit Heads is
mandatory. In the event that it is impossible for a
Section Chief or Unit Head to attend, he will communicate
with the First Assistant at least 24 hours before the staff
meeting and if excused by the First Assistant, he shall
designate an attorney to attend and act in his stead.

Reports:

Reports shall be received from those attending the
staff meeting in the following order:

1. The Administrative Section shall be reported by
the Executive Assistant.

2. Appeals and Research by the chief of that Section.

3. Voting and Elections by the chief of that Section.

4. General Litigation by the Second Assistant until
a chief of that Section is appointed.

> As part of this general report, supplemental
> reports may be made by the unit head of each
> Section in the following order:

273

(a) Federal Custody Unit
(b) Due Process Unit
(c) Equal Protection Unit

5. Special Projects shall be reported by Staff Assistant, A. B. Caldwell.

These shall include matters concerning the monthly report, the Division Manual, and the daily summaries of civil rights information.

Format of Reports:

It shall be the responsibility of each section chief and each unit head to report on the workload of his Section or Unit including the number of cases processed since the last meeting, their type and disposition. Special mention should be made of any unusual or particularly involved matters.

Limitations on Discussion:

Topics or questions sought to be raised at the staff meeting should be formally identified and communicated to the First Assistant not later than the day immediately preceding the particular staff meeting. Each topic should include an estimation of the time required to present such discussion.

CORRESPONDENCE

AB-

The first section (A) has
been modified so that everything
is docketed first and then
the items listed (a) thru (f)
are delivered directly to the
AAG prior to routing. Other
incoming items go to Mr. Ryan
after docketing.

Except for this, the only
thing I can think of off hand
for the manual would be an item
pertaining to "extra" clerical
help - e. g., when someone is
in need of additional help,
they should let me know rather
than find some girl who is free
at the moment and give her the
job.

DJb

CIVIL RIGHTS DIVISION CIRCULAR NO. 2

Mail and Correspondence Procedures

I. INCOMING CORRESPONDENCE

A. HANDLING.

1. All correspondence, reports, memoranda, or other materials pertaining to the following categories will be delivered directly to the Office of the Assistant Attorney General as soon as received:

a. New matters

b. White House and Congressional correspondence

c. Matters emanating from the Office of the Attorney General

d. Matters emanating from the Office of the Deputy Attorney General

e. Matters emanating from the Office of the Solicitor General

f. Matters which while not necessarily new reflect developments of particular interest or importance.

The above described materials will then be forwarded to the Docket Room through the First Assistant to the Assistant Attorney General.

2. All other types of incoming correspondence not described in paragraph one shall, after docketing, be routed through the Office of the First Assistant to the appropriate Sections.

B. DISPOSITION

1. Unless further action is indicated the yellow Record Division copy of the reply should have the incoming correspondence attached to it.

2. In those instances where the responsive letter or memorandum does not constitute a final reply, the incoming correspondence should be appended to the copy which is directed to the person responsible for completing the assignment.

277

3. Original incoming correspondence should be returned to the appropriate office in those instances where the White House, the Attorney General, or his Executive Assistant request a suggested reply.

4. Changes or alterations in file numbers of incoming correspondence should be routed through or handled by the Docket Room to insure uniformity in the various records maintained in the Division and the Records Administration Office.

II. OUTGOING CORRESPONDENCE

A. PREPARATION AND HANDLING

1. Congressional mail is prepared for the signature of the Deputy Attorney General unless otherwise specified or addressed to the Assistant Attorney General in charge of the Division. Such mail, when prepared for the Deputy Attorney General's signature, should be routed through the Docket Room to the First Assistant and the Assistant Attorney General for clearance prior to forwarding to the Deputy Attorney General's mail room. If, however, such mail is carried by hand to the Office of the First Assistant or the Assistant Attorney General for clearance, the Docket Supervisor should be advised.

All Congressional mail should be acknowledged within three days.

2. Correspondence in the following categories should be prepared for the Assistant Attorney General:

a. Congressional mail in accordance with paragraph II, A1 above;

b. Letters to heads of government departments or agencies and members of the Judiciary;

c. Letters to United States Attorneys which concern matters of policy, or relate to decisions at variance with the opinion expressed by the United States Attorney;

d. Letters or memoranda pertaining to policy which in the opinion of the First Assistant should be signed by the Assistant Attorney General;

e. All memoranda to the Director of the Federal Bureau of Investigation regarding investigations and all other memoranda to the heads of other divisions or bureaus within the Department sent in the name of the Assistant Attorney General.

B. INTERNAL ROUTING

1. Without first being routed through the Docket Room---

a. Letters, telegrams, and memoranda prepared in accordance with paragraphs II, A2, and B2 for the signature of the Assistant Attorney General are to be sent direct to the Executive Assistant and the First Assistant for review and initialing and to the Assistant Attorney General for signature;

b. Letters, telegrams, and memoranda signed by the Section Chiefs will be forwarded directly to the First Secretary to facilitate review by either the First Assistant or by the Assistant Attorney General prior to mailing.

2. All outgoing mail, telegrams, and memoranda leaving the Division must be routed through the Docket Room.

C. FORMAT AND STYLE

1. Stationery selection shall conform to the following rules:

a. Assistant Attorney General stationery should be used only for correspondence prepared for the signature of the Assistant Attorney General, the First Assistant, or the Acting Assistant Attorney General.

b. Memoranda prepared for the Attorney General shall be prepared on such stationery. THE BLUE MEMORANDA SHALL NOT BE USED IN THIS CASE.

c. Department of Justice letterhead should be used for all other attorneys in the Division. Correspondence written for the signature of the Attorney General or the Deputy Attorney General should be prepared on appropriate stationery.

2. The file number, when available, the Civil Rights Division docket number (if any), together with the initials of the Assistant Attorney General, the attorney-originator and the secretary should appear on all file copies.

With the exception of memoranda to the Federal Bureau of Investigation, initials should not appear on letters or memoranda going outside the Division which have been prepared for the Assistant Attorney General's signature.

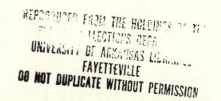

3.   The Government Printing Office Style Manual should be the final authority on any questions of form, punctuation, form of address, and style.

4.   The required minimum and optional number of copies will be as follows:

a.   Required minimum (all copies on white tissue unless otherwise specified)
1 yellow copy for the Records Division
1 green copy for the Civil Rights Division Chrono File
1 copy for the originator
1 courtesy copy on all congressional mail, correspondence to other departments and agencies, and formal memoranda to the Attorney General, etc.
1 copy for the Deputy Attorney General on all correspondence prepared for his signature
1 extra copy on all congressional correspondence
2 courtesy copies to Director of F. B. I.

b.   Optional at discretion of the attorney-originator
1 copy for Bureau of Prisons (Federal Custody Unit only)
1 copy for administrative file on matters pertaining to policy or procedure
1 copy for Appeals & Research Section when giving legal opinion, views on proposed legislation, letters concerning cases on appeal, or matters concerning legal research.

/s/ W. Wilson White
Assistant Attorney General
Civil Rights Division

Department of Justice
Washington

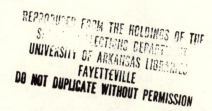

MEMORANDUM FOR THE ATTORNEY GENERAL

Re:

W. Wilson White
Assistant Attorney General
Civil Rights Division

CIVIL RIGHTS DIVISION CIRCULAR NO. 3

Replies to Incoming Correspondence

GENERAL RULES

1. Refer to the incoming letter that is the subject of the reply by date and subject matter. Should the incoming letter be undated, refer either to the time it was postmarked or the time it was received in the Department.

2. Avoid stilted legalistic terminology. Avoid excessive use of the impersonal pronoun, in favor of the personal.
Examples:

(a) In writing to laymen, avoid use of such words or phrases as "in the premises," "allegation," "venue," etc.

(b) Instead of "it is suggested," we suggest.

(c) Instead of "the receipt is acknowledged," say we acknowledge, or we wish to acknowledge.

3. In drafting a letter for the personal signature of the Assistant Attorney General, use the first person singular rather than the impersonal pronoun, or the editorial "we." The tone of the letter should be as though actually dictated by the Assistant Attorney General. This also applies to correspondence drafted for the signature of the First Assistant.

4. In responding to letters with which enclosures were sent, refer to and identify the enclosures.

CITIZEN MAIL

Generally incoming mail that does not involve an inquiry or complaint but merely expresses views or provides information, should be acknowledged. Following are guidelines for handling of such mail:

1. Abusive. Letters to the Department which are abusive in tone and contain no specific complaint or information meriting an answer, need not be acknowledged.

2. Critical. Letters that are critical of Department action or policy but not abusive in their language should be acknowledged. There is no necessity, however, to "thank" the correspondent for his views, nor to even express "appreciation" for his interest in writing. Some courteous but non-committal response such as the following, might be appropriate:

It is always of interest and may often be of value to this Department to receive the views of those who have knowledge of matters with which the Department is concerned.

282

3. <u>Commendatory</u>. Where the correspondent has commended some action or general policy of the Attorney General or any part of the Department, it is entirely appropriate to "thank" him or express "appreciation" on behalf of the particular official to whom the letter is addressed. All expressions of thanks, however, should be moderate and conservative.

4. <u>Informative</u>. Where the correspondent has furnished factual information for the Department in his letter, or has enclosed newspaper clippings, the letter should be acknowledged. Unless the letter or enclosure is abusive in tone it is appropriate to thank the correspondent for his interest in providing us with the information.

INQUIRIES

Generally, if the inquiry is one that can be answered, the answering letter should re-state the inquiry before proceeding with the answer. If the inquiry is one to which the Department cannot give an answer, then it is unnecessary to re-state the inquiry before proceeding with the answer. When the inquiry is ambiguous, re-state it in terms that express what you believe is the real question. In this connection, however, do not state that this "apparently" was what he meant, or that "we assume" he meant to ask such-and-such. No language should be used that could be interpreted as casting reflection on the literary competence of the inquirer.

The following comments apply to particular types of inquiry:

1. <u>For factual information</u>. Factual information that is readily available, such as the citation of cases or statutes, should be provided. If, however, it would take any appreciable amount of time or effort for the Department to obtain or assemble the information requested, the person requesting it should be advised that the Department does not have it "available" or "available for distribution." Where the information is obtainable from another source, such as the Government Printing Office or the Clerk of a Court, the correspondent should be referred to such source. When we are unable to provide information requested it is entirely appropriate to say that we "regret" that we are unable to do so.

2. <u>For legal advice</u>. Normally pure requests for a legal opinion or legal advice shall be referred to the Office of Legal Counsel for handling. However, when a mixed request covers factual information within our specific competency as well as legal advice, after disclosing the factual information the following is an appropriate additional response:

> The Attorney General is authorized by law to render legal opinions only to the President and heads of the executive departments. Accordingly, we cannot give you an answer to your inquiry.

It is appropriate to suggest that the correspondent "seek the advice of private counsel" or "consult with private attorney." It is not necessary, in connection with such suggestion, to stipulate "<u>competent</u> counsel", or "<u>competent</u> attorney."

- 2 -

INQUIRIES - (Continued)

3. **For views.** Requests for the comments or views of the Attorney General or the Department on a general subject such as "segregation," "miscegenation," the "Kohler strike," or the "Little Rock situation," may be ignored. If the letter contains nothing more than such a general request for "views" it need not be acknowledged.

COMPLAINTS

As a general rule all letters which complain of something that the writer believes is a violation of federal law or which ask for action by the Department, should be answered, however abusive the language of the complaint may be or however unfounded it may appear to be from our viewpoint. In answering complaints the following suggestions may be useful:

1. As a general rule, do <u>not</u> re-state the substance of a complaint, as would be done in the case of an inquiry. It is rarely that any re-statement will satisfy the correspondent as being a fair synopsis of the matter of which he actually complains. Furthermore, a re-statement is unnecessary inasmuch as the Department's response will ordinarily be a mere "no violation of federal law" or "the matter will receive our careful consideration."

2. If the Department is taking no action it is well to explain the limits of the Department's jurisdiction.
Example:

In matters such as the one which you describe /assuming it is other than an election case/ this Department can take action only when there has been a violation of a federal criminal statute.

3. In advising the complainant that there is no violation of federal law use unequivocal language. Avoid such words or phrases as "in our opinion," "apparently," and "such as will warrant action." An appropriate response might be:

We have given your letter careful consideration and must advise you that the information given does not indicate any violation of federal law.

4. In cases where the Department is unable to take any action the correspondent should not be referred to another agency, such as a bar association or legal aid society, unless it actually appears that the complaint is one for which they may provide a remedy.

5. There is no need to express "regret" that the Department is unable to take any action. The phrase, <u>unable to take any action</u>, or <u>without authority to take any action</u>, is to be preferred over such phrases as "unable to assist."

6. In those cases where the complainant's letter does indicate a possible violation of federal law the most that he should be advised is that:

This matter will receive our careful consideration and should it develop that a violation of federal law is involved, appropriate action will be taken.

- 3 -

284

CONGRESSIONAL MAIL

Answers to congressional inquiries should be brief, but direct and specific, and should not contain extended legal discussions. Supporting reasons for an answer, if not requested, ordinarily need not be given. Requests for information, however, should be treated with considerably more indulgence than would similar requests from private citizens.

If a Congressman has transmitted to us an inquiry from a constituent our answer should refer to the date of the Congressman's letter as well as the date of the constituent's letter, and the subject matter of his inquiry. Example:

This is in reference to your memorandum to the Attorney General dated February 10, 1958, with which you transmitted a letter of February 4, 1958 addressed to you by John Jones of Chicago, Illinois. In his letter Mr. Jones inquires. . .

In closing the reply, refrain from offers of our services such as: "we will be glad to furnish any future information you may desire." An appropriate closing sentence might be: "we trust that this information will be of assistance to you in answering Mr. Jones' inquiry."

MENTAL PATIENTS

Letters from patients in mental institutions, and from persons who are obviously suffering some mental disturbance, should receive the same consideration and courteous response as letters from other citizens. The response should be directed to the patient himself and not to the head of the institution. In case of repeated letters from the same correspondent it may be appropriate to write him in language similar to the following:

We have received your letter of January 10, 1958, in which you again explain the circumstances of your detention in the Mendicino State Hospital. We can add nothing to our previous reply of December 15, 1957. Further correspondence regarding this matter will serve no useful purpose.

After sending such an answer any further letters from the same correspondent may be filed without acknowledgment.

PRESIDENTIAL MAIL

In answering mail that the White House has sent to the Department for consideration and acknowledgment it is appropriate to begin the response with such language as:

Your letter of January 10, 1958 to the President has been referred to this Department.

It is not necessary to say that the President has referred the letter to us "for reply" or "for consideration and acknowledgment," or for any other reason.

- 4 -

PRISONER LETTERS

State Prisoners. Letters from prisoners in state penitentiaries or county jails should, in the absence of exceptional circumstances, be answered by addressing the reply to the Inmate with a copy to the Warden or head of the institution. The letter should be captioned with the prisoner's name and number, if known.

CIVIL RIGHTS DIVISION CIRCULAR NO. 4.

PROCEDURES FOR PREPARATION OF
COMMENTS ON LEGISLATION

Frequently the Civil Rights Division is requested to comment upon bills introduced in the Congress. Many are replicas of earlier bills upon which we have commented, or involve matters in which we have little or no interest but which are referred to the Division in case of possible interest. Accordingly, the following may be of help to individual members of the staff in preparing comments:

1. Prior reports.

Since a large number of bills, currently submitted for comment are identical with those upon which reports have been submitted by this Division or are similar in substance thereto it is necessary initially to determine whether a prior report has been made by the Division. Such procedure avoids duplication of effort and precludes the possibility of the submission of divergent comments or recommendations. If it be determined that a recommendation differing from a former one should be submitted, it should be done with full knowledge of what our prior position has been.

Several methods of determining whether the Civil Rights Division has commented upon a particular item or type of legislation are as follows:

(a) The Appeals and Research Section maintains a file on comments submitted by the Division, by (1) bill number, (2) name of sponsor, (3) date of introduction, and (4) subject matter.

(b) Pertinent information may also be obtained from the index cards maintained in Mr. Chambers' office by Miss Moore. This will include not only comments by the Division, but also comments by other divisions of the Department.

(c) If the number of the prior bill is known, the Department file may be obtained by calling

287

Mr. Deale or Miss Robinson, extension 3185.
Mrs. Baker, 3171, or Mrs. Donlan, 3191,
also are available to locate Department
files with cognate bills.

(d) Reference to earlier bills on the same subject
can be obtained from the Index to the Congressional Record or from the Commerce Clearing
House Congressional Index. The Commerce
Clearing house Index would appear to be the
more convenient because it appears before
the bound index to the Congressional Record,
and is also contained in one volume, whereas
there are two Congressional Indexes for each
session. In using the Commerce Clearing House
Index, the subject index will indicate whether
a bill with the same general or similar subject
matter has been introduced, and the author
index whether the author of the bill has introduced the same general or similar legislation.
Having obtained the bill number, more detailed
information may be found in the divisions of
the index entitled "House Bills and Senate
Bills." The status tables indicate whether
any hearings or reports are available. They
may be checked for further leads for possible
comments by the Department.

If it be determined that this Division has commented on
the same or similar legislation, it should be sufficient to
advise the Deputy Attorney General's office without more that
the Civil Rights Division has commented upon a similar bill,
referring to the bill by number, giving the date of the comment,
and stating that this Division has no additional of different
views to express. It is also desirable to refer to the letter
from the Department to the Bureau of Budget or to the Congressional Committee concerned, commenting on the bill, if such
exist. If this Division has not commented on the bill but
some other Division of the Department has, and we agree
generally with its comments it should be adequate so to state.

2. <u>New bills not of interest to the Civil Rights Division</u>

If the bill be a new one or one upon which the Department
has notcommented, it should be examined to ascertain whether
it is one in which neither the Department in general nor this
Division in particular have any interest. If it falls within
that category, the bill should be examined only for the following
purposes:

- 3 -

(a) That it is not obviously unconstitutional.

(b) That the draftsmanship of the bill is not obviously faulty.

(c) That it does not contain any clearly observable inaccuracies, such as mistakes in dates and names.

If no comment is appropriate under (a), (b), or (c), the comment should be restricted to a very brief description of the bill and the statement that the Civil Rights Division has no comment.

3. New bills of interest to the Department

If the bill is one in which either the Department in general or this Division in particular has an interest a more extensive memorandum is required. The first paragraph should describe the bill, what it intends to accomplish, and the method by which it seeks to accomplish its purpose. This will, of course, include proposed changes in existing laws. Bills of particular significance should be analyzed section by section.

A bill in this category likewise should be examined for constitutionality, draftsmanship, and accuracy, but with considerably more care. Any adverse comment on draftsmanship should be accompanied by a suggested draft change. If there is any policy question in respect of which the Department or this Division has adopted a position, it should be indicated and discussed, and a potential policy question which is not primarily the concern of the Department or of this Division might well be noted without discussion, so that the attention of persons having interest in that particular policy will be alerted. If we know or have reason to believe that some other department or agency of the Government has an interest in the subject matter of the bill, that fact and the nature of that interest might be set forth.

W. Wilson White
Assistant Attorney General
Civil Rights Division

289

SUGGESTIONS RE DRAFTING OF REPLIES
TO INCOMING CORRESPONDENCE

General Rules

1. Refer to the incoming letter that is the subject of the reply by date and subject matter. Do not omit referring to its date merely because of an undue lapse of time between it and your answer. If the incoming letter is undated there is no need to refer to it as having been "undated." Either refer to the time it was postmarked or received in the Department. Example:

> We wish to acknowledge receipt of your letter of February 10, 1958, in which you describe the circumstances of your arrest and detention by Chicago police officers. ...

2. Avoid stilted legalistic terminology. Avoid the impersonal pronoun, in favor of the personal. Examples:

(a) In writing to laymen, avoid use of such words or phrases as "in the premises," "allegation," "venue," etc.

(b) Instead of "it is suggested," _we suggest_.

(c) Instead of "the receipt is acknowledged," say _we acknowledge_, or _we wish to acknowledge_.

3. In drafting a letter for the personal signature of the Assistant Attorney General, use the first person singular rather than the impersonal pronoun, or the editorial "we." The letter should be drafted as though actually dictated by the Assistant Attorney General.

4. In responding to letters with which enclosures were sent, refer to and identify the enclosures.

Fan Mail

As a general rule fan mail i.e., incoming mail that does not involve an inquiry or complaint but merely expresses views or provides information, should be acknowledged. The following rules of thumb may be used as a guide in

290

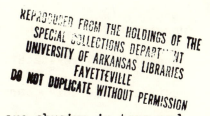

handling fan mail:

1. _Abusive_. Letters to the Department which are abusive in tone and contain no specific complaint or information meriting an answer, need not be acknowledged.

2. _Critical_. Letters that are critical of Department action or policy but not abusive in their language should be acknowledged. There is no necessity, however, to "thank" the correspondent for his views, nor to even express "appreciation" for his interest in writing. Some courteous but non-committal response such as the following, might be appropriate:

> It is always of interest and may often be of value to this Department to receive the views of those who have knowledge of matters with which the Department is concerned.

3. _Commendatory_. Where the correspondent has commended some action or general policy of the Attorney General or any part of the Department, it is entirely appropriate to "thank" him or express "appreciation" on behalf of the particular official to whom the letter is addressed.

4. _Informative_. Where the correspondent has furnished factual information for the Department in his letter, or has enclosed newspaper clippings, the letter should be acknowledged. Unless the letter or enclosure is abusive in tone it is appropriate to thank the correspondent for his interest in providing us with the information.

Inquiries.

Generally, if the inquiry is one that can be answered, the answering letter should re-state the inquiry before proceeding with the answer. If the inquiry is one to which the Department cannot give an answer, then it is

291

unnecessary to re-state the inquiry with any particularity. When the inquiry is ambiguous, re-state it in terms that express what you believe is the real question. In this connection, however, do not state that this "apparently" was what he meant, or that "we assume" he meant to ask such-and-such. No language should be used that could be interpreted as casting reflection on the literary competence of the inquirer.

The following comments apply to particular types of inquiry:

1. **For factual information**. Factual information that is readily available, such as the citation of cases or statutes, should be provided. If, however, it would take any appreciable amount of time or effort for the Department to obtain or assemble the information requested, the person requesting it should be advised that the Department does not have it "available" or "available for distribution." Where the information is obtainable from another source, such as the Government Printing Office or the Clerk of a Court, the correspondent should be referred to such source. When we are unable to provide information requested it is entirely appropriate to say that we "regret" that we are unable to do so.

2. **For legal advice**. An appropriate response to a request for legal advice would be as follows:

> The Attorney General is authorized by law to render legal opinions only to the President and heads of the executive departments. Accordingly, we cannot give you an answer to your inquiry.

It is appropriate to suggest that the correspondent "seek the advice of private counsel" or "consult with a private attorney." It is not necessary, in connection with such suggestion, to stipulate "competent counsel," or "competent attorney."

3. **For views**. Requests for the comments or views of the Attorney General or the Department on a general subject such as "segregation"

"miscegenation," the "Kohler strike," or the "Little Rock situation,"
may be ignored. If the letter contains nothing more than such a general
request for "views" it need not be acknowledged.

Complaints.

As a general rule all letters which complain of something that the
writer believes is a violation of federal law or which ask for action by the
Department, should be answered, however abusive the language of the complaint
may be or however unfounded it may appear to be from our viewpoint. In
answering complaints the following suggestions may be useful:

1. As a general rule, do not re-state the substance of a complaint,
as would be done in the case of an inquiry. It is rarely that any re-statement
will satisfy the correspondent as being a fair synopsis of the matter that he
is actually complaining of. Furthermore, a re-statement is unnecessary
inasmuch as the Department's response will ordinarily be a mere "no violation
of federal law" or "the matter will receive our careful consideration."

2. If the Department is taking no action it is well to explain the
limits of the Department's jurisdiction. Example:

> In matters such as the one which you describe /assuming it
> is other than an election case/ this Department can take action
> only when there has been a violation of a federal criminal statute.

3. In advising the complainant that there is no violation of federal
law use unequivocal language. Avoid such words or phrases as "in our
opinion," "apparently," and "such as will warrant action." An appropriate
response might be:

> We have given your letter careful consideration and must
> advise you that the information given does not indicate any
> violation of federal law.

<u>Complaints</u>, cont'd

4. In cases where the Department is unable to take any action the correspondent should not be referred to another agency, such as a bar association or legal aid society, unless it actually appears that the complaint is one for which they may provide a remedy.

5. There is no need to express "regret" that the Department is unable to take any action. The phrase, <u>unable to take any action</u>, or <u>without authority to take any action</u>, is to be preferred over such phrases as "unable to assist."

6. In those cases where the complainant's letter does indicate a possible violation of federal law the most that he should be advised is that:

> This matter will receive our careful consideration and should it develop that a violation of federal law is involved, appropriate action will be taken.

Congressional Mail

Answers to congressional inquiries should be brief, but direct and specific. No extended legal discussions should be indulged in. Supporting reasons for an answer need not ordinarily be given if not requested. Requests for information, however, should be treated with considerably more indulgence than would similar requests from private citizens.

If a Congressman has transmitted to us an inquiry from a constituent our answer should refer to the date of the Congressman's letter as well as the date of the constituent's letter, and the subject matter of his inquiry. Example:

> This is in reference to your memorandum to the Attorney General dated February 10, 1958, with which you transmitted a letter of February 4, 1958 addressed to you by John Jones of Chicago, Illinois. In his letter Mr. Jones inquires... .

In closing the reply, do not state that "we will be glad to furnish any further information you may desire," or similar offers of our services. An appropriate closing sentence might be: "We trust that this information will be of assistance to you in answering Mr. Jones' inquiry."

Presidential Mail

In answering mail that the White House has sent to the Department for consideration and acknowledgment it is appropriate to begin the response with such language as:

Your letter of January 10, 1958 to the President has been referred to this Department.

It is not necessary to say that the President has referred the letter to us "for reply" or "for consideration and acknowledgment," or for any other reason.

Prisoner Letters

1. Federal Prisoners. Letters from prisoners in federal penal institutions will be answered by the Federal Custody Unit.

2. State Prisoners. Letters from prisoners in state penitentiaries or county jails shouod, in the absence of exceptional circumstances, be answered by addressing the reply to the warden or other head of the institution. The letter should be captioned with the prisoner's name and number, if known. Inasmuch as the reply is going to someone other than the original correspondent it should not commence with such phrases as "we wish to acknowledge" or "this is in reference to." Our reply should commence with some such simple statement as:

This Department has received a letter dated January 10, 1958 from the above inmate, in which he describes the circumstances of his arrest and trial for the charge on which he was sentenced to your institution.

The answer to the prisoner's inquiry or complaint may be prefaced by the phrase: "Please advise Mr. Jones." In each instance the warden should be thanked for his assistance.

Mental Patients

Letters from patients in mental institutions, and from persons who are obviously suffering some mental disturbance, should receive the same consideration and courteous response as letters from other citizens. The response should be directed to the patient himself and not to the head of the institution. In case of repeated letters from the same correspondent it may be appropriate to write him in language similar to the following:

> We have received your letter of January 10, 1958 in which you again explain the circumstances of your detention in the Mendicino State Hospital. We can add nothing to our previous reply of December 15, 1957. Further correspondence regarding this matter will serve no useful purpose.

After sending such an answer any further letters from the same correspondent may be filed without acknowledgment.

PLEADINGS AND FORMS

C O P Y

UNITED STATES OF AMERICA

v.

TOM A. CREWS

Crews v. U.S.
160 F. 2d 746
(C.C.A. 5, 1947)

Case No. 7593 J.

C H A R G E

Gentlemen of the Jury, the United States Attorney has filed in this Court an information against Tom A. Crews, the material part of the information being as follows:

On or about September 21, 1945, in Suwanee County, Florida, and in the Southern District of Florida, Tom A. Crews, who was at the time of the happening of the event complained about, the duly appointed Town Marshal in and for Branford, Florida and the duly elected and qualified and acting Constable in and for District #5, Suwanee County, Florida, and that acting under color of law by virtue of his said offices the said Tom A Crews did wilfully, unlawfully and wrongfully, under color of law, regulations, and customs of the State of Florida and of the Town of Branford in said county, subject and cause to be subjected Sam Askins McFadden, a negro citizen and inhabitant of the State of Florida and the United States of America, to the deprivation of the rights, privileges and immunities secured and protected to the said Sam Askins McFadden by the Constitution and laws of the United States in this to-wit: "The right to be secure in his person and to be immune from illegal assault and battery: the right and privilege not to be deprived of liberty and life without due process of law; the right and privilege not to be denied equal protection of the laws; the right and privilege to be tried upon the charge on which he has been arrested by due process of law, and if found guilty, to be sentenced and punished in accordance with the laws of the State of Florida;" all of said rights, privileges and immunities being secured to the said Sam Askins McFadden by the Fourteenth Amendment to the Constitution of the United States as against any person vested with and acting under the authority of the State of Florida.

Specifically, the charge is that on or about September 21, 1945 the defendant, while acting as Town Marshal and Constable, arrested the said Sam Askins McFadden and forcibly and against his will took and caused to be taken the said McFadden to a point in Suwanee County at or near the Suwanee River in said County and did wilfully, unlawfully and wrongfully whip, beat, abuse and otherwise cruelly mistreat the said McFadden by striking him with a cow whip and striking him upon his head with a pistol and other weapons unknown and that he did then and there, through threats, forcibly cause the said Sam Askins McFadden to jump into the Suwanee River, as the result of which the said McFadden was drowned.

To this information the defendant has entered a plea of not guilty, which makes up the issue that you are to try. The Government by the information filed, charging the accused and the defendant by his plea of not guilty, denying every material allegation of the information.

Notwithstanding this information this defendant, as do all defendants in criminal cases, comes into this court clothed in the presumption of innocence, which presumption of innocence ramains and abides with him throughout the trial, unless and until the Government has, by competent evidence, convinced the minds of every individual juror of the guilt of the accused beyond a reasonable doubt. A reasonable doubt, gentlemen, means just exactly what the term implies - a doubt that would appeal to a reasonable man; a doubt for which you can give yourself a reason. It does not mean an idle, whimsical or fanciful doubt, but a real well-founded doubt.

There are certain matters the court feels it should make clear to you at the outset. The court desires that you clearly understand that the defendant, Tom A. Crews, is not here on trial for a violation of any laws of the State of Florida; for assault, for murder or for any other offense that may be charged against him under the laws of Florida. Neither is the defendant on trial for assault or for murder under any law of the United States of America. He is merely on trial here for depriving Sam Askins McFadden of certain rights, privileges and immunities secured and protected to him by the Constitution of the United States. The Fourteenth Amendment to the Constitution of the United States rpovides that "no State shall deprive any person of life, liberty or property without due process of law, nor deny to any person within its jurisdiction the equal protection

of the laws." This Constitutional provision also provides
that Congress may pass appropriate legislation carrying into
effect the provisions of the Fourteenth Amendment, which I have
just read to you. After the adoption of the Fourteenth
Amendment to the Constitution, many years ago Congress passed
a law which provides that "whoever, under color of any law,
statute, ordinance, regulation or custom, wilfully subjects or
causes to be subjected, any inhabitant of any State, territory
or district, to the deprivation of any rights, privileges or
immunities, secured or protected by the Constitution and laws
of the United States ***" shall be fined not more than
$1,000.00 or imprisoned for not more than one year, or both.

The Constitutional provision which I have just read you
assures to every citizen of these United States the right and
privilege not to be deprived of liberty without due process
of law, under color of any law, statute, ordinance, regulation
or custom of any State. We are also secure in the right not
to be subjected to punishment, pain or penalties other than
those prescribed for every person alike. This includes the
right to be tried upon a charge upon which one may be
arrested - to be brought by due process of law into a court of
the State and if found guilty to be sentenced and punished in
accordance with the laws of the State. All these rights were
secured to McFadden along with you and me and every one else
by the Constitution of the United States, and the Federal

Statute under which this information is filed fixes the penalty for anyone, who, under color of State authority, denies to anyone of us any of these rights.

The court also desires that you clearly understand that the statute upon which this prosecution is based was not intended to cover and does not cover personal and individual acts of a citizen in wrongfully depriving another citizen of the Constitutional rights guaranteed to him by the Fourteenth Amendment. The statute applies only to one who acts under guise or color of authority of State law and thus brings about the illegal deprivation of Constitutional rights. The statute was not designed to reach, and does not reach the personal individual acts of one person towards another, when the act is not done under color of State law, even though the person committing the act is the holder of a public office. However, it is the law that any misuse of power possessed by virtue of State law, made possible only because the wrongdoer is clothed with authority of State law, is action taken under color of State law. It is important that you keep clearly in mind the legal distinction which I have just pointed out to you between the personal and individual acts of a citizen holding a public office and the illegal misuse of power possessed by virtue of his office, in determining the guilt or innocence of this defendant.

This brings us to the question whether or not McFadden was taken into custody by the defendant by virtue of the

302

authority vested in him as an officer of the law. An officer of the law does not have the power to divest himself of his official authority in actions taken by him which on their face appear to be actions taken pursuant to his authority, but his official position does not deprive him of the right to act as an individual in personal altercations with others. However, his official position does not vest in him the power to engage in personal altercations with other citizens. It only vests in him the power to take persons into custody under a claim that such persons have violated some law. So, gentlemen of the jury, in determining the guilt or innocence of the defendant here, you must take into consideration the circumstances under which the defendant took McFadden into his custody and determine whether or not in so doing and in doing what he did, the action taken by him was taken "under color of State law."

If you find from the evidence in this case that the defendant took McFadden into his possession under color of law by reason of the positions he held, then the court charges you that McFadden had the right to be tried upon any charge for which he had been arrested, in a regularly constituted court of justice having jurisdiction and if found guilty subjected to the usual pain and penalties applicable to all persons alike for the offense charged, but not to be subjected to unusual punishment or to be tried by ordeal by the defendant or to be subjected to any extraordinary or unusual pain or punishment because of his race and color. Those were his Constitutional rights and privileges under the Federal Constitution.

Let me repeat the essential issue on this question. As previously stated to you, the Federal Statute under which the defendant is here on trial has no application to a citizen who acts without color of law; that is, of his own personal volition for his own personal reasons. The act applies only when and only to one who acts under the guise or pretense of authority of law and the statute was not designed to reach private personal controversies between two people. So if you find from the evidence that the defendant was not acting under color of law, but solely in his individual capacity, because of personal animosity toward McFadden, then what he did constituted only a violation of the State law, which should be remedied in the State courts of Florida and is not a violation of any Federal law. But, as I said before, if McFadden was taken into custody by the defendant, under color of law, by reason of the positions held by the defendant, then the ordeal to which the defendant subjected McFadden at and near the Suwanee River constituted a violation of the Federal statute.

Your attention is further specifically called to the language of the statute which provides that "whoever, under color of law," etc., does the act prohibited, shall be guilty of the offense defined in the statute. Now color of law means a mere semblance of legal right. So, color of law, as used in the statute, does not necessarily mean the exercise of some specific legal authority vested in an officer of the law, but also semblance,

appearance and pretense and implies, in the language of the
statute, that the act to which it applies need not necessarily
have the real characteristics of a legal act.) Therefore, we
do not have in this case any question as to whether the defendant,
in taking McFadden into custody, acted under authority of any
law of Florida, but whether or not the taking of McFadden into
custody was done under color of law of Florida, state, county,
or municipal, arising out of the official positions held by the
defendant, Crews.

Next, the court calls to your attention the fact that the
statute says, "whoever, under color of any law, statute,
ordinance, regulation or custom, wilfully subjects or causes to
be subjected any individual to the deprivation of any rights,
privileges or immunities secured or protected to him by the
Constitution of the United States and the laws of the United
States, shall be guilty," etc. Now, the word "wilfully" appearing in this statute, has a meaning and a very distinct and
definite meaning that must be carefully considered by you. The
statute provides that the thing done must be done wilfully. In
law the use of the words, "wilful" and "wilfully" implies a
conscious purpose to do wrong. Doing a thing knowingly and
wilfully implies not only a knowledge of the thing done, but a
determination to do it with bad intent or with an evil purpose
or motive. It is not sufficient that the defendant here had
generally a bad purpose in doing the things he did. In order to

convict it is necessary for the Jury to find that the defendant
had in mind the specific purpose of depriving McFadden of a
Constitutional right - that is, to deprive him of the right to
be tried by a court, to be tried in an orderly way and to receive, if found guilty, the usual pains and punishment for an
offense he may have committed.

(The law denies to anyone acting under color of law)...
statute, ordinance, regulation or custom (the right to try a person
by ordeal; that is, for he, himself, to inflict such punishment
upon the person as he thinks the person should receive. Now in
determining whether this requisite of wilful intent was present in
this case you gentlemen of the jury are entitled to consider all
the attendant circumstances; the malice, if any, of the defendant
toward the deceased; the weapons used in the assault, if you find
any were used; and the character and duration of the provocation of
the assault and the time and manner in which it was carried out.) All
these facts and circumstances may be taken into consideration from
the evidence that has been submitted for the purpose of determining
whether the acts of the defendant were wilful and for the deliberate
and wilful purpose of depriving McFadden of his Constitutional
right to be tried by a jury just like everyone else.

The use of the word, "wilfully," in the statute, makes
"intent" a material element of the offenses charged in this case.
Now, "intent" is something that exists in a man's mind. It is
impossible for you to enter into the mind of a defendant to
determine the intent with which he acted. Therefore, his intent

has to be judged at least by his intelligence, as shown by the evidence; by his experience in life, as shown by the evidence, and generally by judging him as reasonably prudent persons, experienced in the affairs of everyday life, judge each other, and it is the law that a person intends the usual consequences of his acts.

The proof of a general intent to do McFadden wrong is not sufficient, but a specific intent to deprive him of a Constitutional right is a burden the law casts upon the Government in this case. In considering whether the defendant had such specific intent you may take into consideration the incident in May, 1945, when the defendant arrested McFadden and took him before the County Judge and the results of that arrest and prosecution and you may also take into consideration what the defendant did on the night when McFadden was again taken into custody by him.

Neither color of law nor specific intent may be presumed by you gentlemen of the jury but both color of law and specific intent must be proven by the government beyond a reasonable doubt.

In concluding this part of the court's charge, let me summarize the questions you have to determine:

1. Did the defendant take McFadden into custody under color of law?

2. Did the defendant specifically intend to deprive McFadden of a Constitutional right guaranteed to him by our Federal Constitution?

3. Has the Government established these two essentials to your satisfaction beyond a reasonable doubt?

If the Government has done so, it is your duty to find the defendant guilty in this case.

If you have a reasonable doubt upon either of the two essentials named above it is your duty to acquit the defendant.

The defendant did not take the stand in this case and it, therefore, becomes the duty of this court to give you an instruction as to the legal effect of his failure to testify. The court instructs the jury that while the statutes of this State permit a defendant to testify he is under no obligation to do so and his failure to do so creates no presumption against him and you are not authorized to draw any distinction from or make any reference to the failure of the defendant to testify, for with his silence you have nothing to do. You are to decide the case with reference alone to the testimony actually introduced without regard to what might have not or might have been shown if the defendant had testified.

Now, gentlemen of the jury, you have heard and patiently listened to the evidence in this case. You are the sole judges of the evidence, its weight and sufficiency and the credibility of the witnesses. It is your duty to seek to reconcile the testimony of the witnesses so as to make each witness speak the truth; but if, after a full and fair consideration of all the testimony, you find an irreconcilable conflict in the testimony then you must determine what testimony is true and reject such

testimony you disbelieve and from the testimony you do believe,
find your verdict.

In passing upon the credibility of a witness it is proper
to take into consideration the manner of the witness on the
witness stand, his candor or want of candor, his intelligence or
otherwise, the reasonableness or unreasonableness of his statements, his interest, if any he has, and all circumstances
surrounding such witness at the time of giving his testimony
and at the time of the happening of the events testified about.
You are the sole and exclusive judges of the evidence and the
credibility of the witnesses and as to what has been proven and
what has not been proven in this case.

In considering this testimony you are to lay aside any
preconceived ideas that you may have as to the wisdom or unwidsom
of the particular statute under which this defendant is being
tried and you are to lay aside and not be influenced by any
prejudice because of race, color or any supposed conflict in
state or federal powers and duties. You and I are under the
sworn obligation to enforce the law as it is given to us by
Congress and it is not within our province to pass judgment upon
the question of whether any particular statute is good or bad.
With the consequences of your verdict you have absolutely nothing
to do. As to what may be the result of your verdict is entirely
beyond your province. All that you are empaneled and sworn to do
is to find a verdict that speaks the truth.

If, after considering all the evidence in this case, you believe from the testimony submitted to the exclusion of and beyond a reasonable doubt that the defendant, Tom A. Crews, is guilty as charged in the information, then you should find the defendant guilty. On the other hand, if you have a reasonable doubt as to the guilt of the defendant, Tom A. Crews, you should find him not guilty.

LEGISLATIVE HISTORIES OF

CIVIL RIGHTS STATUTES

<u>The Civil Rights Act of 1957</u>

This memorandum describes the background of the adoption of the Civil

Rights Act of 1957 and the legislative history of selected aspects of the

act. The aspects selected for treatment relate largely to operational

problems which may be faced by the Civil Rights Commission and the Civil

Rights Division of the Department of Justice.

I. The Background of the Legislation.

Over the years there have been numerous unsuccessful attempts to enact

federal legislation dealing with the franchise, lynching, fair employment

practices and similar subjects regarded as falling under the category of

civil rights. An attempt at an omnibus approach to the problems was made

with the issuance by President Truman on December 5, 1946, of Executive

Order No. 9808 (3 CFR, 1943-1948 Comp., p. 590), "Establishing the

President's Committee on Civil Rights." The Committee, consisting of 15

members under the chairmanship of Mr. C. E. Wilson, was:

> "authorized on behalf of the President to inquire into and to
> determine whether and in what respect current law-enforcement
> measures and the authority and means possessed by Federal, State,
> and local governments may be strengthened and improved to safe-
> guard the civil rights of the people."

The order directed that the Committee

> "shall make a report of its studies to the President in writing, and
> shall in particular make recommendations with respect to the adop-
> tion or establishment, by legislation or otherwise, of more adequate
> and effective means and procedures for the protection of the civil
> rights of the people of the United States."

The report, "To Secure These Rights," was issued in 1947. The Com-

mittee had no subpoena power, and the report indicates (p. XI) that the

information on which it was based was obtained from a series of public

hearings, consultation with witnesses in private meetings, and staff

312

studies. The report contained a long series of recommendations (pp. 151-173). These included the establishment of a permanent Commission on Civil Rights in the Executive Branch of the Government, which was to make a "continuous appraisal of the status of civil rights, and the efficiency of the machinery with which we hope to improve that status" and to "make regular reports which would include recommendations for action in the ensuing periods." It would collect data so as to be in a position to fill in the "huge gaps in the available information about the field" (p. 154). The report did not indicate whether or not the Commission was intended to have subpoena power.

Another recommendation of the Committee involved the elevation of the Civil Rights Section of the Department of Justice to the status of a full division within the Department under the supervision of an assistant attorney general. The report (pp. 120-122) indicated that, because of their sensitivity to local opinion and attitudes, United States Attorneys sometimes failed to prosecute civil rights cases vigorously. It was therefore recommended (pp. 151-52) that the new division operate through regional offices which, apparently, would not be subordinate to the United States Attorneys. It was noted, however, that the Department of Justice had suggested that the heads of the regional offices should have the status of Assistant United States Attorneys.

The Commission further recommended the creation in the Congress of a Joint Standing Committee on Civil Rights (pp. 151, 154). With respect to legislation, it suggested, among other things, the enactment of federal fair-employment practice, anti-lynching and anti-poll tax statutes (pp. 157, 160, 167). It also urged that Congress enact statutes protecting the rights of qualified persons to participate in federal primaries and elections against interference by both public officers and private individuals (p. 160).

The Committee urged that section 51 (now section 241) of Title 18, of the United States Code, be amended so as to impose the same liability upon an individual acting alone as the statute now imposes upon conspirators. It also suggested that section 52 (now section 242) of Title 18, be amended to enumerate expressly the rights intended to be protected (pp. 156-157), and thus meet problems raised by the opinion of the Supreme Court in Screws v. United States, 325 U.S. 91, 103.

In his message to Congress of February 2, 1948 (S. Doc. No. 516, 80th Cong., 2d Sess.), President Truman echoed many of the recommendations earlier made by the Committee. He urged the establishment of a permanent Commission on Civil Rights which would continually review civil rights policies and practices, study specific problems and make recommendations to the President at frequent intervals. He also recommended the establishment by the Congress of a Joint Congressional Committee on Civil Rights and, within the Department of Justice, of a Division of Civil Rights under the supervision of an assistant attorney general. He adopted the recommendations of the Committee with respect to the amendment of 18 U.S.C. §51, and proposed federal legislation covering lynching, fair-employment practices and protection against interference with the right to vote in all federal elections, including primaries. The President suggested that such legislation also apply to state elections insofar as the interference was based on race, color or any other unreasonable classification. However, the President's recommendations were apparently not embodied in any specific legislation, and all that followed was that the House passed anti-poll tax

legislation, which died in the Senate.

The immediate history of the 1957 act probably finds its source in

President Eisenhower's State of the Union message of January 1956, in which

he stated:

> "It is disturbing that in some localities allegations persist that
> Negro citizens are being deprived of their right to vote and are
> likewise being subjected to unwarranted economic pressures. I
> recommend that the substance of these charges be thoroughly examined
> by a bipartisan Commission created by the Congress. It is hoped that
> such a Commission will be established promptly so that it may arrive
> at findings which can receive early consideration. * * *
>
> "We must strive to have every person judged and measured by what
> he is, rather than by his color, race, or religion. There will soon
> be recommended to the Congress a program further to advance the
> efforts of the Government, within the area of Federal responsibility,
> to accomplish these objectives."[1]

Numerous bills dealing with civil rights were introduced during the

first and second session of the 84th Congress, and hearings were held upon

them by a Subcommittee of the House Committee on the Judiciary,[2] by the

full Committee[3] and by the Committee on Rules.[4] On April 9, 1956,

Attorney General Herbert Brownell addressed to the Speaker of the House of

Representatives an "executive communication" relating to civil rights legis-

lation, referring to the President's State of the Union message, and making

a number of specific suggestions.[5] These included the establishment of a

bipartisan commission of six members to be appointed by the President with

the advice and consent of the Senate. The Commission would have a life of

---

[1] H. Rept. No. 2187, 84th Congress., 2d Sess., p. 6
[2] Hearings on "Civil Rights" before Subcommittee No. 2 of the House
Committee on the Judiciary, 84th Cong., 1st Sess.
[3] Hearings on "Civil Rights" before the House Committee on the Judiciary,
84th Cong., 2d Sess.
[4] Hearings on H.R. 627 before the House Committee on Rules, 84th Cong.,
2d Sess.
[5] H. Rept. No. 2187, supra, pp. 11-14.

two years, unless extended by Congress, and would have authority to subpoena witnesses and to take testimony under oath. The communication emphasized that the Commission would be concerned with the extent and means by which the right to vote was being denied and with charges that unwarranted economic or other pressures were being applied to deny fundamental rights safeguarded by the Constitution and the laws of the United States.

The second proposal contained in the communication was for the authorization of an additional assistant attorney general to direct the Government's legal activities in the field of civil rights. The Attorney General indicated that the existing Civil Rights Section of the Department of Justice was but one of a number of sections within the Criminal Division, that more emphasis should be placed upon civil law remedies, and that the civil rights activities of the Department of Justice should not be confined to the Criminal Division.

The third proposal related to the protection of voting rights by civil remedies. The Attorney General pointed out that the existing statute providing such remedies (42 U.S.C. §1971) was limited to the deprivation of such rights by officials acting under the authority of law. He recommended that there be added a section covering intimidation or coercion of individuals in the exercise of the right to vote in general, special and primary elections for federal office. The provision would apply irrespective of whether the intimidation or coercion was by individuals purporting to act under the authority of law. The recommendation also involved authorization of the Attorney General to bring injunction or other civil proceedings on behalf of the United States or the aggrieved person in any case covered by

the statute and the elimination of the requirement that all state administrative and judicial remedies be exhausted before access to the federal
courts would be available.

The fourth recommendation contained in the executive communication
dealt with section 1980 of the Revised Statutes (42 U.S.C. § 1985), which
provides civil remedies for the violation of civil rights, including conspiracies for the purpose of depriving "any person or class of persons of
the equal protection of the laws, or of equal privileges and immunities
under the laws." With respect to this statute it was suggested that the
Attorney General be authorized to initiate civil actions to protect the
rights which it secured.

As a result of the hearings, the House Judiciary Committee reported
favorably H.R. 627[6]/ which had originally been introduced by its chairman,
Mr. Celler, but which was completely re-written by the Committee. On
July 23, 1956, the bill passed the House by a vote of 279 to 126.[7]/ However,
the Senate did not consider it before the termination of the 84th Congress,
and the bill failed to be enacted.

As passed by the House, H.R. 627 bore considerable resemblance to the
Civil Rights Act of 1957 which was ultimately passed by the 85th Congress.
Part I of the bill provided for the establishment of a commission on civil
rights of six members. Like section 104(a) of the bill which was ultimately
enacted, section 104(a) of H.R. 627 described the duties of the Commission
and was divided into three subparagraphs. Subparagraph (1) provided that the
Commission shall:

6/ See H. Rept. No. 2187, supra.
7/ 102 Cong. Rec. 13999. All other references to the Congressional Record
contained in this memorandum are to the daily edition of volume 103 (1957),
relating to the proceedings of the first session of the 85th Congress.

"(1) investigate allegations in writing that certain citizens of the United States are being deprived of their right to vote or that certain persons in the United States are voting illegally or are being subjected to unwarranted economic pressures by reason of their sex, color, race, religion, or national origin; * * *"

It may be noted that this provision would not have required the allegations referred to to be under oath or affirmation or to set forth the facts upon which they were based. The provision contained references to allegations that citizens "are being subjected to unwarranted economic pressures" and that certain persons "are voting illegally." It referred to sex as a basis of deprivation of rights. In these respects subparagraph (1) differed sharply from the bill as ultimately enacted.

Subparagraph (2) of section 104(a) of H.R. 627 directed the Commission to:

"(2) study and collect information concerning economic, social, and legal developments constituting a denial of equal protection of the laws under the Constitution; * * *"

The reference in this provision to economic and social developments was not contained in subparagraph (2) of the law which was enacted. Subparagraph (3) of H.R. 627 was identical with subparagraph (3) of the 1957 act.

Section 102 of H.R. 627 contained provisions relating to the rights of persons adversely affected by testimony and to the protection against disclosure of testimony given in executive session. The other provisions of the bill embodied the suggestions contained in the Attorney General's executive communication. Part II provided for an additional assistant attorney general, and Parts III and IV would have amended 42 U.S.C. § 1985 and 42 U.S.C. § 1971 to effectuate those recommendations.

The failure of the Senate to act on H.R. 627 during the 84th Congress caused further efforts to be made to enact civil rights legislation in the

318

85th Congress. In his State of the Union message of January 10, 1957,

President Eisenhower said:

> "Last year the administration recommended to the Congress a four-
> point program to reinforce civil rights. That program included:
>   In the first part, creation of a bipartisan commission to investi-
> gate asserted violations of civil rights and to make recommendations;
>   Its second provision, creation of a Civil Rights Division in the
> Department of Justice in charge of an assistant attorney general;
>   Its third, enactment by the Congress of new laws to aid in the
> enforcement of voting rights; and
>   Its fourth, amendment of the laws so as to permit the Federal
> Government to seek from the civil courts preventative relief in
> civil rights cases.
> I urge the Congress to enact the legislation."[8]

In the first session of the Congress attention was concentrated in the

House upon H.R. 1151 introduced by Representative Keating and H.R. 2145 in-

troduced by Representative Celler.[9] These were substantially similar to

each other and also resembled the final version of H.R. 627 of the 84th

Congress. In the hearings on the bills, the Attorney General reiterated

the recommendations in the President's State of the Union message and stated

that H.R. 627 had "embodied the administration civil-rights proposals."[10]

The Committee made a number of amendments of H.R. 2145 and approved it as so

amended, but ordered the Chairman to introduce "a clean bill," H.R. 6127.[11]

The Committee noted that H.R. 6127 was, in general, similar to H.R. 627,

but that a number of major variations existed.[12] Thus with respect to the

duties of the Commission subparagraph (1) of section 104(a) was amended to

direct the Commission to investigate "allegations in writing under oath or

---

8/ New York Times, January 11, 1957, p. 10.
9/ H. Rept. No. 291, 85th Cong., 1st Sess., pp. 1-2.
10/ Hearings on "Civil Rights" before Subcommittee No. 5 of the House
Committee on the Judiciary, Serial No. 1, 85th Cong., 1st Sess., p. 589.
11/ H. Rept. No. 291, supra, pp. 2-3
12/ ibid., pp. 3-4.

affirmation" and to require that the writing "set forth the facts." The duty of the Commission to investigate allegations that persons are voting illegally and that citizens "are being subjected to unwarranted economic pressures" was eliminated, as was the reference to sex as a basis of discrimination.

Subparagraph (2) of section 104(a) of H.R. 6127, as reported by the Committee and as ultimately enacted, eliminated the reference in the parallel provision of H.R. 627 to "economic" and "social" developments. It merely conferred the duty upon the Commission to:

> "study and collect information concerning legal developments constituting a denial of equal protection of the laws under the Constitution; * * *."

H.R. 627 contained no territorial limitations upon the authority of the Commission to subpoena witnesses. As introduced, section 102(k) of H.R. 6127 would have prohibited the Commission from issuing any subpoena requiring the presence of the party subpoenaed at a hearing outside the judicial circuit of the United States in which the witnesses is found, resides or transacts business. As enacted, the provision was further restricted so that it would not operate "outside of the State." As introduced and as enacted, section 102(g) of H.R. 6127 would have imposed criminal penalties for the release or use in public without the consent of the Commission of evidence or testimony taken in executive session. Although section 102(g) of H.R. 627 contained a similar prohibition against disclosure, no criminal sanctions were contained in the bill.

Sections 121 and 131 of H.R. 627 would have authorized the Attorney General to institute civil actions for damages or injunctive relief under 42 U.S.C. § 1985 and 42 U.S.C. § 1971 "for the United States, or in the name

of the United States but for the benefit of the real party and interest."
The parallel sections of H.R. 6127 as introduced provided that those actions could be instituted only "for the United States, or in the name of the United States" and would be limited to injunctive or similar relief. They contained no authority for the United States to bring an action for damages on behalf of an aggrieved party. Section 131 of the bill as ultimately passed so provides with respect to 42 U.S.C. § 1971, relating to voting rights. However, as indicated below, the provision relating to 42 U.S.C. § 1985 was ultimately completely deleted by the Senate.

On June 18, 1957, H.R. 6127 passed the House by a vote of 286 to 126 (Cong., Rec. 8538). In the meantime, S. 83, a bill similar to, but not identical with, H.R. 627 had been introduced in the Senate. Extensive hearings on that and related bills were held before the Subcommittee on Constitutional Rights of the Senate Judiciary Committee.[13/] However, the Committee did not report the bill, and on July 16, 1957, a motion was made on the floor of the Senate to take up H.R. 6127. This motion was carried by a vote of 71 to 18. At the same time a motion to refer the House bill to the Senate Committee on the Judiciary in order to obtain a considered Committee report was defeated (Cong. Rec. 10687-10695). As a result, no Senate Committee report on the bill ever issued. After extensive debate and the adoption of amendments, the bill passed the Senate by a vote of 72 to 18 on August 7, 1957 (Cong. Rec. 12644).

The Senate modified the bill in five principal respects. First it amended section 105(a) to provide that the Commission's staff director be

---

13/ Hearings on "Civil Rights--1957" before the Subcommittee on Constitutional Rights of the Senate Judiciary Committee, 84th Cong., 1st Sess.

appointed by the President with the advice and consent of the Senate, that the President consult with the Commission before submitting the appointment, and that the compensation of the staff director be fixed at a rate, not in excess of $22,500 a year, to be determined by the President. Second, it amended section 105(b) to delete the authorization conferred upon the Commission to accept the services of up to fifteen voluntary and uncompensated personnel at any one time. The provision was rewritten to prohibit the use of any such personnel.

The third important amendment adopted by the Senate deleted the provisions of Part III of the bill which would have authorized the Attorney General to institute actions for injunctive relief for violations of 42 U.S.C. 1985. At the same time, the Senate inserted a provision repealing section 1989 of the Revised Statutes (42 U.S.C. § 1993). That statute had authorized the use of the armed forces to aid in the execution of judicial process issued under, or to prevent the violation and enforce the execution of, the provisions of 42 U.S.C. § 1985 and of certain other civil rights statutes.

The fifth important change was the addition of amendments to the Criminal Code relating to criminal contempts. The amendments would have defined such contempts and have conferred the right to a jury trial in all prosecutions for criminal contempt. These provisions would not have been limited to contempts under the Civil Rights Act of 1957, but would have applied generally. Finally, the Senate added a section to the bill to amend 28 U.S.C. § 1861, dealing with the qualifications of federal jurors. The amendment eliminated the then existing disqualification of persons incompetent for jury service under state law.

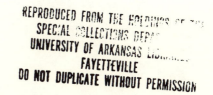

No formal conference was held between the Senate and the House with respect to the Senate amendments, and, accordingly, no conference report was issued. However, on August 27, 1957, the House adopted House Resolution 410 agreeing to all of the Senate amendments other than Amendment No. 7, relating to the use of voluntary personnel, and Amendment No. 15, relating to contempt procedure (Cong. Rec. 14687-14714).

In effect, House Resolution 410 concurred in the Senate's amendment of section 105(b) of the bill to prohibit the use of voluntary employees. It merely provided for the addition to that provision of the language ultimately adopted which makes applicable only to individuals whose services are compensated by the United States the criminal penalties imposed by section 102(g) for unauthorized disclosure of evidence received in executive sessions of the Commission. Resolution 410 amended Senate Amendment 15, by deleting the broad amendments to the Criminal Code which the Senate had adopted and replacing them with section 151 of the bill as enacted, which limits the new contempt procedure to cases arising under the Civil Rights Act.

On August 29, 1957, the Senate agreed to the House amendments, thus completing Congressional action on the bill (Cong. Rec. 15044). It was approved by the President on September 9, 1957.

II. Commission on Civil Rights.

The legislative history of Part I of the Civil Rights Act of 1957, (which creates the new Commission on Civil Rights) is somewhat fragmentary and does not provide substantial help in interpreting the statute. The House Judiciary Committee Report on H.R. 6127 (H. Rept. No. 291, 85th Cong., 1st Sess., p. 5) stated that the Commission was created for the purpose of "investigation and study" of the denial of the right to vote and to "analyze the legal developments in Federal policies and laws involving the constitutional right of equal protection under the laws". The Commission, said the Report (ibid., p. 8), would be "a factfinding and investigatory body" the primary purpose of which would be "to collect and accumulate data so that a more intelligent study of the problem may be made."

The provisions pertaining to the Commission were analyzed in the Report in essentially the language of the bill itself (ibid., pp. 6-8), and the language of the bill as finally enacted is the same in most respects as that reported out by the House Committee on the Judiciary. The principal changes were the insertion of a geographical limitation upon the subpoena power to the State, rather than to the judicial circuit, in which the witness resides, transacts business, or is found (Section 102(k)); the addition of the words "and have that vote counted" in section 104(a)(1); the requirement that the fulltime staff director be a Presidential appointee (section 105(a)); a denial of any authority to utilize the services of voluntary and uncompensated personnel (section 105(b)); and a change in the wording of section 105(b) to make the provision in section 102(g) imposing a penalty for the unauthorized use or release of testimony taken in executive session apply only to persons whose services are compensated by the United States.

The pertinent material relating to the Commission in the legislative history is set forth below under the general headings of (A) Procedure, (B) Duties and (C) Operations.

(A). Procedure. Both Congressman Keating and Congressman Celler explained that the provisions in section 102 containing rules of procedure for the Commission were the same as the rules governing hearings before Congressional committees (Cong. Rec. 7517, 7583, 7588). The House Judiciary Committee minority agreed that the rules of procedure are "substantially those which govern the committees of the House when engaged in an investigative function," but believed them inadequate for the Commission because once the Commission was set up, the Congress would lose control over it.14/ Their complaint about the breadth of the subpoena power was partially satisfied by the subsequent limitation by state instead of by judicial circuit.

One procedural rule not found in the rules governing Congressional hearings was that against disclosure of testimony taken in executive session (section 102(g)); it was inserted to protect persons concerning whom testimony might be given.15/ However, in addition to the belief of Senator Talmadge (Cong. Rec. 10373) that the "secrecy" provision "surrounds testimony given in executive session with an iron curtain of secrecy," several Senators commented that the provision in section 102(g) for the fining or imprisonment of "Whoever releases or uses in public without the consent of the Commission evidence or testimony taken in executive session * * *" was too broad.

14/ H. Rept. No. 291, supra, pp. 52-53. Senator Stennis, however, stated that the Commission could write its own rules, not limited by any requirement that it adhere to judicial decisions relating to Congressional committees (Cong. Rec. 12579).
15/ Cong. Rec. 7588, 7831; Hearings on H.R. 6127 before the House Committee on Rules, "Civil Rights", p. 10.

While Senator Javits submitted a memorandum designed to show that the provision was intended to apply only to Commission personnel, there was widespread fear, expressed by Senators Morse, Ervin and Johnson of Texas and Congressman Dies, that it would be a threat to the press (Cong. Rec. 12623-12624, 12936-12937, 13661, 13387-13388, App. 6745). Senator Javits also agreed that the provision should be corrected (Cong. Rec. 13661). Section 102(g) itself could no longer be amended since there had been no disagreement on that section between the Senate and House versions. Accordingly, Senator Case of South Dakota suggested that the desired result could be accomplished by amending section 105(b) to define the word "Whoever" in section 102(g) as applying only to persons whose services are compensated by the Government. He stated that his proposal would end "doubt of any kind now that the press of the country and the reporters generally are exempted from any applicability of the penalty provided for the unauthorized disclosure of evidence taken before the Commission in executive session." (Cong. Rec. 13791-13792, 15039-15041). This proposal ultimately was adopted by the Senate and accepted by the House.

Nothing useful was found on the pertinency provisions of sections 102(a) and 102(h).

B. _Duties_. The Commission's duties were generally described as the development of reliable information and investigation of the need for further legislation (Cong. Rec. 7588, 11271). Senator Javits (Cong. Rec. 11942) stated also that the Commission would have power to investigate and report on what was going on in the area of civil rights, including all of the civil rights enumerated in the Congressional Record at page 11355. The bill was criticized in the minority House report because of the mandatory language in section 104(a)(1)[16/] (H. Rept. No. 291, supra, p. 43), and on

the same ground by Senator Stennis who stated that the Commission would be

obliged to investigate every complaint submitted to it (Cong. Rec. 12579).

In addition, Senator Eastland contended that the Commission's authority to

hold hearings "for the purpose of carrying out the provisions of this Act"

(see section 105(f)), was broader than its listed duties (Cong. Rec. 12603).

With respect to section 104(a), Senator Thurmond contended that as the

statute was phrased the person making a complaint need not have a direct

interest in the matter (Cong. Rec. 14997). The language "and have that vote

counted" was inserted in section 104(a)(1) in the House after the bill came

out of committee. Mr. Hoffman, favoring the amendment, said it was crucial

since the right to have the vote counted was included in the right to vote

under the Supreme Court's decision in United States v. Classic, 313 U.S. 299

(Cong. Rec. App. 4716). Section 104(a)(1) was said by Mr. McCulloch to

have been limited to investigation of deprivations of the right to vote be-

cause of "color, race, religion, or national origin," in order to insure the

Act's constitutionality (Cong. Rec. App. 4713-4714). While he had opposed

inclusion of the word "religion" in committee (Cong. Rec. App. 4713-4714),

as had the minority report (H. Rept. 291, supra, pp 43-44), others defended

its inclusion as necessary and in accord with the other specified categories

(Cong. Rec. 8084). Congressman Keating also opposed striking out the spe-

cific limitations on the ground that this would open section 104(a) to in-

vestigation of ordinary irregularities concerning such matters as age

---

16/ "The Commission shall (1) investigate allegations . . . that certain
citizens of the United States are being deprived of their right to vote
. . .". (Emphasis supplied).

requirements, literacy tests, the poll tax, etc., matters of State law which were properly for State consideration (Cong. Rec. 8081).

The Commission's duty to study and collect information concerning legal developments constituting a denial of equal protection of the laws (section 104(a)(2)), was described by Congressman Celler in a colloquy with Congressman Davis as including the power to investigate deprivations of the right to vote on broader grounds than those mentioned in section 104(a)(1) (Cong. Rec. 8081). It was Congressman Celler's view that the "legal developments" provision must be read together with the provisions on deprivation of voting rights in the preceding paragraph (Cong. Rec. 8091). The same view that the duties under section 104(a)(2) are broader than race, color, religion, or national origin, was expressed by Congressman Willis at the House Rules Committee hearings, p. 54.

Mr. Vanik, supporting a move to bring H.R. 6127 to the floor, said the Commission would be able to "investigate, study, and collect information concerning economic, social and legal developments which constitute a denial of equal protection of the laws * * *", (Cong. Rec. 5497). Senator Eastland's view was that the Commission's duties on this score would be as broad as the desires of the Commission (Cong. Rec. 10217, 12604).

Other critics of the provision denounced it as vague and intended "to do a hatchet job on the South," and as making the Commission the investigatory arm of the Civil Rights Division (Cong. Rec. 10125, 10451-10452). Senators Morse and Kefauver stressed that the purpose of the Commision was to obtain facts upon which legislation might be based, and Senator Kefauver did not favor creating the Commission in the Executive Branch (Cong. Rec. 10823, 10826-10827).

There was no material of great value concerning the Commission's duty to appraise the laws and policies of the Federal Government with respect to equal protection of the laws (Section 104(a)(3)). Senator Johnston of South Carolina believed it to be vague (Cong. Rec. 10125), and the minority of the House Judiciary Committee thought that such laws and policies should also be analyzed from the standpoint of the 10th Amendment (H. Report, No. 291, supra, pp. 53-54).

C. Operations. As reported by the House Committee, H.R. 6127 provided for utilization by the Commission of not more than 15 voluntary and uncompensated persons (ibid., pp. 20-21). The minority report objected to the use of any such personnel (ibid., p. 43), as did Senator Russell, who considered it likely to undermine the integrity of the Commission (Cong Rec. 10422-10423). As finally adopted, the Act specifically prohibits the utilization of voluntary or uncompensated personnel (section 105(b)); Senator Knowland, who introduced Senate Amendment No. 7, making this change, stated its purpose to be to make sure that persons with a particular interest would not be employed "and that any persons employed on a voluntary /sic/ basis will carry on their work on an impartial basis." (Cong. Rec. 12212).

With respect to the requirement (section 105(e)) that "All Federal agencies shall cooperate fully with the Commission to the end that it may effectively carry out its functions and duties," there was some disagreement about whether this would include the Federal Bureau of Investigation. Senator Johnston believed it would (Cong. Rec. 10124), while Attorney General Brownell, testifying at the hearings before the subcommittee on Constitutional Rights of the Senate Judiciary Committee on S. 83, stated that the F.B.I. could only investigate matters involving criminal statutes (p. 13). The House Committee stated "The subject matter which the Commission is directed to investigate and study is beyond the authority of the Federal Bureau of Investigation." (H. Rept. No. 291, supra, p. 8).

III. OTHER PROVISIONS

This section of this memorandum reviews those aspects of the legislative history of the Civil Rights Act of 1957 which concern (A) the establishment and functions of the Civil Rights Division of the Department of Justice, (B) the additional protections relating to voting rights which were enacted, (C) the elimination of Part III of the Act, (D) the repeal of R. S. § 1989, relating to the use of military force, and (E) the amendment of 28 U.S.C. § 1861 concerning the qualifications of federal jurors.

A. Civil Rights Division. While Part II of the Act provides merely for the appointment of an additional assistant attorney general in the Department of Justice, with no specification as to his functions and duties, the Attorney General repeatedly stated, and even pledged, and the Congressional committees involved as well as other members of both Houses of Congress fully understood, that this official would head a Civil Rights Division with functions, duties, and powers in the general field of the enforcement of civil rights and civil liberties. Hearings before Senate Subcommittee on Constitutional Rights on S. 83, pp. 11-12. The reasons given for not spelling out the jurisdiction of the head of the Civil Rights Division were historical and functional. Instead of specifying the duties of the new assistant attorney general, Congress followed its normal practice of providing by statute merely for the appointment of the official involved without rigid description of duties, so as to leave full operational responsibility of all activities in the Department of Justice in the hands of the Attorney General. Congress' power over money appropriations, it was emphasized in the hearings, insures faithful adherence to any understandings between the executive and the legislative branches with respect to the scope of the functions of each division chief; while on the other hand lack of specificity in the enabling legislation permits administrative flexibility and fixes responsibility in the head of the Department. _Ibid_, p. 11.

Although, because of these considerations, the language of the Act is singularly uninformative as to the import of Part II, there clearly was this basic understanding that the intent of this Part was to create a Civil Rights Division, and there further was agreement -- at least among the proponents of the legislation -- as to the purposes and functions of such a Division.

Four prime factors were cited repeatedly in justification of the establishment of a separate Division within the Department of Justice to deal with the problem of civil rights: (1) complexity and delicacy of the problem, (2) necessity of giving additional prestige to the unit dealing with civil rights, (3) anticipated increase in the workload, (4) incongruity of retaining as a part of the Criminal Division an activity with so many civil aspects.

According to the House Judiciary Committee, the most important factor leading to the creation of a Civil Rights Division was that the problems involved in the area of civil rights had grown so complex and delicate that there was required "a centralized responsibility in the person of an eminently qualified attorney with the prestige of a Presidential appointment behind him." House Rept. No. 291, _supra_ p. 9. Attorney General Brownell indicated that in his opinion it was illogical to retain jurisdiction of the enforcement of civil rights laws in the Criminal Division since enforcement of these laws involved a great many purely civil aspects. Hearings before House Judiciary Subcommittee, p. 569.

In colloquy with Rep. Hillings he agreed that among the other reasons for

having a separate Division handle this responsibility were an anticipated

increase in the workload and the necessity for additional prestige which

an assistant attorney general at the head of a full Division would provide.

Ibid, p. 587. And Congressman Keating emphasized (Cong. Rec. 7588) that in

his opinion:

> "The problems involved in civil rights legislation
> and litigation * * * require the attention of
> personnel trained especially in this field. More-
> over, if the proposed bill becomes law, there will
> be involved not so much criminal prosecutions as
> civil remedies. For these reasons a separate
> Division on Civil Rights should be established,
> separate and apart from the Criminal Division."

While actual discussion in regard to the functions of the Civil Rights

Division was sparse, Sen. Case of South Dakota inserted into the record

(Cong. Rec. 10694-95) a letter written by the /then/ Deputy Attorney General

Rogers to Sen. Eastland in connection with civil rights bills introduced

in the 84th Congress. This letter lists the statutes under the jurisdiction

of the Civil Rights Section of the Criminal Division which would be

transferred to the jurisdiction of the Civil Rights Division, and then goes

on as follows:

> "The Civil Rights Division probably would also be
> responsible for the formulation of legal and policy
> approaches involving constitutional and civil rights
> within the Department of Justice, and would serve as
> liaison between the Department and other Government
> departments, agencies, and commissions in such matters.
> For example, the new division might assist the
> President's Committee on Government Contracts in its
> program to diminish discriminatory practices in its
> field; advise the State Department in connection
> with human rights problems involving the United Nations;

or assist other Government establishments in
maintaining equality of opportunity in employment
in their staffs. The Civil Rights Division would
also be responsible for keeping the Attorney
General informed of developments in constitutional
law affecting the basic rights of the people, and
it would participate in cases before the courts
involving important civil-rights issues.

"After further consideration of the problem and
experience in the operation of the Civil Rights
Division, additional statutes and functions,
might be transferred to the Division and
reassignments might well be made. The foregoing
tentative list of statutes and outline of
functions, however, should indicate the scope
and nature of the proposed Division's authority
and duties."

Beyond that, the feeling was expressed in Congress that the functions

and duties of the Division were not definitely defined and accordingly

would encompass whatever matters might ultimately be included by the courts

within the scope of civil rights. Cong. Rec. 11254. Senator Johnston of

South Carolina stated, referring to the Senate Report on S. 902, 84th Cong.,

a predecessor bill, that the Division would keep under scrutiny organizations

and individuals fomenting racial tension (apparently much as the Internal

Security Division keeps surveillance over subversive organizations). Cong.

Rec. 10201-2.

The only point in respect of the Division's functions upon which there

was more than negligible comment had to do with the problem of the actual

handling of civil rights cases before the courts. There was fairly general

agreement between proponents and opponents of the bill that attorneys from

the new Division rather than local United States Attorneys would handle all,

or at least the bulk of, civil rights cases in the courts. Rep. Willis

(N. C.), House Rules Committee hearings pp. 57, 66; Rep. Delaney (N. Y.),

House Rules Committee hearings, pp. 70-1; Minority Report of House Judiciary Committee, H. Rept. 291, supra, pp. 59-60. While the Division thus would be handling a considerable number of cases in many States (Rep. Celler, Rules Committee hearings, p. 16), this was thought to be quite justified, in view of the fact that its personnel, being experts in the field, could handle the cases more properly and expeditiously, in the proven pattern of Departmental handling of anti-trust and tax cases. Rep. Delaney (N.Y.), Rules Committee hearings, pp. 70-1.

B. Additional Protections Relating to Voting Rights

Prior to enactment of the Civil Rights Act of 1957, the only statute providing a civil remedy in cases of voting rights violations was 42 U.S.C. § 1971 which provided that:

> "All citizens of the United States who are otherwise qualified by law to vote at any election by the people in any State, Territory, district, county, city, parish, township, school district, municipality, or other territorial subdivision, shall be entitled and allowed to vote at all such elections, without distinction of race, color or previous condition of servitude; any constitution, law, custom, usage, or regulation of any State or Territory, or by or under its authority, to the contrary notwithstanding."

Part IV (section 131) of the new Act gave the subsection designation "(a)" to what had previously been section 1971, and added to such section four new subsections, (b) through (e). Basically, subsection (b) prohibits the intimidation of or the attempt to intimidate any person in his voting rights in any general, special, or primary election involving federal office. Subsection (c) permits the Attorney General of the United States to institute an injunctive action in any case where a person has engaged, or where there are reasonable grounds to believe he is about to engage, in any of the acts prohibited by subsections (a) or (b). Subsection (d) grants jurisdiction to federal district courts in proceedings under section 1971, without regard to whether the person aggrieved has exhausted any administrative or other remedies that may be provided by law. And subsection (e) provides for counsel for persons tried for contempt in connection with section 1971.

The clearly expressed purpose of these amendments was to permit the Government to protect citizens' voting rights other than by way of criminal proceedings which, since they can be used only after the event, usually come too late effectively to protect the right involved. Testimony of Attorney General Brownell on H.R. 627, 84th Cong., House Judiciary Sub-committee hearings, pp. 570-3; Senator Douglas, Cong. Rec. 7675.

To accomplish this purpose, the Act adds an injunctive remedy safeguarding the right to be free from threats in connection with the exercise of voting rights in elections for federal office to the previously existing remedies safeguarding the right not to be interfered with in any election, federal or state, for reason of race, color or previous condition of servitude. In addition, for the first time the Attorney General, acting "for the United States, or in the name of the United States," is permitted to apply for injunctive relief to secure both of these rights.

While there was some dispute during the debates as to the scope of this legislation insofar as it might affect purely local elections, it appears from the context that any confusion was more semantic than substantive. Thus, Representative Celler stated that Part IV did not deal with intimidation or coercion in connection with a purely local election for local office. Rules Committee hearings, p. 42. On the other hand, Rep. Forrester, also a member of the Judiciary Committee, indicated that in his opinion the amendments to section 1971 had to do with both federal and purely local elections. Rules Committee hearings, p. 163. Indeed he stated that the bill "refers to all primaries; it refers to every election: State, county, municipal, township, school district; it applies to the election of a common justice of the peace. Does anyone want to challenge that? I say it does." Cong. Rec. 7775.

What the gentlemen apparently were referring to is that per se the Act specifically creates a new substantive remedy only in subsection (b) of section 1971, and that this new remedy deals only with federal elections. But insofar as subsection (c) also creates a remedy by granting the Attorney General powers of enforcement with respect not only to § 1971 (b) but also with respect to § 1971 (a) -- which does cover local and federal voting matters in cases of racial discrimination -- it has an impact both on federal and on local elections. Attorney General Brownell was addressing himself specifically only to primary elections, but what he said was applicable to general and special elections as well, when he testified that under the bill the Government could act with respect to elections in two situations: (1) where, regardless of whether or not a federal office is involved, persons acting under color of law deprive a citizen of his right to participate in an election because of his race or color, and (2) where federal offices are included in the election and citizens are deprived of their right to vote or to have their vote counted by means of threat or intimidation. House Judiciary Subcommittee hearings, supra, pp. 606-7.

This latter category, according to a number of Senators, is not limited to racial discrimination under the 14th or 15th Amendments. Rather, it rests on the constitutional guaranty of the right of all citizens to cast a free and untrammeled ballot. Senators Russell, Yarborough, Eastland, and Thurmond, Cong. Rec. 11619, 11926, 11679.

It should be noted that under Part IV of the Act the Attorney General has the power both to intervene in an action brought by an aggrieved person, and to file an independent action without the consent of, indeed without the knowledge of, such person. Attorney General Brownell in House Judiciary Subcommittee hearings, supra, p. 599. An amendment by Sen. Ervin which would have required prior written authorization from the person for whose benefit the action is brought was defeated in the Senate. Cong. Rec. 12230, 12232. Representative Keating indicated that in his opinion the United States could sue even if only a single individual were aggrieved, although this would probably not be the usual situation. Cong. Rec. 7591.

A substantial difference between previous civil rights bills and the present Act is that 42 U.S.C. § 1971 (b) contains the proviso that no person whether acting under color of law or otherwise may interfere with certain voting rights. The generally understood purpose of the italicized words was to cover the actions of both public officials and private persons. Cong. Rec. 11679; House Report No. 291 supra, pp. 11, 47-8. This remedies what to the Attorney General seemed the most obvious defect in the old civil rights bills. House Judiciary Subcommittee hearings, 84th Cong., 1st Sess., pp. 570-3.

Another substantial change in existing law is that embodied in 42 U.S.C. § 1971 (d), which provides that the federal district courts would exercise jurisdiction without regard to any failure to exhaust State administrative or other remedies. See comment by Sen. Carroll, Cong. Rec. at 11792. According to Sen. Javits, this provision was inserted so as to prevent the tying up of a litigant in administrative remedies until after the primary or general election. Cong. Rec. 11792. Without this provision, it was felt by proponents of the bill, the primary purpose -- to prevent harm before it occurs -- would have been defeated. Cong. Rec. 7589. An amendment by Sen. Case of South Dakota to give district courts discretionary instead of mandatory jurisdiction in cases of non-exhaustion of State remedies was rejected by roll call vote. Cong. Rec. 12213-15. The effect of this vote is to reaffirm the mandatory jurisdictional feature of section 1971 (d). Another amendment, by Rep. Ray, to deprive federal courts of jurisdiction if there is a plain, speedy, and efficient State remedy, likewise was defeated. Cong. Rec. 8400-06. In other words, the efficacy or lack of efficacy of State remedies is immaterial.

On the other hand, § 1971 (d) does not appear to suspend the traditional authority of State judges to pass summarily on voting complaints arising on election day. Proponents of the bill felt that its provisions would apply only in cases of intimidation, threats or coercion, or attempts at such acts, and that in other respects State tribunals were fully competent. Cong. Rec. 7587.

There was only very limited discussion on the meaning of the concept of the threats and the coercion referred to in section 1971 (b), particularly with reference to the question of economic boycotts. Rep. Celler, testifying before the House Rules Committee, stated that in his opinion a mere refusal to sell would not violate the Act, but that a threat of individual or organized economic boycott or reprisal would constitute a violation if it were directly linked with an election to federal office. Rules Committee hearings, pp. 44-6.

C. **Elimination of Part III, which would have conferred broader authority on the Attorney General.** Part III of H.R. 6127, as passed by the House, conferred upon the Attorney General remedial powers similar to those conferred upon him by Part IV, dealing with voting rights. Part III, (§ 121) authorized the Attorney General to institute suits for injunctive relief to prevent violations of R.S. § 1980, 42 U.S.C. § 1985. That section provides a civil damage remedy against any person who conspires (1) to interfere with federal officers in the discharge of their duties and as a result injures or deprives another of his rights or privileges as a citizen of the United States (subsection (a)); (2) to intimidate or injure parties, witnesses, or jurors involved in any court matter or to obstruct the due course of justice in any state court with intent to deny to a citizen the equal protection of the laws (subsection (b)); and (3) to deprive another of the equal protection of the laws or of equal privileges and immunities under the law, or of the right to vote in elections affecting federal offices (subsection (b)). According to the House Committee on the Judiciary (H. Rept. No. 291, supra, p. 10):

> "The effect of the provisions of the proposed
> bill on existing law as contained in title 42,
> United States Code, section 1985 is not to
> expand the rights presently protected but
> merely to provide the Attorney General with
> the right to bring a civil action or other
> proper proceeding for relief to prevent acts
> or practices which would give rise to a cause
> of action under the three existing subsections."

A minority of the committee characterized the provisions of Part III as "truly shocking" and stated the effect on state and local law enforcement officers as follows: "police officers will be faced with the threat of a

Federal injunction. That can only mean the chaos which must result from the breakdown of law and order." (<u>Ibid</u>., pp. 45-46) The minority also adverted to the fact that the committee had already eliminated the "unprecedented proposal whereby the Attorney General * * * would represent private litigants in a civil action to recover damages." (<u>Ibid</u>., p. 55; see also P. 4 and remarks of Representative Celler, Cong. Rec. 7582-7583).

The attacks on Part III were renewed in the debates in the Senate. The principal objections raised by the opponents of Part III may be summarized as follows: (1) Since 42 U.S.C. § 1985 covered the whole field of civil rights the Attorney General's authority would be similarly extensive; (2) in particular, Part III would authorize the Attorney General to institute suits to compel the integration of the public schools. The proceedings on Part III may be described in greater detail as follows:

At the hearings on S. 83, 85th Congress, which was substantially similar to H.R. 6127, Attorney General Brownell testified (See Hearings before Subcommittee on Constitutional Rights of Senate Judiciary Committee, p. 50):

> "We will file with you a list of the civil rights
> of our citizens that are protected by the Federal
> Constitution, and whenever an occasion arises where
> we think that any of those rights, which are
> protected by the Constitution, have been violated,
> that is the type of case in which we would act."

This list, as submitted, included the following: Right to vote in federal elections and to have the ballot fairly counted; right to vote in any election free from discrimination by a state on account of race or color; right to inform a federal officer of a violation of federal law; right to testify in a federal court; right to be free of mob violence while in federal custody, right to be secure from unlawful searches and seizures; right to assemble peaceably, free from unreasonable restraints by state or local officials; freedom of religion, speech, and of the press; right not to be discriminated against in public employment on account of race or color; right not to be denied the use of governmentally-owned facilities on account of race or color; right not to be subjected to racial segregation under compulsion of state authority; right not to be denied due process of law or equal protection of the law "in other regards"; right to a fair trial; right not to be held in peonage (Hearings, supra, pp. 245-247; see also, Cong. Rec. 10927-28).

With respect to school integration, the Attorney General stated that he could not envisage any frequent use of the civil remedies proposed by Part III; he thought, however, that those remedies could be useful in the Hoxie type case, involving interference by private individuals with the attempts of local school boards voluntarily to eliminate segregation (id., pp. 7-8).

Many of the Senators from the southern states challenged what in their opinion were the unduly broad provisions of Part III. Thus Senator Ervin stated (Cong. Rec. 9910):

> " * * * section 1985 is concerned in general terms with all rights arising under 'the privileges or immunities' and 'the equal protection of the laws' clauses of the 14th amendment, and in specific terms with definite rights arising under 'the due process of law' clause of the 14th amendment and other articles of the Constitution. These things being true, the bill covers in substantial measure the entire spectrum of civil rights."

And, subsequently he remarked (Cong. Rec. 9913):

> "Under the bill, particularly under part 3, which gives the Attorney General the power to bring suit

> in the name of the United States at the expense of
> the taxpayers in all of the numerous cases that are
> to be covered by subsections 1, 2, and 3, of
> section 1985, of title 42, the Attorney General of
> the United States could bring suits virtually un-
> limited in number and nature. * * *. I cannot
> conceive of a broader power being given to one
> public official."

According to Senator Hill the enactment of Part III would permit the
Attorney General to intervene in state labor cases (Cong. Rec. 10230).
Senator Stennis stated that Part III, "by amending existing statutes, would
extend the operation of the bill to all conceivable kinds of cases which
could be dumped in the general category of Civil Rights" (Cong. Rec. 10362).
Senator Ellender argued that "Within the broad and nebulous field of civil
rights, the authority in part III would vest police powers in the Federal
Government" (Cong. Rec. 10453). Senator Eastland asserted that Part III,
under recent decisions of the Supreme Court, would enable the Attorney
General "to apply his coercive power to all publicly operated recreational
facilities, including swimming pools, golf courses, community theatres,
public stadiums, hotel facilities and State parks, and many, many more
areas. The injunctive weapon would be employed against all public transportation systems of every kind and character throughout the South,
regardless of the provisions of State constitutions and legislative enactments" (Cong. Rec. 10219). Senator Russell expressed a similar concern
(Cong. Rec. 9711-14).

Part III was also objected to because it was viewed as enabling the
Attorney General to go into court and obtain an injunction compelling a
local school board anywhere in the country to adopt a plan of integration.
According to Senator Eastland, to deny the right to attend a nonsegregated

school would be a violation of 42 U.S.C. § 1985; what the Attorney General would do "would be to bring suit for an injunction * * *." He would get a decree to integrate the school and give the child the right to attend a nonsegregated school. If the decree were violated, he would have two remedies. First, the person who violated it could be brought into court under an attachment, tried without a jury, and put in jail for criminal contempt. Second, under section 1993 of title 42 of the United States Code the President of the United States could use the Armed Forces to enforce judgments rendered under section 1985" (Cong. Rec. 9983-84). [17] Similar views were expressed by Senators Ervin (Cong. Rec. 9904-10089) and McClellan (Cong. Rec. 10468-69).

The proponents of Part III did not attempt particularly to dispute its probable scope, except as to the use of armed force to compel compliance with court decrees, but defended it on the ground that it merely added a needed additional remedy in the civil rights area. See Cong. Rec. 8839, 9717-18, 10104-05, 10428, 10663-64, 10918, 10983, 11115-16, 11117, 11244. And ultimately they agreed to the elimination of the provisions of Part III conferring authority on the Attorney General to bring injunction suits (See Cong. Rec. 11344-78). The amendment striking section 121 of Part III was adopted by a vote of 52 to 38 (Cong. Rec. 11378). The deletion of Part III was supported by a number of northern Senators who were in general in favor of the bill. These included Senators Anderson, Aiken, Saltonstall, O'Mahoney, Mundt, and Smith of New Jersey. See Cong. Rec. 10480, 10678, 10681-82, 10811-13, 10818, 10912-35, 11099, 11106-07, 11343-44.

---

[17] The question of 42 U.S.C. § 1993 is treated separately, infra.

D. Repeal of R.S. § 1989 (42 U.S.C. § 1993) relating to use of military

force. This section, originally enacted in 1866, 14 Stat. 29, authorized

the President --

> "or such person as he may empower for that purpose,
> to employ such part of the land or naval forces of
> the United States, or of the militia, as may be
> necessary to aid in the execution of judicial
> process issued under any of the preceding provisions
> /42 U.S.C. §§ 1981-1983, 1985-1992/, or as shall be
> necessary to prevent the violation and enforce the
> due execution of the provisions of this Title
> /42 U.S.C. §§ 1981-1983, 1985-1994/."

The section was repealed by § 122 of the Civil Rights Act of 1957

because of the argument advanced by southern Senators opposing the bill

that it would permit the use of military force to compel compliance with

injunctions obtained by the Attorney General under the provisions of

Part III. It will be noted that Part III, § 121, of H.R. 6127 proposed

to amend 42 U.S.C. § 1985, so as to authorize the Attorney General to sue

for injunctive relief to prevent violations of § 1985. 18/   Since § 1985

is one of the statutes specified in R. S. § 1989, it was claimed that the

latter could be used in connection with Part III of the bill. This was

developed during the Senate debate on the bill as follows:

On June 19, 1957, Senator Johnston of South Carolina, in objecting to

consideration of the bill by the Senate, asserted that in order to enforce

its provisions the bill gave the President "the power of using the Army

and Navy." (Cong. Rec. 86601). Senator Ervin commented to the same effect.

(Cong. Rec. 8838). Senator Russell spearheaded opposition to the bill on

the same ground, asserting that "the bill is cunningly designed to vest in

---

18/ As pointed out above, that section provides a civil damage remedy against
persons who, inter alia, conspire to deprive another of the equal protection of
the laws. This, it was asserted, covered a broad area, including the right of
an individual to attend a non-segregated public school.

the Attorney General unprecedented power to bring to bear the whole might of the Federal Government, including the Armed Forces if necessary, to force a commingling of white and Negro children in the State-supported public schools of the Sourth," and that "the unusual powers of this bill would be utilized to force the white people of the South at the point of a Federal bayonet to conform to almost any conceivable edict directed at the destruction of any of the local customs, laws, or practices separating the races in order to enforce a commingling of the races throughout the social order of the South" (Cong. Rec. 9709.) He then went on to "demonstrate by explaining part III of the bill that the talk about voting rights is a smokescreen to obscure the unlimited grant of powers to the Attorney General of the United States to govern by injunction and Federal bayonet." (Cong. Rec. 9710). Thus, § 1985 "the old reconstruction law creating the right to sue for damages, is specifically mentioned in this authorization /42 U.S.C. § 1993/ of the use of military force * * *;"" ** the voting section * * is not tied in with the use of military forces, whereas that section which will be utilized to force the mixing of the races in the schools and in the public places of amusement is tied in with the statute authorizing the use of military forces" (Cong. Rec. 9712). Senator Russell's views were supported by others: Senator Ervin (Cong. Rec. 9904), Senator Eastland (Cong. Rec. 9984-86), Senator Fulbright (Cong. Rec. 9985), Senator Johnston of South Carolina (Cong. Rec. 10203), Senator McClellan (Cong. Rec. 10461), Senator Thurmond (Cong. Rec. 11122-25), Senator Long (Cong. Rec. 11133).

Senator Dirksen denied that the bill was drafted to permit the use of military force in order to force integrated schools on the south; he asserted that the President under § 1993 already had the "ultimate authority to employ the land and naval forces to aid in the enforcement of desegregation decrees," and, apart from § 1993, the President was authorized to use the military forces under 10 U.S.C. (Supp. IV) §§ 332-333 (Cong. Rec. 10105, 10107). [19/] However, he could not imagine an occasion arising calling for the use of the military "to enforce civil-rights decrees." (Cong. Rec. 10105-10106). Senator Ervin replied that there was a material distinction between the President's power under 10 U.S.C. §§ 332 and 333 and his power under 42 U.S.C. § 1993 (Cong. Rec. 10107-08):

> "I submit that under the other statutes /10 U.S.C.
> §§ 332, 333/ the situation has to be in a much more
> drastic condition. It practically must amount to
> an insurrection. In this instance the President
> can call the troops out to enforce one judgment
> in a case. * * * In order for that power to
> exist it would not be necessary for any 'cain' to
> be raised. * * *. All that it would be necessary
> to do under title 42, section 1993, would be to
> obtain a judgment against me or my constituents
> under title 42, section 1985, but we would have
> to be in more or less of a state of insurrection
> before action could be taken under the other
> statutes. That would be the fundamental difference.."

According to Senator Eastland, the two statutes were separate and conferred separate and distinct powers on the President, "one of which could be used

---

19/ 10 U.S.C. § 332 authorizes the President to use military force whenever he considers that unlawful obstructions, combinations, or assemblages, or rebellion against the authority of the United States, make it impracticable to enforce the laws of the United States in any state or territory by ordinary judicial proceedings. 10 U.S.C. § 333 vests similar authority in the President with respect to insurrections or domestic violence in a state involving a deprivation of federal rights or obstructing the execution of federal laws or impeding the course of justice under those laws. The President's proclamation of September 23, 1957, and his executive order of September 24, 1957, authorizing the use of the military in the Little Rock situation, cited 10 U.S.C. §§ 332 and 333.

in case of rebellion and insurrection, and the other /of/which could be
used at the discretion of the President at any time in the aid of the
execution of judicial processes. * * *. That statute /§ 1993/ remains
on the books to be used by any despot, or strong figure on horseback."
(Cong. Rec. 10215). And, he subsequently argued that § 1993 might be used
"in the absence of rebellion"; that the President would not have to wait
"until there was defiance, or until the temporary injunction had been
violated. The Armed Forces could go in forthwith in order to enforce the
injunction." (Cong. Rec. 10220).

Senator Humphrey, a supporter of the bill, stated that § 1993 was
unnecessary since "/t/here is plenty of other appropriate law, besides
Reconstruction law, available for the President's use." (Cong. Rec. 10816).
Senator Anderson, another of the bill's supporters, stated (Cong. Rec. 10817):

> "The plain language of part III asserts that
> judicial decrees can be invoked to enforce
> anything termed civil rights. It also asserts
> that these decrees can be backed by the full
> weight of the Army, the Navy, and the militia."

Senators Knowland and Humphrey then offered an amendment to repeal 42 U.S.C.
§ 1993 (Cong. Rec. 10835). Senator Javits, in discussing the amendment, said
that there appeared to be no persuasive reason for retaining § 1993: Under
Title 10 the President had "all the power he needs in order to keep order"
"in the event of some large-scale breach of public order * * * regardless of
this particular provision of the bill." (Cong. Rec. 10934-10935).
Senator Long stated that even if § 1993 should be repealed "under the
Constitution and other sections of the law the use of Federal troops, including
the use of bayonets, to enforce such measures /viz. integration/ will still
be available." (Cong. Rec. 11133). Senator Russell, announcing his support of
the amendment, stated (Cong. Rec. 11134):

"Senators may differ as to the general authority of
the President of the United States to employ the
military forces, but I assert that the adoption of
the amendment will eliminate from our law the specific
power of the President to delegate the authority to
employ troops to execute specific judicial process in
specific cases.

"There is a vast difference between the employment of
troops under a specific statute to carry out a specific
judgment of a court, and the general powers of the
President of the United States to quell insurrection within this
land. It should be unnecessary to dwell upon that difference."

The amendment to repeal § 1993 was adopted without dissent (90-0)

Cong. Rec. 11137).

E. Amendment of 28 U.S.C. § 1861 dealing with the qualifications of federal

jurors. Section 152 of the Civil Rights Act of 1957 amends the federal juror

statute, 28 U.S.C. § 1861, by eliminating the fourth ground of disqualification

for jury service, namely, that the individual "is incompetent to serve as a

grand or petit juror by the law of the State in which the district court is

held." This change was offered by Senator Church as an amendment to the jury

trial amendment, on behalf of himself and a group of other supporters of the

bill "to eliminate whatever basis there may be for the charge that the efficacy

of trial by jury in the Federal courts is weakened by the fact that, in some

areas, colored citizens, because of the operation of State laws, are prevented

from serving as jurors. Thus the argument has been made that no jury trial

should be permitted in civil rights cases, even in a proceeding for criminal

contempt, because such cases concern relationships between the races, and in

the South they would be tried by an all-white jury. * * *. There is no reason

why Congress should not modify Federal law so as to safeguard against dis-

crimination on the basis of race, color, or creed, in the selection of jurors

who are to serve in Federal Courts." (Cong. Rec. 11933). Moreover, this would

establish uniform qualifications for federal jurors. (_ibid_.). After
discussion along similar lines (see Cong. Rec. 11934, 12059-60, 12065-66,
12071, 12097-99, 12114, 12138-39, 12147), the Church proposal was adopted
(Cong. Rec. 12178).

Public Law 85-315
85th Congress, H. R. 6127
September 9, 1957

AN ACT

71 Stat. 634.

o provide means of further securing and protecting the civil rights of persons within the jurisdiction of the United States.

Be it enacted by the Senate and House of Representatives of the United States of America in Congress assembled,

Civil Rights
Act of 1957.

PART I—ESTABLISHMENT OF THE COMMISSION ON CIVIL RIGHTS

SEC. 101. (a) There is created in the executive branch of the Government a Commission on Civil Rights (hereinafter called the "Commission").

(b) The Commission shall be composed of six members who shall be appointed by the President by and with the advice and consent of the Senate. Not more than three of the members shall at any one time be of the same political party.

(c) The President shall designate one of the members of the Commission as Chairman and one as Vice Chairman. The Vice Chairman shall act as Chairman in the absence or disability of the Chairman, or in the event of a vacancy in that office.

(d) Any vacancy in the Commission shall not affect its powers and shall be filled in the same manner, and subject to the same limitation with respect to party affiliations as the original appointment was made.

(e) Four members of the Commission shall constitute a quorum.

RULES OF PROCEDURE OF THE COMMISSION

SEC. 102. (a) The Chairman or one designated by him to act as Chairman at a hearing of the Commission shall announce in an opening statement the subject of the hearing.

(b) A copy of the Commission's rules shall be made available to the witness before the Commission.

(c) Witnesses at the hearings may be accompanied by their own counsel for the purpose of advising them concerning their constitutional rights.

(d) The Chairman or Acting Chairman may punish breaches of order and decorum and unprofessional ethics on the part of counsel, by censure and exclusion from the hearings.

(e) If the Commission determines that evidence or testimony at any hearing may tend to defame, degrade, or incriminate any person, it shall (1) receive such evidence or testimony in executive session; (2) afford such person an opportunity voluntarily to appear as a witness; and (3) receive and dispose of requests from such person to subpena additional witnesses.

(f) Except as provided in sections 102 and 105 (f) of this Act, the Chairman shall receive and the Commission shall dispose of requests to subpena additional witnesses.

(g) No evidence or testimony taken in executive session may be released or used in public sessions without the consent of the Commission. Whoever releases or uses in public without the consent of the Commission evidence or testimony taken in executive session shall be fined not more than $1,000, or imprisoned for not more than one year.

Evidence or testimony. Release.

(h) In the discretion of the Commission, witnesses may submit brief and pertinent sworn statements in writing for inclusion in the record. The Commission is the sole judge of the pertinency of testimony and evidence adduced at its hearings.

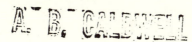

351

71 Stat. 635.

(i) Upon payment of the cost thereof, a witness may obtain a transcript copy of his testimony given at a public session or, if given at an executive session, when authorized by the Commission.

Witness fees.   (j) A witness attending any session of the Commission shall receive $4 for each day's attendance and for the time necessarily occupied in going to and returning from the same, and 8 cents per mile for going from and returning to his place of residence. Witnesses who attend at points so far removed from their respective residences as to prohibit return thereto from day to day shall be entitled to an additional allowance of $12 per day for expenses of subsistence, including the time necessarily occupied in going to and returning from the place of attendance. Mileage payments shall be tendered to the witness upon service of a subpena issued on behalf of the Commission or any subcommittee thereof.

(k) The Commission shall not issue any subpena for the attendance and testimony of witnesses or for the production of written or other matter which would require the presence of the party subpenaed at a hearing to be held outside of the State, wherein the witness is found or resides or transacts business.

COMPENSATION OF MEMBERS OF THE COMMISSION

SEC. 103. (a) Each member of the Commission who is not otherwise in the service of the Government of the United States shall receive the sum of $50 per day for each day spent in the work of the Commission, shall be reimbursed for actual and necessary travel expenses, and shall receive a per diem allowance of $12 in lieu of actual expenses for subsistence when away from his usual place of residence, inclusive of fees or tips to porters and stewards.

(b) Each member of the Commission who is otherwise in the service of the Government of the United States shall serve without compensation in addition to that received for such other service, but while engaged in the work of the Commission shall be reimbursed for actual and necessary travel expenses, and shall receive a per diem allowance of $12 in lieu of actual expenses for subsistence when away from his usual place of residence, inclusive of fees or tips to porters and stewards.

DUTIES OF THE COMMISSION

SEC. 104. (a) The Commission shall—

(1) investigate allegations in writing under oath or affirmation that certain citizens of the United States are being deprived of their right to vote and have that vote counted by reason of their color, race, religion, or national origin; which writing, under oath or affirmation, shall set forth the facts upon which such belief or beliefs are based;

(2) study and collect information concerning legal developments constituting a denial of equal protection of the laws under the Constitution; and

(3) appraise the laws and policies of the Federal Government with respect to equal protection of the laws under the Constitution.

Reports to President and Congress.   (b) The Commission shall submit interim reports to the President and to the Congress at such times as either the Commission or the President shall deem desirable, and shall submit to the President and to the Congress a final and comprehensive report of its activities, findings, and recommendations not later than two years from the date of the enactment of this Act.

Termination of Commission.   (c) Sixty days after the submission of its final report and recommendations the Commission shall cease to exist.

POWERS OF THE COMMISSION

SEC. 105. (a) There shall be a full-time staff director for the Commission who shall be appointed by the President by and with the advice and consent of the Senate and who shall receive compensation at a rate, to be fixed by the President, not in excess of $22,500 a year. The President shall consult with the Commission before submitting the nomination of any person for appointment to the position of staff director. Within the limitations of its appropriations, the Commission may appoint such other personnel as it deems advisable, in accordance with the civil service and classification laws, and may procure services as authorized by section 15 of the Act of August 2, 1946 (60 Stat. 810; 5 U. S. C. 55a), but at rates for individuals not in excess of $50 per diem. *Staff director.*

(b) The Commission shall not accept or utilize services of voluntary or uncompensated personnel, and the term "whoever" as used in paragraph (g) of section 102 hereof shall be construed to mean a person whose services are compensated by the United States.

(c) The Commission may constitute such advisory committees within States composed of citizens of that State and may consult with governors, attorneys general, and other representatives of State and local governments, and private organizations, as it deems advisable.

(d) Members of the Commission, and members of advisory committees constituted pursuant to subsection (c) of this section, shall be exempt from the operation of sections 281, 283, 284, 434, and 1914 of title 18 of the United States Code, and section 190 of the Revised Statutes (5 U. S. C. 99). *62 Stat. 697 et seq.*

(e) All Federal agencies shall cooperate fully with the Commission to the end that it may effectively carry out its functions and duties.

(f) The Commission, or on the authorization of the Commission any subcommittee of two or more members, at least one of whom shall be of each major political party, may, for the purpose of carrying out the provisions of this Act, hold such hearings and act at such times and places as the Commission or such authorized subcommittee may deem advisable. Subpenas for the attendance and testimony of witnesses or the production of written or other matter may be issued in accordance with the rules of the Commission as contained in section 102 (j) and (k) of this Act, over the signature of the Chairman of the Commission or of such subcommittee, and may be served by any person designated by such Chairman. *Hearings, etc.* *Subpenas.*

(g) In case of contumacy or refusal to obey a subpena, any district court of the United States or the United States court of any Territory or possession, or the District Court of the United States for the District of Columbia, within the jurisdiction of which the inquiry is carried on or within the jurisdiction of which said person guilty of contumacy or refusal to obey is found or resides or transacts business, upon application by the Attorney General of the United States shall have jurisdiction to issue to such person an order requiring such person to appear before the Commission or a subcommittee thereof, there to produce evidence if so ordered, or there to give testimony touching the matter under investigation; and any failure to obey such order of the court may be punished by said court as a contempt thereof.

APPROPRIATIONS

SEC. 106. There is hereby authorized to be appropriated, out of any money in the Treasury not otherwise appropriated, so much as may be necessary to carry out the provisions of this Act.

PART II—To Provide for an Additional Assistant Attorney General

SEC. 111. There shall be in the Department of Justice one additional Assistant Attorney General, who shall be appointed by the President, by and with the advice and consent of the Senate, who shall assist the Attorney General in the performance of his duties, and who shall receive compensation at the rate prescribed by law for other Assistant Attorneys General.

PART III—To Strengthen the Civil Rights Statutes, and for Other Purposes

62 Stat. 932.

SEC. 121. Section 1343 of title 28, United States Code, is amended as follows:

(a) Amend the catch line of said section to read,

"§ 1343. Civil rights and elective franchise"

(b) Delete the period at the end of paragraph (3) and insert in lieu thereof a semicolon.

(c) Add a paragraph as follows:

"(4) To recover damages or to secure equitable or other relief under any Act of Congress providing for the protection of civil rights, including the right to vote."

Repeal.

SEC. 122. Section 1989 of the Revised Statutes (42 U. S. C. 1993) is hereby repealed.

PART IV—To Provide Means of Further Securing and Protecting the Right To Vote

SEC. 131. Section 2004 of the Revised Statutes (42 U. S. C. 1971), is amended as follows:

(a) Amend the catch line of said section to read, "Voting rights".

(b) Designate its present text with the subsection symbol "(a)".

(c) Add, immediately following the present text, four new subsections to read as follows:

"(b) No person, whether acting under color of law or otherwise, shall intimidate, threaten, coerce, or attempt to intimidate, threaten, or coerce any other person for the purpose of interfering with the right of such other person to vote or to vote as he may choose, or of causing such other person to vote for, or not to vote for, any candidate for the office of President, Vice President, presidential elector, Member of the Senate, or Member of the House of Representatives, Delegates or Commissioners from the Territories or possessions, at any general, special, or primary election held solely or in part for the purpose of selecting or electing any such candidate.

"(c) Whenever any person has engaged or there are reasonable grounds to believe that any person is about to engage in any act or practice which would deprive any other person of any right or privilege secured by subsection (a) or (b), the Attorney General may institute for the United States, or in the name of the United States, a civil action or other proper proceeding for preventive relief, including an application for a permanent or temporary injunction, restraining order, or other order. In any proceeding hereunder the United States shall be liable for costs the same as a private person.

"(d) The district courts of the United States shall have jurisdiction of proceedings instituted pursuant to this section and shall exercise the same without regard to whether the party aggrieved shall have exhausted any administrative or other remedies that may be provided by law.

71 Stat. 637.

"(e) Any person cited for an alleged contempt under this Act shall be allowed to make his full defense by counsel learned in the law; and the court before which he is cited or tried, or some judge thereof, shall immediately, upon his request, assign to him such counsel, not exceeding two, as he may desire, who shall have free access to him at all reasonable hours. He shall be allowed, in his defense to make any proof that he can produce by lawful witnesses, and shall have the like process of the court to compel his witnesses to appear at his trial or hearing, as is usually granted to compel witnesses to appear on behalf of the prosecution. If such person shall be found by the court to be financially unable to provide for such counsel, it shall be the duty of the court to provide such counsel."

71 Stat. 638.

PART V—TO PROVIDE TRIAL BY JURY FOR PROCEEDINGS TO PUNISH CRIMINAL CONTEMPTS OF COURT GROWING OUT OF CIVIL RIGHTS CASES AND TO AMEND THE JUDICIAL CODE RELATING TO FEDERAL JURY QUALIFICATIONS

SEC. 151. In all cases of criminal contempt arising under the provisions of this Act, the accused, upon conviction, shall be punished by fine or imprisonment or both: *Provided however*, That in case the accused is a natural person the fine to be paid shall not exceed the sum of $1,000, nor shall imprisonment exceed the term of six months: *Provided further*, That in any such proceeding for criminal contempt, at the discretion of the judge, the accused may be tried with or without a jury: *Provided further, however*, That in the event such proceeding for criminal contempt be tried before a judge without a jury and the sentence of the court upon conviction is a fine in excess of the sum of $300 or imprisonment in excess of forty-five days, the accused in said proceeding, upon demand therefor, shall be entitled to a trial de novo before a jury, which shall conform as near as may be to the practice in other criminal cases.

Criminal contempt. Penalties.

This section shall not apply to contempts committed in the presence of the court or so near thereto as to interfere directly with the administration of justice nor to the misbehavior, misconduct, or disobedience, of any officer of the court in respect to the writs, orders, or process of the court.

Nonapplicability.

Nor shall anything herein or in any other provision of law be construed to deprive courts of their power, by civil contempt proceedings, without a jury, to secure compliance with or to prevent obstruction of, as distinguished from punishment for violations of, any lawful writ, process, order, rule, decree, or command of the court in accordance with the prevailing usages of law and equity, including the power of detention.

SEC. 152. Section 1861, title 28, of the United States Code is hereby amended to read as follows:

62 Stat. 951.

"§ 1861. Qualifications of Federal jurors

"Any citizen of the United States who has attained the age of twenty-one years and who has resided for a period of one year within the judicial district, is competent to serve as a grand or petit juror unless—

"(1) He has been convicted in a State or Federal court of record of a crime punishable by imprisonment for more than one year and his civil rights have not been restored by pardon or amnesty.

"(2) He is unable to read, write, speak, and understand the English language.

"(3) He is incapable, by reason of mental or physical infirmities to render efficient jury service."

Short title.   SEC. 161. This Act may be cited as the "Civil Rights Act of 1957".

Approved September 9, 1957.

GPO 86139

BIBLIOGRAPHY OF LAW REVIEW ARTICLES AND OTHER PUBLICATIONS
CONCERNING CIVIL RIGHTS FUNCTIONS OF THE DEPARTMENT OF JUSTICE

"Federal Protection of Civil Rights" - Robert Carr (1947)

"The Constitution and Civil Rights," pp. 64-66, 71, 83 ff., 88 -
Milton Konvitz (1947)

"To Secure These Rights." p. 114 ff. - Report of the President's
Committee (1947)

"Civil Rights in America," p. 2 - Annals of the American Academy of
Political and Social Science, edited by Carr, article by Cushman,
(May issue, 1951)

"Civil Rights in the United States in 1951," p. 33 - American Jewish
Committee and NAACP Pamphlet

"Civil Liberties Under Attack," 9. 29 - Wilcox, editor, article by
Carr (1951) *University of Penn, Press. (1951)*

"Political and Civil Rights in the United States," pp. 44, 86-96-
Emerson and Haber (1952)

"Social Work Yearbook," pp. 114, 565, 570 (1954)

"Civil Liberties and the Vinson Court," p. 215 - C. Herman Pritchett
(1954)

"The Supreme Court in the American System of Government," p. 71 -
Robert Jackson (1955)

"Freedom Reader," pp. 95, 96, 184, 188, 190 - Newman, editor (1955)

"Civil Liberties in the United States," pp. 118, 124 - 128, 146
Robert Cushman (1956)

"Racial Desegregation and Integration," p. 12 - Annals of the
American Academy of Political and Social Science, article by L. W.
Logan (March issue, 1956)

*Freedom from Fear on the Home Front:
29 Iowa Law Review, Page 415, - Vol 29-1943-4*

CASES

Irvine v. California, 347 U.S. 128 (1954) Douglas dissent. Lists prosecutions under 241-4 in Civil Rights Section. Cites articles by Tom Clark and Henry Putzel.

Screws, 325 U.S. 159 Roberts dissent. Quotes Attorney General and "policy of strict limitation" of Justice Department in prosecutions under Civil Rights statutes.

Additions to June 21, 1956 List of References to Civil Rights Section

Rogge, O. John (Assistant Attorney General, Criminal Division),
    ABA Journal, Vol. 25, p. 1030 (1939).

Grossman, Eugene, "Federal Courts - Jurisdiction over Violations
    of Civil Liberties by State Governments and Private Indivi-
    duals," Michigan Law Review, Vol. 39, p. 284 (1940).

Cushman, Robert, "Safeguarding Our Civil Liberties," Public
    Affairs Pamphlet #43, p. 28 (1941).

Carr, Robert K., "Screws v. United States," Cornell Law Quarterly,
    Vol.   , p. 48 (Sept. 1945).

Clark, Tom, "A Federal Prosecutor Looks at the Civil Rights Statute,"
    Columbia Law Review, Vol 7, p. 175 (1947).

Report on Legal and Illegal Forms of Forced Labor in the U.S. -
    Presented to Ad Hoc Committee on Slavery, ECOSOC - U.N. 1951
    p. 4 - refers to need for enforcement of anti-slavery laws -
    The Civil Rights Section of the Department of Justice with its
    6 lawyers and no power of independent investigation is in
    sharp contrast to the Antitrust Division with its 320 lawyers
    and full investigative powers.

Stanford Law Review, Vol 7. p. 76, "State Police, Unconstitutionally
    Obtained Evidence, and Section 242 of the Civil Rights Statute,"
    (Dec. 1954).

Abrams, Charles, "Forbidden Neighbors," p. 376 (1955).

McKay, Robert B., "With All Deliberate Speed," A Study of School
    Desegregation. N.Y.U. Law Review, Vol. 31, #6, pp. 991-1090.
    p. 1074 Re: Proposed legislation to change Civil Rights Section
    to Division (1956).

The Civil Rights Crisis in the South. Lawyers Guild Review, Summer
    1956, Vol. XVI #2, p. 64. Says Civil Rights Section should be
    enlarged.

Readers Digest, September 1956, p. 50, Crooks Who Steal Your Vote.

Law Review Articles Prepared by Members of the Civil Rights Section

"Interpreting the Hatch Act," 3 Federal Bar Association Journal 407 (Nov. 1939). - Henry A. Schweinhaut

"The Civil Liberties Section of the Department of Justice," 1 Bill of Rights Review 206 (Spring, 1941) Henry A. Schweinhaut

"Criminal Enforcement of Federal Civil Rights," 2 Lawyers Guild Review 18 (May, 1942). - Victor W. Rotnem

"Clarification of the Civil Rights Statutes," 2 Bill of Rights Review 252 (Summer, 1942) - Victor W. Rotnem

"Recent Restrictions upon Religious Liberty," 36 American Political Science Review 1053 (Dec. 1942) - Victor W. Rotnem and Fred G. Folsom, Jr.

"The Federal Civil Right 'Not to be Lynched, '" 28 Washington Law Quarterly 57 (Feb. 1943). - Victor W. Rotnem

"A Slave Trade Law in Contemporary Setting," 29 Cornell Law Quarterly, 203 (Nov. 1943). - Fred G. Folsom, Jr.

"Civil Rights during the War: The Role of the Federal Government" 29 Iowa Law Review 415 (March 1944). - Victor W. Rotnem

"Federal Privileges and Immunities; Application to Ingress and Egress," 29 Cornell Law Quarterly 489 (June 1944) - Sylvester P. Meyers

"Enforcement of Civil Rights," 3 National Bar Journal 1 (March 1945). Victor W. Rotnem

"Federal Civil Rights Enforcement: Current Appraisal," 99 University of Pennsylvania Law Review 439 (January, 1951). Henry Putzel, Jr.

"Federally-Secured Right to be Free from Bondage." 40 Georgetown Law Journal 367 (March, 1952). Sydney Brodie

U. S. COMMISSION ON CIVIL RIGHTS

THE CIVIL RIGHTS ACT OF 1960

Public Law 86-449

A Legislative History and Analysis

September 1960

THE CIVIL RIGHTS ACT OF 1960

Table of Contents

A. B. CALDWELL

SENATE PASSAGE OF H.R. 8601: Congressional Record, p. 7267.

Remarks of Senators (references are to volume 106 of Congressional Record -- daily edition).

Allott:	7087	Humphrey	7266
Bible:	7262	Javits	7260
Bush:	7218	Johnston (SC)	7193, 7203
Case (S.D.)	7219	Keating	7223
Clark	7224	Kefauver	7266
Dirksen	7263	Kuchel	7169
Douglas	7261	McClellan	7221
Eastland	7193	McNamara	7190
Ellender	7229	Morse	7274
Ervin		Russel	7193
Fulbright	7165	Sparkman	7118
Gruening	7225	Stennis	7126, 7262
Holland	7259	Thurmond	7127-69, 7208

U. S. Commission on Civil Rights
September, 1960

FOR OFFICIAL USE ONLY

THE CIVIL RIGHTS ACT OF 1960

Public Law 86-449

A Legislative History and Analysis

I. The Birth of the Bill:

Early in 1959 a variety of civil rights bills was introduced and discussed in the House. These bills provided the basis for the lengthy deliberation and final passage of the Civil Rights Act of 1960.

Certain of the final provisions of H.R. 8601 - The Civil Rights Act of 1960 - were submitted to Congress on February 5, 1959 by President Eisenhower in a special message. (H. Doc. No. 75, 86th Cong., 1st Sess.). [1/] This message urged:

1. Legislation to strengthen the law dealing with obstructions of justice. This provision would

---

[1/] 105 Cong. Rec. 1884. (References to volume 105 of the Congressional Record are to the bound volumes. All other references to the Congressional Record are to the daily edition of volume 106 (1960) relating to the proceedings of the second session of the 86th Congress.)

deter acts of violence designed to obstruct the
effectiveness of court decrees in school desegregation cases. In its final form, Title I of the
1960 Act was broadened to include protection of all
court orders.

2. Legislation "to confer additional investigative
authority on the FBI" in cases involving the
destruction of schools or churches where the
culprit has fled from one state to another to
avoid prosecution. "Such recommendation when
enacted would make it clear that the FBI has
full authority to assist in investigations of
crimes involving bombings of schools and churches."
Title II of the 1960 Act accomplishes this by
creating a "rebuttable presumption" that the
explosives were transported in interstate commerce.
It was broadened to include destructions of any
building or "other real or personal property."

3. Legislation to permit the Attorney General to
inspect Federal election records and to require
their preservation for "a reasonable period of
time." A similar provision was recommended by the
Commission on Civil Rights in its September 1959

report. [2/] In both instances the recommendation was made because of past difficulty in gaining access to local election records. As was stated by the President, "State or local authorities, in some instances, have refused to permit the inspection of their election records in the course of investigations." Under the 1960 Act, these records must be preserved for a period of twenty-two months and are made available to the Attorney General at his request, in the office of the local election official.

4. Legislation "to provide a temporary program of financial and technical aid to State and local agencies to assist them in making the necessary adjustments required by school desegregation decisions." No action has been taken on this point.

5. Legislation to provide for the education of children of members of the Armed Forces when local State schools are closed because of desegregation orders. This provision is contained in the 1960 Act.

2/ Report of the U.S. Commission on Civil Rights 1959, at 138. (Hereafter noted, 1959 Report) "the Commission recommends that the Congress require that all State registration and voting records shall be public records and must be preserved for a period of 5 years, during which time they shall be subject to public inspection..."

6. Establishment of a statutory Commission on Equal Job Opportunity under Government Contracts. No action has been taken on this recommendation.

7. Extension of the Commission on Civil Rights for two years. This was effected by Congress on the 28th of September, 1959. [3]

One week after the President's message, Representative McCulloch (R-Ohio) introduced H.R. 4457. In essence this bill embraced the seven recommendations of the President. His bill, with a similar bill, H.R. 3147, introduced by Representative Celler (D-N.Y.), and 37 other bills, dealing with every facet of civil rights, were referred to the House Committee on the Judiciary. Between March 4 and May 1, 1959, a subcommittee conducted hearings on these bills. [4] For the most part testimony was limited to H.R. 3147 and H.R. 4457.

Emanuel Celler, the Chairman of the subcommittee, in opening the hearings, noted: "The very nature of these bills plainly bespeaks how very far we are from granting to all our citizens equality of opportunity." [5] Upon conclusion of the hearings in early May, the subcommittee met in executive session to consider H.R. 3147. It deleted from that proposal

---

[3] P.L. 86-383; 73 Stat. 724.

[4] Hearings on Civil Rights Before Subcommittee No. 5 of the House Committee on the Judiciary, 86th Cong., 1st Sess., ser. 14.

[5] Id. at 146.

all but the enacting clause, and substituted its own bill
which contained all seven of the President's recommendations.
The full committee adopted five of the recommendations of its
subcommittee, concerning: 6/

1. Obstruction of court orders.

2. Flight to avoid prosecution.

3. Preservation of Federal election records.

4. Extension of the Commission on Civil Rights for two
years.

5. Education of children of members of the Armed Forces.

The Chairman of the Judiciary Committee then introduced
a clean bill, H.R. 8601, containing all of the above items.
This bill was reported by the committee on August 20, 1959. 7/
In its general statement the committee report noted: "the
hearings conducted on this legislation clearly indicate the
need for additional legislation to implement the enforcement
of civil rights . . . . H.R. 8601 is designed to assist in

6/ Those recommendations of the President calling for the
establishment of a statutory Commission on Equal Job
Opportunity and a program of financial aid to State agencies
adjusting to desegregation decisions were deleted.

7/ 105 Cong. Rec. 16621. For Congressman Celler's analysis
of the bill, see id. at 18663.

the achievement of the great American goal of equal rights for all under the law by strengthening the law enforcement functions of the Federal Government." [8/]

H.R. 8601 then went to the House Rules Committee where it remained until February of 1960.

Meanwhile, the Subcommittee on Constitutional Rights of the Senate Committee on the Judiciary held hearings off and on during March, April and May. [9/] On July 15, 1959, it reported to the full committee S.2391, providing for the preservation of voting records and for the extension of the Commission on Civil Rights. When Congress adjourned in mid-September, the committee was still considering this bill. In response to mounting pressures to continue the first session in order to enact civil rights legislation, Senate leaders informally agreed to begin debate on the civil rights issue around the middle of February of 1960. [10/]

8/ H. Rept. No. 956, 86th Cong., 1st Sess.

9/ Hearings on Civil Rights Before the Subcommittee on Constitutional Rights of the Senate Committee on the Judiciary 86th Cong., 1st Sess., pts. 1-4.

10/ 105 Cong. Rec. 19429, 19436.

II. The Registrar Proposal of the Commission on Civil Rights:

In 1957, in passing the first civil rights act in eighty-two years, Congress had given significant assurance to all citizens that their right to vote is basic to the democratic process. By this act, [11/] the Attorney General was empowered to seek court injunctions to enforce the right to vote when an individual is deprived of his voting rights. But civil rights proponents argued that the 1957 law did not go far enough in protecting voting rights. The main issue of the 1960 debate was to center on what kind of provision should be added to the 1957 Act to insure further the constitutional right to vote.

The United States Commission on Civil Rights was one of the first to urge the enactment of additional legislation in the field of voting. In its 1959 report, the Commission revealed that large numbers of Negroes in certain Southern areas were being denied their right to vote. For example, the Commission cited sixteen counties in which Negroes constituted a majority of the population, yet not a single Negro was registered; and in forty-nine other counties in which Negroes constituted a majority, less than 5% of the voting-age Negroes were registered. [12/] On the basis of

---

11/ Civil Rights Act of 1957, 71 Stat. 634.

12/ 1959 Report at 52.

its investigations, hearings, and its evaluation of the effectiveness of the 1957 Act, the Commission concluded that "the
existing remedies under the Civil Rights Act of 1957 are
insufficient to secure and protect the right to vote..." [13]
Therefore, the Commission [14] reported, "Some method must be
found by which a Federal officer is empowered to register
voters for Federal elections who are qualified under State
registration laws but are unable to register." [15] Specifically,
it made a recommendation calling for the appointment of temporary federal registrars. The system as proposed would have
operated as follows:

The President of the United States would receive sworn
affidavits from persons who claimed that:

1. They believed themselves to be qualified to vote
   under State law;

2. They had been unable to register with the proper
   officials;

3. They had been denied this right because of their
   race, color, or national origin.

When nine or more persons from any one political subdivision
of a State sent such an affidavit to the President, it would

13/ Id. at 141.

14/ Governor Battle dissented; for his statement see id. at 142.

15/ Id. at 141.

then be referred to the Commission on Civil Rights for authentication. Once the Commission found the complaint to be substantial, the President could appoint a Federal officer or employee in the area to act as a temporary registrar. The temporary registrar would qualify Negroes to vote in Federal elections when the State registrar refused registration. Voting certificates would be issued to the qualified applicants, permitting the holder to participate in Federal elections.

Following the publication of the report, numerous bills containing the recommendations of the Commission on Civil Rights were introduced in Congress. The essential feature of these bills was to provide a mechanism different from the 1957 Act to enable great numbers of Negroes to register. Basically, the registrar plans had two chief characteristics:

1. They were limited to Federal elections;

2. they provided for an administrative procedure, with the temporary registrar to be appointed by the President.

Because of time limitations, no serious consideration was accorded these bills until the second session of the 86th Congress. During this 1st session, the only positive legislative accomplishment in the field of civil rights was the extension for two years of the Commission on Civil Rights in September 1959. [16]

---

[16] See p. 3, supra.

III. Registrar or Referee?

The second session of the 86th Congress opened in an
election year with the question of civil rights legislation
its most controversial issue. The first session had adjourned
with a long record of civil rights hearingsand debates, but
with little accomplishment. Senate leaders had promised to
begin debate on a civil rights bill on or about the 15th of
February. 17/

On January 7, 1960, the President delivered his State
of the Union Message. 18/ Speaking generally on the issue
of civil rights, the President stated:

> "Early in your last session, I recommended
> legislation which would help eliminate
> several practices discriminating against
> the basic rights of Americans. The Commis-
> sion on Civil Rights had developed additional
> constructive recommendations. I hope that
> these will be among the matters to be seriously
> considered in the current session."

The President, however, did not single out any one of the
recommendations of the Commission and at this time it was
not clear if he supported the registrar proposal. However,
several days later, at a news conference, President Eisenhower said that he was not sure of the constitutional
validity of the registrar plan. 19/

17/ See note 10, supra.

18/ H. Doc. 241 (106 Cong. Rec. 135).

19/ See N.Y. Times, January 17, 1960 p.1.

At this point, neither body of Congress had a bill of its own to consider. The House Civil Rights bill (H.R. 8601) still awaited clearance from the Rules Committee, while its Senate counterpart (S.2391) remained in the Senate Judiciary Committee. Because of this, a number of bills were introduced in both houses. Certain of the Senate bills embracing the registrar recommendation of the Commission on Civil Rights, were referred to the Senate Committee on Rules and Administration for hearings. [20]

For several days testimony was given on the pros and cons of the registrar plan. Then, on January 26th, Attorney General Rogers issued a press release in which he proposed a somewhat different plan. [21] Instead of an administrative procedure as provided in the registrar plan, the Attorney

---

[20] The significance of this unusual procedure should be noted. In the past, civil rights bills have been referred to the Senate Judiciary Committee where there rarely was any positive action taken. By exercising its jurisdiction and deciding on hearings of its own, the Senate Rules Committee created the necessary momentum and interest in civil rights legislation that eventually led to the final passage of the 1960 Civil Rights Act.

[21] Hearings on Federal Registrars Before the Senate Committee on Rules and Administration, 86th Cong., 2nd Sess., 167. (Hereafter noted, Hearings on Federal Registrars.)

General recommended that court-appointed referees be utilized
to register qualified Negroes after a successful judicial
proceeding under the 1957 Civil Rights Act. [22] The basic
purpose of both proposals was to provide a mechanism to
register qualified Negro voters denied that right because
of discriminatory practices. However, under the referee
plan the Attorney General would bring a suit to enjoin a
State registrar from discriminating against voters because
of their race. If the court found a pattern or practice of
discrimination to exist, it could appoint a special master,
to be called a voting referee, to receive complaints, determine whether the complainants were qualified to vote under
State law, and report findings to the court. The report of
the referee would then become part of a court order, unless
"clearly erroneous," and would be binding on State officials
under pain of contempt of court.

22/ On February 14, 1960, a number of law professors and
legislators participated in a Conference on Civil Rights
at the Notre Dame Law School. The various right-to-vote
proposals were discussed and certain recommendations and
improvements suggested. These proceedings are reprinted
in 106 Cong. Rec. A1706 (February 29, 1960). See also
Wooford, "Notre Dame Conference on Civil Rights", 35
Notre Dame Lawyer 328 (1960).

Testifying before the Committee on Rules and Administration on February 5, Mr. Rogers pointed out that his plan "has the full support of the administration" [23/] and "is thoroughly consistent with the spirit of the recommendation of the Civil Rights Commission." [24/] And in a letter submitted to the Rules Committee, Dr. Hannah, the Chairman of the Commission on Civil Rights, acknowledged that the essential difference between the proposals of the Commission and of the Attorney General was "only in the choice of means." In Dr. Hannah's words, "the desired result is a situation in which all citizens are permitted and encouraged to register and vote regardless of race, color, creed, or national origin." [25/] Vice-Chairman Storey, in a companion letter, reaffirmed the view of the Commission: "We are not advocates of any particular legislation but trust the good judgment and wisdom of the Congress to prepare and pass appropriate legislation based upon our factfinding and recommendations." [26/]

23/ Hearings on Federal Registrars, 337.

24/ Id. at 339.

25/ Id. at 371-72.

26/ Id. at 372.

Civil Rights Commissioner Johnson listed three objectives which both proposals were intended to accomplish: [27]

> "The first of these is to provide for a determination as to whether in a particular area discrimination is in fact being practiced with regard to permitting citizens to exercise the right to vote. This determination would be a jurisdictional determination, in the sense that it beings into play the machinery for remedying such discrimination where it is found to exist. The second essential feature is this remedial machinery itself; that is, a procedure providing for prompt and effective registration of those who have been excluded from participation in the voting process. The third essential feature is a provision for enforcement."

As sponsor of the administration's referee plan, Mr. Rogers stated that in his belief, it "would be more effective than the Federal Registrar proposals and would avoid many of the serious and practical problems connected with the Federal registrars." [28] In his January 26th statement, Mr. Rogers outlined the advantages of the administration's proposed referee system:

1. It would cover both State and Federal elections.

2. It would operate witin the established framework of judicial powers, supplementing the 1957 Act.

27/ Id. at 93 (supplemental statement of George M. Johnson Feb. 5, 1960).

28/ Id. at 167-68 (Attorney General's press release).

3. It would be enforceable through contempt powers of the courts.

4. It would cover the whole election process.

5. It would interfere with State voting procedures to a minimum.

During his testimony before the Committee, Mr. Rogers amplified the advantages of the referee proposal as opposed to the registrar plan. In so doing, he cast some doubt on the constitutionality of the registrar plan. ("The constitutional problem is apt to be much more complicated and difficult under the Federal registrar proposal.") [29] Further, he felt that the registrar proposal might, in its effect, operate "to establish a system of separate and unequal voting." [30] He pointed out that a State "might retain consolidated ballots for persons qualified under State laws . . . to vote both for State and Federal officers, and provide separate ballots /for Federal elections only7 for those qualified by the Federal registrars." This would result in destroying "the basic concept of a secret ballot." [31]

29/ Id. at 348.

30/ Id. at 347.

31/ Ibid.

Mr. Rogers favored the contempt provisions of the referee plan to insure its workability, asserting that the certificate to be given by the Federal registrar to a Negro would be worth "just about as much as a ticket to the Dempsey-Firpo fight."[32/]

Even before Mr. Rogers had completed his testimony, some Southern Senators aired objections. One of their most outspoken, Senator Talmadge (D-Ga.), protested that the Attorney General's bill "amounts to nothing more than the wildest dreams of Thaddeus Stevens reincarnated,"[33/] and he argued, "it has been established beyond question that the Attorney General of the United States modeled his Federal election referee bill after one of the infamous Reconstruction Acts."[34/]

It now became apparent that there was a general bipartisan agreement among most legislators that something should be done to provide equal voting rights for Negroes. The debate had crystallized over the method to be adopted to assure the right to vote.

32/ Id. at 358.

33/ Cong. Rec. 1357 (Jan. 28, 1960).

34/ Id. at 1497 (Feb. 1, 1960).

With two differing plans under consideration, several compromise bills were proposed. Senator Keating (R-N.Y.) attempted to effect "a marriage" between the registrar plan and the referee proposal by providing for both procedures in one bill. [35] Asked what his view on this sort of merger would be, Attorney General Rogers quipped: "It can be considered a shotgun wedding so far as I am concerned." [36] A further consolidation offered by Senator Hennings (D-Mo.) called for presidentially appointed Federal enrollment officers. [37] Including sections from both the registrar and referee plans, the essential feature of the Hennings proposal was that it relied upon an administrative official not connected with the court to register qualified Negores. Like the administration's referee plan, the procedure could begin with an action by the Attorney General under the 1957 Civil Rights Act. If the court found discrimination against Negro voters, the President would be empowered to appoint Federal enrollment officers to help Negroes register. As an alternative, the Presidential appointment could be based upon a finding of discriminatory denial of the right to vote by the Commission on Civil Rights.

35/ Id. at 1896 (Feb. 4, 1960). Sen. Javits (R-N.Y.) and Sen. Douglas (D-Ill.) introduced a similar comprehensive bill, id. at 2336 (Feb. 16, 1960).

36/ Hearings on Federal Registrars, 363.

37/ For Senator Hennings' analysis of his plan, see Cong. Rec. 5198-9 (Mar. 15, 1960).

One of the chief advantages of the Hennings plan was that
judicial review would have been postponed until after the
casting of the ballot by the federally-qualified registrants.
Courts also would be empowered to issue injunctions in connection with the procedure. This proposal, like that favoring
a court-appointed referee, would apply to both Federal and
State elections. But like Senator Keating's proposal Senator
Hennings' never received much support.

IV. <u>House Action</u>:

On January 28, Rep. McCulloch (R-Ohio) introduced H.R. 10034, a duplicate of the Attorney General's January 26th draft. On February 9th and 16th the House Judiciary Committee held hearings on it and three similar bills.[38] Deputy Attorney General Walsh testified in behalf of the administration's proposal, emphasizing, for the most part, the fact that the referee plan would affect both Federal and State elections.

On February 16th, Mr. Walsh sent the Committee a new draft of the administration's bill which made various technical changes in the original bill. One week later, Rep. McCulloch introduced a revised bill, H.R. 10065, including these changes.[39] The original administration bill, H. R. 10035, had left the procedure to be followed by the referee completely to the discretion of the judge. Rep. McCulloch's revised bill, H.R. 10625, specified that the applicant should be heard before the referee in a non-adversary or ex parte proceeding. The revised bill further

---

[38] Hearings on Proposals for Voting Rights Before the House Committee on the Judiciary, 86th Cong., 2d Sess. (ser. No. 15). (Hereafter noted, <u>Hearings House Judiciary Committee</u>.)

[39] Cong. Rec. 3029, 3034 (Feb. 23, 1960).

set out the procedure before the referee, as described by
Rep. McCulloch: [40]

> "by specifying that the applicant's statement
> under oath 'shall be prima facie evidence as
> to his age, residence, and his prior efforts to
> register or otherwise qualify to vote' and that
> his written or oral answers given to prove his
> 'literacy' or 'understanding of other subjects'
> shall be included in the referee's report to the
> court."

When introducing this bill, Rep. McCulloch stated that he would
attempt to incorporate it as an amendment to H.R. 8601, the
original House Civil Rights bill. [41]

Between August 20, 1959, and February 18, 1960, H.R. 8601
remained in the Rules Committee without either referee or
registrar amendment. A petition to discharge that committee
of its jurisdiction had been introduced in August by Rep.
Celler and was gaining support. [42] But when only ten names
were lacking from the petition, the Rules Committee, on February
18th, decided to end its six-month blockade and refer H.R. 8601
to the floor. Rules Committee Chairman Smith (D-Va.) announced
that the bill would not be called up on the House floor until
March 10th and then only under a rule providing for 15 hours
of general debate before amendments could be offered. [43]

---

[40] Id. at 5091 (Mar. 14, 1960).

[41] Id. at 3030 (Feb. 23, 1960).

[42] 105 Cong. Rec. 17632, 17092, 18406, 18652. A total of 219
signatures, one more than half the House members is necessary.

[43] Cong. Rec. D124 (Feb. 18, 1960).

On March 10th, the House adopted the rule for debate
(312-93), resolved itself into the Committee of the whole
House on the State of the Union, and began its first full
consideration of H.R. 8601. [44]

General debate continued until March 14th, at which time
a number of amendments were offered to the bill. Rep. Lindsay
(R-N.Y.) offered as an amendment, the original referee proposal
(H.R. 10035), [45] which had been introduced on January 28, by
Rep. McCulloch as a separate bill. Then, H.R. 11160, described
as H.R. 10625 with improvements, was offered as a substitute
by Rep. McCulloch. [46] Although this substitute bill modified
the original administration proposal, it did not change its
fundamental approach. It added a provision that after a court
finding of a pattern or practice of discrimination, and before
applying to the referee, the applicant first must attempt to
register with the State official. The purpose of adding this
requirement was to insure "that the State will have the first
opportunity to correct its errors." [47] It further provided
that the referee must be a qualified voter of that judicial
district. Both of these additions are contained in the 1960
Act.

---

[44] Id. at 4696 (Mar. 10, 1960).

[45] Id. at 5079 (Mar. 14, 1960).

[46] Id. at 5080, 5113 (Mar. 14, 1960).

[47] Id. at 5081 (Mar. 14, 1960).

On March 15, Rep. Kastenmeier (D-Wis.) offered an amendment to Rep. McCulloch's substitute based on Sen. Hennings' earlier proposal for Federal enrollment officers. [48/] The events surrounding the vote on whether to adopt this as a substitute for Rep. McCulloch's referee bill vividly portray the tactics utilized during the debate. When the moment for the vote arrived, the Norther Democrats, advocating the amendment, and Republicans opposing it, filed down the aisle to indicate their preference. Rep. Smith (D-Va.) held back his group of Southern stalwarts as the vote neared a deadlock.

Finally, in a surprise move, [49/] the Southerners voted in favor of the ultra-liberal amendment, and it carried 152-128. [50/] But then on a vote as to whether to adopt this amendment as an amendment to H.R. 8601, Rep. Smith and his colleagues switched sides, joined the Republicans, and defeated the amendment 170-143. [51/] Rep. McCulloch then attempted to offer

---

48/ Id. at 5133 (Mar. 15, 1960).

49/ Anthony Lewis, writing in the N.Y. Times (Mar. 16, 1960) described the scene as follows:

> "Then, at the last moment Judge Smith nodded his head and marched down at the head of his troops. He touched the arm of the Democratic teller, Rep. Emanuel Celler of Brooklyn, an old foe, thus signaling that the Southerners were voting for the ultra-liberal amendment.
>
> Laughter and then applause rang through the House as the members and the reporters in the gallery realized what the Judge was up to."

50/ Cong. Rec. 5142 (Mar. 15, 1960).

51/ Id. at 5143 (Mar. 15, 1960).

a new substitute, [52] identical to H.R. 11160, with one change:
the previous bill specifically stated that the court was
authorized to direct voting referees to attend election places
and report whether persons qualified by the court to vote were
being denied that right. This was eliminated and instead a
provision was submitted that allowed the court to authorize
the referee "to take any other action appropriate or necessary
to carry out the provisions of this subsection and enforce its
decree." However, the clerk inadvertently read the amendment
without the change. Rep. Celler then re-offered the new
substitute containing the proper language. Rep. Smith argued
that this was out of order, since the provision was almost
identical to that already considered and defeated, but he was
in turn ruled out of order. [53]

The House now had before it a refined referee provision.
Created on January 26th, and first introduced two days later,
it had been modified by two Rep. McCulloch substitutes and
the final substitute offered by Rep. Celler. One final
modification in the House was offered and adopted on March 16th.
Proposed by Rep. O'Hara (R-Mich.), this section provided "that
in the case of any application filed 20 or more days prior to
an election which is undetermined by the time of such election
the court shall issue an order authorizing the applicant to

52/ Ibid.

53/ Id. at 5146 (Mar. 15, 1960).

vote provisionally." [54/] The purpose of this addition, was
to insure that judicial delay would not "nullify the right
to vote of those who had applied to the referee." [55/]

From this point, until the final passage of the act
one week later, a number of amendments designed to weaken the
referee section were discussed. On Friday, March 18, H.R.
8601 faced one of its severest tests. With a number of
Northern congressmen indulging in a long weekend, Rep. Budge
(R-Idaho) offered an amendment to limit the use of the
referee machinery to Federal elections only. [56/] Since one
of the chief assets of the referee proposal was its application to both State and Federal elections, this amendment
would have greatly reduced the referee's utility. It was
narrowly defeated by three votes. [57/]

On March 23, the House finally approved the referee proposal; [58/] the following day, H.R. 8601 passed the House
and was sent to the Senate.

At this point, H.R. 8601 included the following provisions: [59/]

54/ Id. at 5337 (Mar. 16, 1960). This provision was to cause
considerable argument in the Senate. See the following
section for further comment.

55/ Id. at 5337.

56/ Id. at 5582 (Mar. 18, 1960).

57/ Id. at 5593 (Mar. 18, 1960).

58/ Id. at 5943 (Mar. 23, 1960).

59/ Id. at 6039 (Mar. 24, 1960).

1. Criminal penalties against persons who obstruct Orders in school desegregation cases.

2. Criminal penalties against persons fleeing from one State to another to avoid prosecution for destroying any building.

3. A requirement that election officials retain records relating to primary or general elections for Federal officers for two years, and make them available to the Attorney General.

4. Federally-subsidized education for children of members of the Armed Forces where local schools are closed due to desegregation orders.

5. Voting referee machinery.

6. Authorization for members of the Commission on Civil Rights to administer oaths.

This last provision, although not included in President Eisenhower's original recommendations, appeared as part of H.R. 8601 as approved by the Judiciary Committee on August 20, 1959. It was originally part of that section extending the Commission for two years. When the extension was granted in 1959, this added authority remained as a separate title.

V. The Senate Debate:

As had been promised, February 15th marked the commence-
ment of the civil rights debate in the Senate. Without a
bill favorably reported from committee, Majority Leader Lyndon
Johnson (D-Tex.) called up a minor House-passed bill, H.R.
8315, and invited Senators to offer civil rights amendments.
This provoked a heated argument over Senate procedure, with
Southern Senators attempting to postpone any action. On
February 16, the Senate defeated Senator Russell's motion
(61-28) to delay consideration of civil rights legislation
for one week. [60]

The next day, Senator Dirksen (R-Ill.) introduced a series
of amendments to add a new title to H.R. 8315 to be known as
"Civil Rights Act of 1960." [61] For the next month, the Senate
debated the necessity and the constitutionality of civil
rights legislation. On February 29, the debate blossomed into
a full-fledged filibuster. During these around-the-clock
sessions, there were a total of 50 quorum calls, and 13 roll-
call votes, [62] and on March 8, the Senate was still officially
on the legislative day of February 15.

_____

[60] Id. at 2392 (Feb. 16, 1960).

[61] Id. at 2488 (Feb. 17, 1960).

[62] Congressional Quarterly. May 6, 1960. "Special Report,"
at 770.

On March 24, the Senate received the House-passed civil rights bill. It thereupon abandoned consideration of its own bill, and referred H.R. 8601 to the Committee on the Judiciary, with binding instructions to report it by midnight of March 29. [63/] The Committee's unusually short report neither favored nor opposed the referee plan. [64/] Four members of the Committee endorsed the Federal enrollment officers plan of Senator Hennings. [65/] The Committee adopted fifteen amendments, affecting every section of the bill, the most substantial being that of Senator Kefauver (D-Tenn.) adopted 7-6. The bill as it was passed by the House provided:

> In a proceeding before a voting referee, the applicant shall be heard ex parte.

The Kefauver amendment "would change the procedure from an ex parte proceeding to provide that the hearing shall be held in a public place and the referee shall give the county or State registrar two days' written notice of the time and place of the hearing, and the State or county registrar or his counsel shall have a right to appear..." [66/] The purpose of this amendment was said to insure public hearings and to avoid what some labeled as a possible "Star Chamber" proceeding.

63/ Cong. Rec. 5982-5 (Mar. 24, 1960).

64/ Senate Report No. 1205, Mar. 29, 1960. 86th Cong., 2nd Sess.

65/ The four were Senators Hennings, Hart, Dodd, and Carroll. See Senate Report No. 1205, Part 2, Apr. 1, 1960.

66/ Cong. Rec. 6415 (Mar. 30, 1960). (Remarks of Sen. Keating.)

A number of Senators, notably Senators Javits, Carroll, and Douglas, vigorously opposed the Kefauver amendment. On April 1, the Senate adopted a substitute amendment introduced by Senator Carroll (D-Colo.). The clause now read:

> In a proceeding before a voting referee, the applicant shall be heard ex parte at such times and places as the court shall direct.

This language offered by Senator Carroll (underscored above) was designed to remove any impression that the hearings were to be clandestine. [67]

On April 7, the Senate adopted a second important amendment to the referee provision. The House had adopted the O'Hara amendment providing that in the case of an individual applying 20 or more days before an election, if his application was still pending by election day, the court must allow him to vote provisionally. Some Southern congressmen particularly objected to this clause, [68] contending that it would supplant State laws that require registration 30 or 60 days before the day of election. They arued this would be giving Negroes

---

[67] Id. at 6432, also 6624-5 (Apr. 1, 1960). (Remarks of Sen. Carroll) for adoption of Carroll Amendment. See Id. at 6640. (Apr. 1, 1960).

[68] Id. at 5339 (Mar. 16, 1960); remarks of Rep. Smith (D-Va.) See also id. at 7007 and 7015 (Apr. 7, 1960) remarks of Sen. Ellender (D-La.) and Sen. Robertson (D-Va.).

an unfair advantage over whites. This provision was there-

fore amended by the added qualification: [69]

> Provided, however, that such applicant shall
> be qualified to vote under State law.

Two of the sponsors disagreed on the meaning of this

proviso. Senator Carroll (D-Colo.) argued that if there be

a court finding of a pattern or practice of discrimination,

even in a suit commenced after expiration of the registration

period, an otherwise qualified applicant would nevertheless

be permitted to vote. He presented this situation: [70]

> "Let us assume that 10 or 15 or 20 people
> came into a Federal Court of equity ot protect
> their constitutional rights under this law.
> Suppose they get a decree that there is a pat-
> tern or practice of discrimination."

He then posed this query to the chamber:

> "Do Senators believe that a federal court
> is going to allow any registration law to
> stand in their way if they have been victims
> of a pattern or practice of discrimination
> perhaps by the maladministration of these
> very same laws?"

---

[69] For evidence of the confusion in the Senate at the time
of the vote, See id. at 7061. The provision was adopted
by a vote of 70-12; most Southern Senators voted for the
amendment, while Sens. Javits, Keating, Hart, Humphrey,
and Douglas were among those voting against it.

[70] Cong. Rec. 7059 (Apr. 7, 1960).

Senator Dirksen disagreed, stating that the 20-day provision
would not supersede a State law requiring registration in 30
or 60 days before an election. [71]

Before the House passed the Senate amended bill, Reps.
O'Hara, McCulloch, and Lindsay engaged in a colloquy designed
to establish the legislative intent. Rep. Lindsay asked Rep.
O'Hara: [72]

> "Does the gentlmen from Michigan contemplate
> that an applicant before the Federal court must
> have attempted to register within the time per-
> mitted by State law even when registration has
> been closed before the court finds the pattern
> or practice of discrimination?" (Emphasis added)

This was answered as follows:

> "When a court finds a pattern or practice of
> discrimination it has also, in effect, found
> that it would have been futile for the appli-
> cant to have attempted to register at any
> time prior thereto, and, if registration had
> already closed, the applicant has had no
> opportunity to meet any such requirement after
> the finding of a pattern or practice of
> discrimination."

Rep. O'Hara continued:

> "Since this is a suit in equity, equitable
> doctrine should apply, including the rule that
> persons asking relief need not have attempted
> a clearly futile act as a condition precedent
> to receiving relif. ...I believe that the
> court could and should examine the circum-
> stances in each case and not exact a require-
> ment of prior application to the local offi-
> cials within the time permitted by state law."

71/ Id. at 7060 (Apr. 7, 1960).

72/ Id. at 7896 (Apr. 21, 1960).

Sens. Javits and Keating (both R-N.Y.) voted against the amendment stating that a court might construe the clause to provide an occasion for a full-scale trial on the applicant's qualifications. [73/]   Sen. Javits also believe that a court might say: [74/]

> "I am sorry; I cannot find that this applicant is qualified. I have not had enough of a trial. I have not had enough time or heard enough evidence. And, not withstanding that the law says I shall issue an order authorizing an applicant to vote provisionally, I cannot meet this particular provision that I find that the appli- is qualified to vote."

Also during the final week of Senate debate, the following major changes to the House bill as recommended by the Judiciary Committee were adopted:

1. Broadening Title I, Obstruction of School Orders, to include any Federal court order. This, the Lausche Amendment, was approved by the Senate on March 30. [75/]

2. Eliminating a provision that would make it a criminal offense to give false bomb tips. [76/]

73/ Id. at 7057-59 (Apr. 7, 1960).

74/ Id. at 7056 (Apr. 7, 1960).

75/ Id. at 6452 (Mar. 30, 1960).

3. Reducing the time period for retention of election records from two years to twenty-two months. [77/]

4. Requiring the Attorney General to examine election records in the office of the election officials, instead of making the local official take the records to a place designated by the Attorney General. The purpose of this change was to lighten the financial burden of local officials in routine cases. [78/]

5. Making it a crime to transport explosives with the knowledge that they will be used to destroy a building. [79/]

On April 7, the bill as amended was read for a third time and ordered to be engrossed. [80/] The following day the formal end to the 1960 Senate civil rights debate was marked by the passage of the bill, 71-18.

77/ The reason for this change turned on the use of the containers in which ballots are stored. Since the containers are needed for elections every two years, the 60-day grace period allows the officials sufficient time to dispose of the ballots, instead of requiring purchase of a new container by every election district in the county. See remarks of Sen. Hruska id. at 6452.

78/ Id. at 6454 remarks of Sen. Hruska.

79/ Id. at 6452 (Mar. 30, 1960).

80/ Id. at 7071 (Apr. 7, 1960).

Retracing its steps, H.R. 8601 was sent back to the House and referred to the Rules Committee. On April 21, the House approved the bill, and on May 6, 1960, the measure was signed into law by President Eisenhower.

Bibliography

VOTING REFEREE PROVSISION

1. Hearings on Federal Registrars Before the Senate Committee on Rules and Administration. 86th Cong., 2d Sess. 1960 (Attorney General's Press Release, p. 167).

2. Hearings on Voting Rights Before the House Committee on the Judiciary. 86th Cong., 2d Sess. ser. No. 15, 1960.

3. Hearings on Civil Rights Act of 1960 Before the Senate Committee on the Judiciary. 86th Cong., 2d Sess., 1960.

4. U.S. Code Congressional and Administrative News. (Advance Sheet) No. 5; April 20, 1960. pp. i-iii (yellow sheets).

5. Id., No. 6. May 5, 1960. pp. 9-51 (blue sheets). Senate Report No. 1205 and House Report No. 956 (to accompany H.R. 8601).

6. Congressional Quarterly. Weekly Report No. 8. (Week ending 2/19/60).

7. Id., Special Report on Civil Rights Legislation. Supplement to May 6, 1960 weekly report.

8. Proceedings of the Civil Rights Conference at the Notre Dame Law School, February 14, 1960. Reprinted in the Congressional Record, p. A1706 et seq.

9. Notre Dame Lawyer. "Notre Dame Conference on Civil Rights", by Harris Wofford, Jr., p. 328. May 1960.

10. "Report on the Administration's Civil Rights Proposals." Department of Justice's mimeographed blue book. Undated /Confidential Source.7

11. Memorandum by Norman J. Small, dated 3/10/60. "Comments on Certain issues submitted as Likely to Arise in the Administration of an Pertaining to the Validity of Proposed "Voting Referee" Registration."

12. New York Times. April 22, 1960. p. 1.

13. California Law Review. Vol. 48, No. 2. May 1960. "Federal Remedies for Voteless Negores." by Ira Michael Heyman.

14. Catholic University Law Review. May 1960.

VI. The Voting Referee Provision

A. The Procedure:

The voting referee provision is in the form of an amendment to the 1957 Civil Rights Act. Before any person can benefit by this section, the Attorney General must first bring an action under the 1957 Act, 42 U.S.C. 1971 (c), [81] to enjoin a State registrar from discriminating against voters because of their race or color. Subsection (b) of the referee section allows the suit to be brought against the State if the local registrar resigns or "has been relieved of his office." [82]

Under the terms of the 1957 Act, the Attorney General may bring such an action "whenever . . . there are reasonable grounds to believe that any person is about to engage /or has engaged7 in any act or practice which would deprive any other person . . ." of his right to vote because of his race or

---

[81] See U.S. v. Raines, __ U.S. __ , (1960)(constitutionality of this section upheld as applied to racial discrimination by State officials).

[82] This subsection resolves the issue presented in U.S. v. Alabama, __ U.S. __ , (1960). The United States had brought an action under the 1957 Act against the members of the Macon County (Ala.) Board of Registrars. When they resigned, the State of Alabama was joined as a defendant. A Federal district court held (171 F. Supp 720) that the State was not a "person" who could be sued under the act. (aff'd 267 F. 2d 808). The United States Supreme Court decided the case after the enactment of the 1960 Civil Rights Act, holding that the State could be joined as a party defendant.

color. [83/] In such a proceeding, the Attorney General would cite in the complaint the names of certain individuals deprived of their right to vote because of their race or color. [84/] The injunction sought by the Attorney General would not be limited to protection of the individuals so named, but would enjoin the defendants from continuing to engage in discriminatory practices "in any other case of any other individual even those not named in the lawsuit." [85/] Once the injunction is issued, the named individuals, and all other qualified voters should be allowed to register and vote. [86/]

If the court finds that there has been a denial of voting rights because of racial discrimination, and the Attorney General so requests, the court "shall" make a finding as to whether the discrimination was "pursuant to a pattern or practice." Presumably the court would issue an injunction under the 1957 Act when it finds a denial, but it is possible that the injunction might be issued at a later date. The issuance

---

83/ 71 Stat. 634.

84/ See remarks of Attorney General Rogers. Hearings on H.R. 8601 Before the Senate Committee on the Judiciary, 86th Cong., 2d Sess., 52-53 (March 28-29, 1960). (Hereafter noted, Hearings, Senate Judiciary Committee.)

85/ Id. at 53.

86/ Id. at 76. (Testimony of Deputy Attorney General Walsh.)

of an injunction is not, however, a condition precedent to the
finding of a pattern or practice. The finding of a pattern
or practice follows from the finding that there has been a
denial of the right to vote because of race or color.

If the court finds a pattern or practice of discrimination
to exist, then persons of the same race or color as those who
were found to have been discriminated against, and who reside
in the area administered by that election official, may apply
to the court for an order declaring them qualified to vote
in "any election", State or Federal. [87]

Persons seeking such an order may apply for at least
one year after the finding of a pattern or practice, "and
thereafter until the court finds that such a pattern has
ceased." The court order will be issued "upon proof" by the
applicant,

1. That he is qualified to vote under State law;

2. That he has tried to register since the court
   finding of a pattern or practice, but;

3. That he has been deprived of the opportunity
   to register or has been found not to be qualified
   "by a person acting under color of law."

---

[87] The Act states: "Such order shall be effective as to any
election held within the longest period for which such
applicant could have been registered or otherwise qualified
under State law at which the applicants' qualifications
would under State law entitle him to vote."

Applicants may be heard by the court itself, or the
court in its discretion may appoint one or more qualified
voters in that judicial district, to be known as voting
referees who will have "all the powers conferred upon a
master by Rule 53(c) of the Federal Rules of Civil Procedure."[88]
These referees would in effect perform the same duties as the
State registrar, that is they would test the applicants as to
literacy and review other qualifications for voting prescribed
by State law.

---

[88] Rule 53 (c) states in part: "Subject to the specifications
and limitations in the order, the master has and shall exercise the power to regulate all proceedings in every hearing
before him and to do all acts and take all measures necessary or proper for the efficient performance of his duties
under the order. He may require the production . . . of
all books, papers, vouchers, documents and writings. . . .
He may rule on the admissibility of evidence . . . and has
the authority to put witnesses on oath and may himself
examine them and may call the parties of the action and
examine them upon oath. . ."

In effect, The 1960 referee provision broadens the scope

of Rule 53 which permits the appointment of masters only

in limited situations.

Rule 53 (a) provides in part: "Each district court with
concurrence of a majority of all the judges thereof, may
appoint one or more . . . masters. . ."

Rule 53 (b) States: "A reference to a master shall be
the exception and not the rule. In actions to be tried by
a jury, a reference shall be made only when the issues
are complicated; in actions to be tried without a jury,
save in matters of account, a reference shall be made
only upon a showing that some exceptional condiction
requires it."

If a referee is appointed, applicants are to be heard in an ex parte proceeding, to be held "at such times and places as the court shall direct." This is to be a non-adversary hearing, "without notice to the other side."[89] However, since the court would have to notify the applicants of the time and place of the hearing (possibly by advertisement), the other side would in all probability obtain the same information. But, even if defendant is present, there is to be no cross-examination and he has no right to be heard.

The referee is to assist the court by making preliminary findings. But, as has been noted, the court is not required to utilize the referee procedure. If the court does not a appoint a referee but hears the applicant itself, it is not clear whether its own hearing would be ex parte. In either case, the act provides that whether or not a referee is appointed, applications are to be heard within ten days and are to be determined "expeditiously."

Those persons seeking a court order to enable them to vote, must come before the referee or the court at the designated time and place. They must show that they are qualified to vote but have been denied the opportunity to register, or else have been found not qualified, since the finding by the court of a pattern or practice of discrimination. Presumably, applicants must also show that they are of the same race or

---

89/ Cong. Rec. 6626 (Apr. 1, 1960); remarks of Senator Javits.

color as those the court found to have been discriminated against. The applicant's statement under oath "shall be prima facie evidence as to his age, residence, and his prior efforts to register or otherwise to qualify to vote." However, the applicant need not show that the reason he was denied his right to vote was on account of his race or color. This is conclusively presumed [90]/ from the finding of a pattern or practice of discrimination, the fact that he is of the same race or color as those against whom the discrimination exists, and the fact that although he is qualified to vote, he has been denied the opportunity to register since the finding off a pattern or practice, Deputy Attorney General Walsh stated that Congress was justified in establishing the conclusive presumption that the pattern or practice of discrimination

---

[90]/ "A legislative presumption" according to Rep. McCulloch; Cong. Rec. 5081 (Mar. 14, 1960). See also testimony of Deputy Attorney General Walsh. Hearings on Voting Rights Before the House Committee on the Judiciary, 86th Cong., 2d Sess., ser. no. 15, at 21. (Hereafter Noted, Hearings, House Judiciary Committee).

91/

was the basis for the denial.

If the referee conducts a hearing, he must report to the court which applicants are qualified under State law but have been deprived the opportunity to register or were found not qualified. Where the State requires a literacy test, the applicant's statements given to prove his literacy are to be included in the referee's report. When it receives the report, "the court shall cause the Attorney General to transmit a copy thereof to the State attorney general" and to all appropriate State officials, with an order to show cause "why an order of the court should not be entered in accordance with such a report." If the court itself holds the hearing, it would presumably draft findings of fact and transmit them in the same way. The defendants then have ten

---

91/ During the Hearing before the House Judiciary Committee, Walsh testified:

"If you found a pattern or practice against Negroes and (t)he (applicant) is a Negro, I think Congress is justi-fied in jumping the gap and establishing a conclusive presumption that that is the reason for his troubles."

Congressman Celler then asked:

"You mean that Congress can justify that presumption?"

Walsh answered as follows:

"Yes, sir. I think it is a reasonable presumption. I think if you have had a pattern found, the like-lihood of any other reason for refusing to let him register even though he was qualified is nil . . .

"Not only is it reasonable, but it is necessary, because for an individual to prove (in) each case that he had been a victim of prejudice is very difficult. Therefore, I think he needs Congress' help in that regard." Hearings, id. at 21.

days "or such shorter time as the court may fix" to challenge

the report. A memorandum of law must accompany exceptions to

matters of law. Exceptions to all matters of fact must be

accompanied by a "verified copy of a public record or by affi-

davit of persons having personal knowledge of such facts."

A hearing on an issue of fact shall be held only if the proof

so offered presents "a genuine issue of material fact." [92]

There might be an issue of fact if the defendant contests the

applicant's age, residence, prior efforts to register or vote

or literacy. As to his literacy, however, no additional

evidence can be offered before the judge either by direct or

on cross-examination because the statute states that the

applicants literacy shall be determined solely on the basis

of his answers to the referee. The defendants might contend

that the applicant's answers given before the referee do not

establish his literacy, but he cannot be retested again in

court. "The applicant is to have no opportunity to expand

/his answers/ ... and say something new before the judge,

neither is he to be cross-examined before the judge . . ." [93]

regarding the substance of his answers before the referee.

---

[92] This is the same standard provided in Rule 56 (c) of the
Federal Rules of Civil Proceudre for a motion for a summary judgment.

[93] Hearings, Senate Judiciary Committee. 45; (remarks of
Deputy Attorney General Walsh.)

Presumably, however, the applicant could be required to testify again as to his age, residence, or prior efforts to vote, if a genuine issue of fact has been raised as to any of these points.

Under the original administration bill, the court was to accept the findings in the voting referee's report, "unless clearly erroneous." This standard, part of Rule 53 of the Federal Rules of Civil Procedure, was deleted in one of the earlier revisions. 94/ The act does not state what standard of proof must now be applied in ruling on exceptions to referee's findings. The burden of proof, however, will be on the State and the standard is possibly lower than that of "clearly erroneous".

If the State does not challenge the referee's findings within ten days, or if exceptions are filed but the court after a review is satisfied with the findings, then the court shall enter an order pursuant to the report, specifying those persons qualified to vote. The Attorney General is to transmit copies of this order to the local election officials. A refusal by the State or local officials to permit such persons to vote "shall constitute contempt of court." 95/

94/ For a most valuable chart depicting the major changes in referee bill, see Cong. Rec. 5851 (Mar. 22, 1960).

95/ See remarks of Rep. McCulloch. Id. at 5082 (Mar. 14, 1960).

The court order will be effective for as long a period as the applicant would have been qualified to vote if registered under State law.

The court, or the referee, "shall" issue to each applicant who has been declared qualified, a certificate, identifying the holder as the person so qualified. The exact form of these certificates is not prescribed in the act.

The court may authorize the referee "to take any other action, appropriate or necessary to carry out the provisions of this subsection and to enforce its decrees." Under this provision, a referee could be authorized to be present at the balloting and to make sure that the ballot is counted. 96/

If an application filed 20 or more days prior to an election is challenged and remains undetermined by election day, "the court shall issue an order authorizing the applicant to vote provisionally:

96/ This clause in the referee section might cause some speculation. It is not entirely clear whether the referee could get an injunction from the court if the applicant is intimidated or refused the right to vote by the local registrar. It would seem certain that the referee could get the Department of Justice to prosecute for obstruction of a court order, or he might seek the aid of a U.S. marshall. But it would appear that if the local election official disobeys the court order in the referee's presence, then this would be a violation in the court's presence. Therefore, it might be argued that the court could summarily punish the official without a jury.

Provided, however, that such applicant shall be qualified to vote under State law." In such cases, the applicant's ballot is to be impounded pending final determination of his application. [97/]

B. Analysis:

A number of views have been expressed as to whether the referee provision will prove to be effective. It is not the purpose of this analysis to weigh the various criticisms, but rather to point out certain aspects of the referee provision that may create problems when the section is utilized.

1. Pattern or Practice:

The finding by a court that a pattern or practice of discrimination exists is the key to the referee section. If the Attorney General is successful in a proceeding under the 1957 Act, and if the Attorney General so requests, it is mandatory on the court to make a finding as to whether a pattern or practice exists. Some critics have raised doubts as to the effectiveness of this mandatory instruction to the court. Senator Hennings (D-Mo.) argued that under article III of the Constitution, [98/]

97/ For a discussion of the provisional voting section, see supra at 24-26.

98/ Cong. Rec. 4850 (Mar. 11, 1960); (memorandum of Senator Hennings).

"Congress may not impose upon the courts an
obligation to render any decisions which are
not necessary to the resolution of a case or
controversy which has been properly brought
before it."

The Department of Justice takes the view that the original d

decree does not end the case or controversy, since in such

a suit the case or controversy arises from the public interest

to insure complete freedom from discrimination. The Depart-

ment argues that the primary purpose of such a proceeding

"is not necessarily to redress grievances of specific iddi-

viduals . . ." but rather "to pry open to non-discriminatory

voting an area that has been closed by the illegal acts of

the defendants." 99/

Professor Harris Wofford cites a more practical obstacle.

He questions whether a southern judge would make such a finding

even if requested. 100/

"Some of the Federal district judges in the very
black belt areas of the Deep South which are
most involved are southerners who share many of
the attitudes of the local officials for whom a
substitute is required . . . .

Considerable court resistance to finding of . . .
a pattern over and above a finding of discrimination in individual instances can be expected."

99/ "Report on the Administration's Civil Rights Proposals."
(Department of Justice's mimeographed Blue Book, undated.)
/Confidential Source.7

100/ Cong. Rec. A1706 (Feb. 29, 1960); (reprint of the proceedings
of the Congerence on Civil Rights at the Notre Dame Law
School on Feb. 14, 1960).

Requiring certain of these judges to make a finding of a pattern or practice, comments Professor Wofford, "provides a second opportunity for any judicial bias against civil rights suits . . . to manifest itself."[101]

An even more difficult problem is the meaning of the words "pattern or practice." Testifying before the Senate Rules Committee, Attorney General Rogers stated that the issue regarding the pattern or practice has to be one that the judge is convinced is "not moot."[102] Later, Deputy Attorney General Walsh explained to the House Judiciary Committee,[103]

> "Pattern or practice would have their generic meanings. In other words the court finds that the discrimination was not an isolated or accidental or perculiar event; that it was an event which happened in the regular procedures followed by the state officials concerned."

Senator Keating (R-N.Y.) defined pattern or practice as "not merely an isolated instance of racial discrimination."[104]

101/ Wofford, "Notre Dame Conference on Civil Rights," 35 Notre Dame Lawyer 342-43 (1960). This same objection is noted by Heyman, "Federal Remedies for Voteless Negroes." 48 Calif. L. Rev. (1960).

102/ Hearings on Federal Registrars, 354.

103/ Hearings, House Judiciary Committee, 13.

104/ Cong. Rec. 7223 (Apr. 8, 1960).

He then cited four examples of what would constitute a pattern or practice within the meaning of the act: [105/]

> "A challenging system which operated to strike
> Negroes from the voting rolls while leaving
> enrolled white persons who were equally subject
> to challenge would constitute a pattern or
> practice of discrimination. Similarly, if State
> registration officials applied more stringent
> qualification tests to Negroes than to white
> citizens, or attempted to frustrate Negro enroll-
> ment by failing to hold registration sessions,
> such dereliction of duty would constitute a pat-
> tern or practice. Moreover, a single act such
> as enactment of a statute directed at Negroes
> would in itself constitute a pattern or practice
> of discrimination."

2. Qualifications of the Applicant:

a) Prior Registration

Critics of the referee provision maintain that requiring the Negro to attempt to register with the local officials after the court finding of a pattern and before coming to the referee will render the whole procedure ineffective. Senator Hart (D-Mich.) has stated that the referee provision will cause only "delay, danger, and discrouagement:" [106/] "delay" from the slow process to which the Negroes have been

---

105/ The Department of Justice's mimeographed Blue Book states:

> "A conclusion that a pattern or practice exists would
> involve the finding that the racially discriminatory
> treatment engaged in by the defendants was more normal
> than extraordinary--the rule not the exception. Cf.
> Snowden v. Hughes, 321 U.S. 1. For example, . . ."

It then proceeds to cite the first three examples noted

by Senator Keating.

106/ Cong. Rec. 4853 (Mar. 10, 1960).

and probably will be subjected in trying to register; "danger"[107]
from possible economic reprisals[108] and excessive publicity;
and "discouragement" from the inevitable delays and possible
dangers. For these reasons, the requirement has been cited
as a very likely deterrent to effective application of the law.[109]

The statute itself clearly specifies that the applicant
must have attempted to register "since" the finding of a pattern
or practice and before applying to the court. But a review
of the Congressional debated and hearings raises some doubts
as to whether this will always be required. At one point Attorney
General Rogers seemed to indicate that this would be a mandatory
requirement:[110]

107/ As Senator Douglas put it: "The weak Negro must first
apply to what is generally a hostile set of registrars."
Cong. Rec. 5336 (Mar. 15, 1960).

108/ Recently, the NAACP reported that Negroes in Fayette County
(Tenn.) were suffering economic reprisals for attempting to
register to vote. See Jackson (Miss.) Clarion-Ledger,
July 17, 1960, sec. 5, p. 20. On September 13, 1960, the
Justice Department brought suit in Memphis under the 1957
Civil Rights Act charging 27 persons and 2 banks in Hay-
wood County (Tenn.) with using economic pressures to keep
Negroes from voting. (Haywood County neighbors Fayette
County.) N.Y. Times, September 14, 1960. p.1, 46.

109/ Heyman, op. cit. supra note 22.

110/ Hearings, Senate Judiciary Committee, 58.

"after the order enjoining State officials from discriminating was made by the court, that /those/ Negroes who are not involved in the litigation would be required to attempt to vote, attempt to register with State officials, and if they were denied that right then they would go to a referee." (Emphasis added.)

But these proceedings are before an equity court, and a maxim of equity is that a vain or futile act will not be required. If the pattern or practice of discrimination is of such a nature that it would be pointless (if not dangerous) for a Negro to attempt to register, will a court insist on this requirement? Deputy Attorney General Walsh stated that in such a situation a court might dispense with it, [111/] noting that the act states:

> This subsection shall in no way be construed as a limitation upon the existing powers of the court. So too, if the time for registration had terminated, and the registration books were closed, the court probably would not require an impossible act.

However, there are convincing arguments in the legislative history that the requirement is mandatory. Judge Walsh himself stated that this step in the procedure is "the heart of the bill's equity." [112/] And sponsors of the referee bill pointed out that this requirement gives the State an opportunity to correct its errors, [113/] the presumption being that local registrars will abide by the original court injunction. With this provision in the bill having such importance, it is conceivable

---

111/ Id. at 66.

112/ Id. at 63.

113/ Cong. Rec. 5081 (Mar. 10, 1960);(remarks of Rep. McCulloch).

that a court will insist that an applicant attempt to register before coming to the court.

If this requirement is not waived, what must the individual have done in trying to register? The act states that he must show that since such a court finding he has been denied or deprived of an opportunity to vote or found not to be qualified by a local official. This clearly implies that he must have attempted to register. But does it mean that if a county conducts registration for Negroes at a very slow rate, the candidate must stand in line day after day until he is admitted into the registration room? [114] And what if the registration board neglects to notify Negroes whether they have passed? How long must a Negro wait for an answer until it can be presumed that he has been found not qualified? And what happens if a registration board has resigned and has not as yet been replaced? [115] A court might make the applicant await the reappointment of a registration board and give the new board the prior opportunity to register the voter.

_____

[114] William P. Mitchell of the Tuskegee (Ala.) Civic Association states that the present policy of the Macon County registrars is to take application only from one Negro citizen per registration day. See Birmingham (Ala.) News. July 21, 1960 p. 46.

[115] See Gomillion v. Lightfoot. 270 F. 2d 594 (5th Cir. 1959).

b) Proof of Qualifications:

Another difficulty might arise from proving to a biased referee or judge that the applicant has tried to register but has been denied, and is qualified under State law to vote. Just as Professor Wofford has pointed out that the judge might indulge in "judicial bias", it is possible that the referee might be as biased as the local election officials and apply the laws just as stringently.

3. Possibility of Delay:

Some critics of the referee provision argue that its major shortcoming will prove to be the number of delays, inherent in the judicial process. [116] To a great extent this problem turns on the number and timing of the appeals that may be taken during the proceeding.

Essentially, there are six steps in the judicial process of the referee section:

Step One: The court may find that an individual's right to vote has been denied because of his race or color. On the basis of this finding, either simultaneously or at a later date, the court will ordinarily issue an injunction (pursuant to the provision of the 1957 Act) to enjoin such further deprivations.

116/ See discussion supra, p. 40.

Step Two: If the court finds such denial, and if requested by the Attorney General, it must find whether this discrimination was pursuant to a pattern or practice.

Step Three: Assuming the finding of a pattern or practice the court may, in its discretion, appoint a voting referee to make preliminary findings.

Step Four: The referee must receive any applications and conduct ex parte hearings to determine which of the applicants are qualified to vote. The referee reports his preliminary findings to the court, and the parties to the proceeding are notified of his findings. (If no referee is appointed, the court itself would make all findings and notice would be given to all parties in the same fashion.)

Step Five: After giving both parties an opportunity to present exceptions to the preliminary findings (whether of the referee or of the court itself) and if appropriate, holding a hearing upon such exceptions, the court will enter an order upon the basis of the preliminary findings. If any exceptions to the preliminary findings have been successfully presented, the court may modify the preliminary findings or discard them altogether.

<u>Step Six</u>: The court may take any other action and may
authorize the referee to take any other action
appropriate or necessary to carry out its
orders.

a) Delays Inherent in the Litigation:

The proceedings under 1960 Act, like any judicial proceeding,
will be subject to certain inevitable delays. Aside from the
necessary time that would elapse between the receipt of a complaint by the Department of Justice and the actually filing
of a suit under the act, there will be at least a delay of
twenty days between the filing of a complaint and the defendant's
answer. Pretrial discovery, and preliminary motions might well
cause additional delay before the trial actually commences.
Between the start of the trial and the court's determination
there will be a further lapse of days or possibly weeks. Even
more time may be taken up in presenting proof and argument on
the request for findings as to a pattern or practice; and there
may also be an argument on the request to appoint a referee.

Applications must be heard within ten days and "determined
expeditiously." If the provision for a referee is utilized,
he must prepare his preliminary findings and submit them to
the court. Ten days (or perhaps less) then elapse to allow
the defendant time to file exceptions. Further time presumably
would elapse before holding a hearing on the exceptions and
before the court issues an order upon the basis of the hearings.

These steps may be condensed and expedited to some degree, and the arrangement for provisional voting may cure some of the ills of undue judicial delay. But in many cases it can be expected that the whole process may be a lengthy one, and in some cases this delay may be extended by the use of delaying procedural tactics. The true effectiveness of the referee section may very well hinge on the period of time that the entire process will take.

b) The Right to Appeal:

Important to this analysis is a recognition of the fact that there are different individuals concerned in the initial and final steps. At Step One, the Attorney General is seeking an injunction under the 1957 Civil Rights Act "whenever any person has engaged or there are reasonable grounds to believe that any person is about to engage in any act or practice which would deprive any other person" of his right to vote. In the event an injunction is issued, it would be directed against a particular person or persons for example against registrar X of a specific district. In such a suit, individuals who have been deprived their right to vote are not formal parties, although they might be mentioned by name in the complaint. However, an additional purpose of this procedure is to lay a basis for assisting other persons similarly denied their right to vote because of their race or color, but not as yet identified to the court. Once the court finds that this discrimination was pursuant to a pattern or practice (Step Two),

other persons, not directly involved in Step One, may apply
to the court for an order declaring them qualified to vote.
If the court chooses to appoint a referee (Step Three), the
referee will receive applications, conduct ex parte hearings,
and report to the court those found to be entitled to a court
order. (Step Four). After hearing the defendant's exceptions
to the preliminary findings of the referee, the court will
then enter its own findings and issue an order specifying
those qualified (Step Five). Additionally, the court may take
any other steps necessary to carry out its order (Step Six).
Clearly, when the court issues its order at Step Five, it
might, at that time, include supplemental orders, which would
then become part of the Step Five order.

The injunction issued at Step One goes against only the
person engaged in the discriminatory practice, (probably the
local State registrar). The court order at Step Five on the
other hand, is effective against any State official who has
notice of the order. Any official with notice of the order
who refuses to honor the order, would be in contempt of court.
In any case brought pursuant to this section, the State may
be joined as a party defendant. Throughout this proceeding,
therefore, the parties remain constant (U.S. v. State Y or
Registrar Y) while the individuals concerned vary from Step
One to Step Five.

If either the Attorney General or the defendant desires to appeal at any time during this process, it must do so at one of the above identified steps.

a) At Step One, the court may find that one or more persons have been denied their right to vote. This is a mere finding by a court, and an appeal would not appear to be allowed from such a finding. Title 28 U.S.C. 1291 (1958) provides for appeal only from "final decisions of the district courts," except in specified circumstances not material here. This section has been interpreted by the Supreme Court "to disallow appeal from any decision which is tentative, informal or incomplete." [117] However, if this finding is implemented by an injunction, that would appear to be a final order and therefore an appeal would lie at that moment. Likewise, if the court refused to grant an injunction, and refused to find any instance of discrimination, that would be a final decision and an appeal could be taken by the U.S. Attorney General. Furthermore, if the court found discrimination as to A, B, and C, but no discrimination as to D, an appeal as to A, B, or C by the State and as to D by the Attorney General would be permissible when an order was issued. However, the issuance or refusal to issue an injunction at Step One, is but one phase of the entire procedure outlined in the act. The Supreme Court has stated that section 1291 does not:[118]

---

[117] Cohen v. Beneficial Industrial Loan Corp. 337 U.S. 541, 546 (1949).

[118] Ibid.

> "permit appeals, even from fully consummated decisions, where they are but steps towards a final judgment in which they will merge. The purpose is to combine in one review all stages of the proceedings that effectively may be reviewed and corrected if and when final judgment results."

Since in this process, there must be a Step One before there can be a Step Two, Three, Four, or Five, a court might envision the whole process to be one proceeding, and therefore allow only one appeal at the end of Step Five. However, this would be most unlikely, for a Step One injunction would be a final decision as to the particular persons cited in the complaint and as to the particular persons thereby enjoined.

Significant to this discussion, is a consideration of whether an appeal, if allowed at Step One, would actually result in any "judicial delay." Such delay, if any, would result not from the appeal itself but from a stay of the order or a stay of further proceedings (or both). The grant of a stay in proceedings is discretionary on the court and not automatic.[119] If a stay of the order were granted, it might be limited in such a fashion as to allow the original complainants to vote, at least to vote provisionally, in an election taking place before final determination of appeal.[120]

119/ See Masses Publishing Company v. Patten, 245 F. 102; there is some authority that once an appeal is considered, the trial court is without jurisdiction to proceed further until there has been an appellate determination. See Rogers v. Consolidated Rock Products, Inc. 114 F. 2d 108 (9th Cir. 1940).

120/ See Remarks of Attorney General Rogers. Hearings, Senate Judiciary Committee. 26

If an appeal were allowed, it might attack the findings but a stay in proceedings might only go to the order of the court, i.e., the injunction. It should be noted that the successive steps are dependent not on the issuance of an injunction, but on the finding of a denial. There would be a public interest not to halt all proceedings at Step One, since a principal interest is to assist other applicants at Step Five. If a stay were issued, it would probably be entered by the Court of Appeals, although the trial court could grant it itself.

2) At Step Two the court makes a finding as to whether the discrimination was pursuant to a pattern or practice. Since this would be only a finding, it should not in itself be appealable. However, the evidence as to pattern or practice would in large part have been presented in the original trial. Such additional evidence as was necessary to establish the pattern or practice could also probably be presented in that trial. If this were done, then the determination as to pattern or practice could be obtained at the same time as the determination of individual discrimination. In such a case, the two determinations would be appealable simultaneously - when the Step One injunction is issued. From a tactical point of view, it may be desirable to combine the proof on the two points (individual discrimination and pattern or practice) in the same trial. For one thing, this would save

time by avoiding separate hearings. For another, it would allow the Attorney General to get an early determination of pattern or practice, before any appeal has been taken (and to get this determination reviewed at an early state). And finally, it might avoid constitutional problems as to whether the finding of pattern or practice is within the "case or controversy" requirement of article III of the Constitution.

If at Step One the court does not issue an order, but merely finds a denial and finds that the denial was pursuant to a pattern or practice, then, since such a finding would not be a final order, it would not be appealable. If at either Step One or Step Two, the court finds that there was no pattern or practice of discrimination, the Attorney General would undoubtedly be allowed to appeal. This would be a final determination of the matter since later steps cannot be pursued unless there is such a finding. 121/

121/ The legislative history of the 1960 act is somewhat ambiguous with respect to Congress' intention regarding the problem of finality. Rep. Celler (D-N.Y.) was not sure whether the decree finding a pattern or practice to exist was a final order upon which an appeal would lie. He stated, somewhat obscurely, that it would all depend on the circumstances. (Cong. Rec. 5854). Rep. Curtis (D-Mass.) expressed the view that only the order declaring the applicant qualified to vote /at Step Five/ is the final order, and not the finding of a pattern or practice. (Cong. Rec. 5853.) Rep. McCulloch stated (Cong. Rec. 5854):

> "It is my opinion, if there be a finding of a pattern or practice which is followed by an order or decree with the court implementing that finding, that that is such a final order, or decree, that would be reviewable upon appeal or otherwise." (Continued)

3) At Step Three, the court may, in its discretion, appoint a referee to make preliminary findings, or the court may make such findings itself. If the court chooses to appoint a referee, such an action would most likely not be appealable, since the court clearly has such discretion. Furthermore, such an appointment does not decide anything on the merits of the case. [122/] Conversely, a decision by the court to hold ex parte hearings itself would probably not be appealable.

The only possible review of such a decision would not be by appeal but by writ of mandamus. In La Buy v. Howes Leather Co. [123/] for instance, the Supreme Court held that a Court of Appeals could properly issue a writ of mandamus to compel a district judge to vacate his order referring an antitrust case for trial before a master under Rule 53 (b) of the Federal Rules of Civil Procedure. But, mandamus lies only to review

---

121/ (Continued)

Rep. Lindsay agreed that in a proceeding brought under the 1957 act, "a finding by the court stating that individuals have been denied the right to vote is a final order, and therefore would be appealable." But he went on to add:

"if in such a proceeding the court should go on to find that there was a pattern or practice of voting discrimination, such a finding would be part of the same proceeding and therefore appealable."

122/ I. & I. Holding Corp. v. Greenberg, 151 F. 2d 570 (2d Cir. 1945).

123/ 352 U.S. 249.

an abuse by the trial judge of his discretionary powers:
"a usurpation of judicial power," [124/] as in La Buy where
both parties opposed the appointment of a master. But the
1960 Civil Rights Act, clearly states that a court may appoint
a referee, i.e., it has discretion whether or not to do so.
It should be noted that the appointment of the referee might
take place at Step One or at Step Two.

4) At Step Four, the referee receives applications,
conducts ex parte hearings, and reports its findings to the
court. These actions by the referee would be merely intermediary steps, and no appeal or review would lie. It is
conceivable, however, that one of the parties might attempt
to get the court to intervene in these hearings on the grounds
that the referee's conduct is improper. If this were to
happen, it would seem logical that either the Attorney General
or the applicant could seek some remedy from the court.

A question of constitutional law might arise if the
State registrar, acting in good faith, has found that the
applicant is not literate, but then the referee finds him
to be literate.

5) At Step Five, the court having reviewed the preliminary findings and challenges thereto, and perhaps having
heard arguments, adopts modifies, or rejects the findings or

[124/] 352 U.S. at 314; and see cases cited therein.

portions thereof and issues an appropriate order. Since this would be a final decision, an appeal would lie at this point by either the defendant or the Attorney General. If the State appeals, and if it has not previously been able to, it could attach an appeal to the Court's determination at Steps One and Two.

6) At Step Six, the court may issue additional, ancillary orders. Whether or not these are upheld depends on the nature of the stays issued at Step Five. However, the imminence of the election would have an important bearing and the court might issue an order authorizing the applicant to vote provisionally if the State appealed at Step Five, and the appeal was undecided by election day.

4. Length of Time for Which Registration Would be Effective:

The act states that the order of the court declaring an applicant to be qualified to vote "shall be effective as to any election held within the longest period for which such applicant could have been registered or otherwise qualified under State law at which the applicant's qualifications would under State law entitle him to vote."

The effectiveness of the referee section as to a given applicant may depend entirely on the meaning of this section of the statute. The entire referee process may be completed, and the applicant registered, but the State might, in the meanwhile, purge all its voters and require re-registration

for every election. These State actions might prove to be
cumbersome to all the State's residents, but they might prove
as well to be an effective obstacle to the successful application of this statute.

5. Rights of Original Complainants:

The legislative history of the 1960 Civil Rights Act points
out that it was enacted to benefit applicants subsequent to
the original suit. In many respects it was assumed that the
rights of the original complainants for whom the Attorney
General has brought an action, would be settled by the issuance
of an injunction. But this order does not necessarily have to
register anyone. [125/] These persons might have to return to
the registrar and be registered in the normal way. True, the
State registrar is under a court injunction not to deprive
these individuals of their right to vote because of their
race or color. But, if the registrar defies the court and
continues to deny registration, must these complainants then
apply to the referee or the court? Or, if the court issues
such an injunction and the complainants return to register,
what course should they follow if, for example, they cannot
get into the registration room? Finally, would these complainants, having once established their qualifications, be

---

125/ But in the first (and only) case filed in which the
    Attorney General has utilized the referee provision,
    the District Judge directed the registrars to place
    the complainants on the rolls within ten days. See
    N.Y. Times, Sept. 14, 1960, p. 46.

entitled to obtain an order and certificate directly entitling them to vote; or would they first have to prove to the referee their qualifications, already determined by the court itself?

A narrow construction of the statute and of the court's jurisdiction could mean considerable delay before these complainants actually exercise their right to vote. However, if the court broadly construes its equitable powers to fashion an appropriate remedy, then the original complainants should speedily obtain their rights.

VII. Preservation of Election Records: *

A. Procedure

Title III of the 1960 Civil Rights Act requires the retention and preservation of all records relating to any Federal election for a period of 22 months. Any election officer or custodian who willfully violates the terms of this section may be fined $1,000, imprisoned for a year, or both. Section 302 provides a penalty against "Any person . . . who willfully steals, destroys, conceals, mutilates, or alters" any such record. These records are to be made available in the office of the election official upon demand in writing by the Attorney General.

B. Analysis

To date this provision of the 1960 Civil Rights Act has been utilized in about 17 counties in Georgia, South Carolina, Alabama, Mississippi, Florida, and Louisiana. There have been at least three instances in which a Federal District Judge has ordered the production of voting records by recalcitrant election officials. [126]

---

* /For additional information, see the Department of Justice memo in the voting files./

[126] On August 11, a Federal Judge struck down a June 6th Alabama State court injunction and ordered Montgomery County to produce its voting records within 15 days. (Birmingham News, Aug. 11, 1960). In Louisiana, Federal District Court Judge J. Skelly Wright has ordered the East Feliciana Parish registrar of voters to make his records available to the Attorney General. (New Orleans Times-Picayune, July 19, 1960.) Similar action has transpired in Bienville Parish. (Id., July 28, 1960).

There has not as yet been an instance in which the Attorney General has sought to examine records, but has been denied by a Federal Court. How effective the information discovered by the Attorney General will be, cannot be adjudged at this time. However, it is expected that this section will overcome problems met by the Commission on Civil Rights and the Justice Department in their investigations of voting denials. 127/

Section 303 allows the Attorney General "or his representative" to inspect the records. Section 304 allows disclosure of the contents of the records to Congress, any Committee of Congress, or to any government agency.

1. The Nature of the Demand:

This section of the act states that the records are to be made available to the Attorney General, "upon demand in writing . . . .This demand shall contain a statement as to the basis and purpose therefor."

The proposed letter to a registrar from the office of the Attorney General requesting inspection of the records, states:

> "This demand is based upon information in the possession of the Attorney General tending to show that distinctions on the basis of race or color have been made with respect to registration and voting within your jurisdiction.

127/ See 1959 Report. 137-38.

"The purpose of this demand is to examine the aforesaid records in order to ascertain whether or not violations of Federal law in regard to registration and voting have occurred."

Senator Keating stated that the Attorney General could demand to see the records even if his reason was merely to discover any possible violations. 128/

2. Preservation of Records:

There may be further difficulty encountered in this section if a State enacts a statute requiring the destruction of all election records, or declares that there shall be no records. Clearly, in such a case, the issue would again be before the courts to resolve.

128/ Cong. Rec. 7223 (Apr. 8, 1960).